Edited by Elizabeth M. Banister,
Bonnie J. Leadbeater, and E. Anne Marshall

Knowledge Translation in Context

Indigenous, Policy, and Community Settings

UNIVERSITY OF TORONTO PRESS
Toronto   Buffalo   London

ISBN 978-1-4426-4179-2

Printed on acid-free, 100% post-consumer recycled paper with vegetable-based inks.

Library and Archives Canada Cataloguing in Publication

Knowledge translation in context : indigenous, policy, and community settings / edited by Elizabeth M. Banister, Bonnie J. Leadbeater, and E. Anne Marshall.

Includes bibliographical references.
ISBN 978-1-4426-4179-2

1. Knowledge management.   2. Knowledge management—Social aspects.
3. Indigenous peoples—Communication.   I. Banister, Elizabeth M.
II. Leadbeater, Bonnie J. Ross, 1950–   III. Marshall, E. Anne, 1951–

HD30.2.K66 2011   658.4'038   C2010-906759-2

University of Toronto Press acknowledges the financial assistance to its publishing program of the Canada Council for the Arts and the Ontario Arts Council.

 Canada Council
for the Arts   **Conseil des Arts**
du Canada

University of Toronto Press acknowledges the financial support for its publishing activities of the Government of Canada through the Book Publishing Industry Development Program (BPIDP).

Contents

Part Two: Knowledge Translation in Policy Contexts

Part Three: Knowledge Translation in Indigenous Contexts

Foreword

BUDD HALL

The publication of this book is a most valuable contribution to what we are beginning to think of as the knowledge movement, an emergence over the past fifty years towards the recovery or strengthening of a knowledge commons. The creation and use of knowledge lies at the heart of all human activity. In the millions of years before we institutionalized knowledge structures, knowledge was intimately linked to the natural world and survival. There was no separation between the ecological or environmental commons and the knowledge commons. Spirit, health, access to food and shelter, reproduction, the land, other living creatures, and knowledge were integrated, holistic, and natural. Over time, knowledge became more specialized – and just as we began to divide the natural commons with private ownership, feudal territorial claims, or even modern nation states, we also fragmented the knowledge commons. We now have universities, research laboratories, government-supported think tanks, and corporate research and development units where it is assumed that the bulk of knowledge is 'created.'

The beginning of the search for the reconnections of knowledge to the world in recent history can be traced to the work of Kurt Lewin at the Tavistock Institute and action research in the 1940s. I think of the work of Tandon, Freire, Fals Borda, and their majority world participatory research of the 1970s. I think of the emergence of the Science Shop movement in the Netherlands in the late 1970s and 1980s. But all holistic approaches to understanding the role of knowledge in the world – including Indigenous approaches to knowledge, arts-based knowledge construction, or even quantum physics – are moving us in these new directions. I use the concept of the *knowledge commons* (Hardin, 1968; Hess & Ostrom, 2006; Joranson, 2008) to mean a conceptual space where the boundaries between diverse locations of knowledge creation, forms of knowledge, and uses of knowledge are diminished in the interest of enhancing knowledge strategies for their application to the complex economic and social issues that confront us in Canada and around the world. The proposition is that lowering the barriers that separate knowledge domains is desirable.

Dialogues, discourses, and practices of a knowledge commons have attracted increased interest and visibility in academic, policy, civil society, philanthropic, and private sector settings in recent years. These discussions are spoken and written about in many ways. We speak of *knowledge translation/transfer/mobilization/exchange, impact* or *utilization, social innovation, community-based research, engaged scholarship, Indigenous-centred research, open* or *democratic knowledge sources,* and so on. What has emerged is the recognition that knowledge creation is not a monopoly of academics. It is created and co-created in community agencies working on green economic alternatives, in health clinics supporting persons living with HIV/AIDS, in engineering departments working on adaptive technologies for children with special needs, in financial institutions finding innovative ways to create affordable housing, in First Nations' controlled adult education classrooms sustaining and revitalizing Indigenous languages and cultures, in cities and towns using community mapping, applied theatre, and just plain talking to plan healthier and more liveable communities, and so much more.

Elizabeth Banister, Bonnie Leadbeater, and Anne Marshall have crafted a timely and important book that moves the discourse of linking knowledge to action forward in some new ways. (I particularly like the five dimensions of knowledge transfer outlined in chapter 9.) They are each experienced and insightful scholars whose leadership in community-based research is well known. In this book, they bring together scholars working in the broad social determinants of health field to give us what is collectively the broadest range of perceptions yet published about what knowledge translation in the fields of health actually means. The book builds on a deep experience and commitment to community-based research at the University of Victoria, an experience that has resulted in the creation of a university-wide structure (the Office of Community-Based Research) to support and enhance the visibility and effectiveness of scholars such as Banister, Leadbeater, and Marshall.

They have done a terrific job of bringing together a remarkable collection of engaged scholars from elsewhere in Canada, the United States, England, Australia, and Aotearoa New Zealand.

There are a number of critical issues that this collection illuminates:

The importance of context. This is one of the vital contributions of this collection. The ways in which knowledge is used depends almost entirely on the context within which one is working and the objectives of the work. Benoit and her co-authors in chapter 2 make this point when working with vulnerable groups. In fact, all of the writers in this book point us away from a cookbook approach to knowledge translation.

The recovery of Indigenous ways of knowing and knowledge translation. As we know, long before European knowledge structures and Western science and disciplinary knowledge strategies emerged, there were entire knowledge systems that had been created by place-based Indigenous peoples. We will not create a new knowledge commons where knowing and doing are reconnected unless we draw on these earlier epistemological traditions. Kuapapa Māori research, Cree ways of knowing, Coast Salish, and more are referred to in this collection. Much more work in this area is both necessary and welcome.

Power and knowledge. One of the underlying themes of the entire collection is that there are power differences among those who may share an interest in health knowledge. Many of the chapters refer to this either directly in terms of issues like accessibility and user-led reviews (chapter 8), the concept of ethical space (chapter 11), or the work done with sex workers (chapter 2). I think that more time and space is needed to further discuss the issues of power and knowledge. This fact is evident because in spite of the millions of dollars going into knowledge transfer and community-based research and the like, very few service agencies working with the most vulnerable have seen their capacities grow in terms of knowledge creation and translation/exchange. What counts as evidence is largely determined by a battle between scholars and policymakers, with the latter making 90 per cent of the decisions. When one considers areas such as biomedical health research with its industrial base and marketing structures, the power to disseminate knowledge about public health issues such as flu pandemics becomes even more tilted in favour of existing power relations.

Achieving recognition within the academy for knowledge transfer and engaged research. With work being done by organizations such as the Community Campus Partnerships for Health, the Canadian Federation of the Humanities and Social Sciences, and many individual university efforts, the recognition of excellence in knowledge translation and related areas of partnership development is beginning to be discussed. Chapter 7 makes specific mention of this issue, and it is implied in other chapters. How do we measure excellence in knowledge transfer? How should this be recognized for merit, tenure, and promotion matters? Should we be including community 'peers' in a new era of 'peer' review?

Using knowledge strategies for transformation or social change. The literature discussing population health or social determinants of health draws attention to the disparities of health status in our communities. There is a sense that the gap between those with the best health and those with a heavy burden of complicating health conditions is either widening or remaining static. Chapter 6 notes that working with advocacy coalitions is an effective way to propel research into policy and action spaces. To what degree can we structure both our research processes and our knowledge transfer processes in ways that strengthen the voices of those most in need of health action? Research and knowledge transfer in the field of HIV/AIDS research comes to mind when thinking of the relationship between social movement activism and knowledge. The Canadian Institutes of Health Research, for example, supports not only community-based research in HIV/AIDS but also funds movement and community-based research facilitators. The HIV/AIDS movement many years ago moved directly into areas of education and research. This book offers some insights into how such connections might be made.

Moving forward. We have come far over the past thirty to forty years in understanding the responsibilities academic researchers have to the communities they seek to serve. We have a long road forwards as well. The editors and authors of this volume provide road maps and signposts for many of the appropriate destinations.

REFERENCES

Hardin, G. (1968). The tragedy of the commons. *Science, 162*(3859), 1243–1248.
Hess, C., & Ostrom, E. (Eds.). (2006). *Understanding knowledge as a commons: From theory to practice.* Cambridge, MA: MIT Press.
Joranson, K. (2008). Indigenous knowledge and the knowledge commons. *The International Information & Library Review, 40*(1), 64–72.

Acknowledgments

The editors wish to thank the Canadian Institutes of Health Research, the Social Sciences and Humanities Research Council of Canada, the UVic Centre for Youth and Society, the BC Child and Youth Health Research Network, and the University of Victoria for their funding and support. Special thanks goes to each of the chapter authors who gave generously of their time and who often travelled long distances to create the face-to-face exchange of interdisciplinary ideas that made this book possible. This collaboration was a once in a lifetime opportunity for us all. We also appreciate our community partners who took time from their already overextended schedules to engage in research with the chapter authors. Thanks to Budd Hall for crafting a thoughtful foreword. Thanks also to Shelley Booth and Sara McLaughlin who organized the international conferences that began this work, and to Sharyl A. Yore for the great care she took in editing the first draft of this manuscript.

KNOWLEDGE TRANSLATION IN CONTEXT:
INDIGENOUS, POLICY, AND COMMUNITY SETTINGS

1 How-What-We-Know-Becomes-More-Widely-Known Is Context Dependent and Culturally Sensitive

BONNIE J. LEADBEATER, ELIZABETH M. BANISTER,
AND E. ANNE MARSHALL

Living in a culture that depended on snow for food, housing, and transportation, it may not be surprising that the Inuit, Aivilik, and Igloolik languages coined unique words for soft snow: soft deep snow, fresh soggy snow, watery snow, compressed snow, pink snow, drifting snow, snow that has melted and refrozen, expected snow, snow falling on water, snow on the ground, falling snow, snow for drinking water, snow bricks for building, snowdrift on a steep hill, snow at dawn and more.

Our knowledge-dependent cultures are in a similar struggle to name the process of how-what-we-know-becomes-more-widely-known for the benefit of our societies. This process, which we call *knowledge translation* (KT), is the subject of this book. Knowledge translation goes by many different names[1] with nuanced meanings (Graham et al., 2006; Landry, Amara, Pablos-Mendez, Shademani, & Gold, 2006). The terms coined to describe this process have proliferated dramatically over the last two decades and include knowledge transfer, translation, management, exchange, uptake, mobilization, utilization, use, and so on. We use knowledge translation as a generic term that includes all of these meanings. Would-be contributors to the field of research on this topic struggle to grasp the most up-to-date conceptual frameworks and terminology under the pressure of the field's fast-paced evolution, but the nuances carried by these different frameworks and terms do matter. The chapters in this book show how different types and mechanisms of KT are emerging from various settings and cultural contexts in which knowledge is used. We need to know about the context-based differences in KT in order to be able to replicate and support successful efforts to apply research-based knowledge to benefit society, in particular, to alleviate health and social problems.

What is meant by the term *knowledge* is also debated, as we attempt to include under a single-umbrella term diverse sources of knowledge, including research evidence, scientific evidence, what is common knowledge, and experiential wisdom. This book focuses mainly on diverse sources of knowledge that address societal concerns with the health and welfare of its populations. The authors are an international group of scholars from Canada, the United Kingdom, Australia, New Zealand, and the United States. In all countries, gaps exist in the access certain groups have to science-based knowledge that could benefit health and social welfare and its use. While much of this research is publicly funded, social disparities which determine who benefits from this knowledge are also widely apparent. This reality underscores the urgency to understand research knowledge utilization processes and how they intersect with knowledge production.

One definition of KT for health researchers states that health knowledge translation is 'a dynamic and iterative process that includes the synthesis, dissemination, exchange, and ethically sound application of knowledge to improve the health of Canadians, provide more effective health services and products and strengthen the healthcare system' (Tetroe, *2007*). This definition points to several mechanisms of KT – synthesis, dissemination, exchange, and application – but how and where these mechanisms are successful in moving knowledge-to-action to improve health and social welfare has not been widely studied (Davies & Nutley, 2008; Straus, Tetroe, & Graham, 2009). We adopt this definition in this volume, replacing *Canadians* with *populations*.

Existing conceptual frameworks that describe KT mechanisms draw attention to the many, often iterative, and non-linear steps that lead from research-based knowledge to health and social welfare benefits (Gabbay & le May, 2004; Landry et al., 2001; Lavis et al., 2003; Weiss, 1979). However, these models are typically not tailored to the different characteristics and needs of specific contexts (Walter, Nutley, & Davies, 2005). Reviewing what we have learned about how research-based knowledge is employed, Davies and Nutley (2008) note that 'we need to understand more about the structures, processes, and cultures within which individuals are embedded in order to understand their engagement with research-based knowledge' (p. 7). This book addresses this gap by showing how effective KT processes operate within a variety of settings and cultural contexts.

The chapters in this book present case studies that highlight contextual differences and variations in the infrastructures or mechanisms needed to set KT in motion. They describe current efforts to enhance KT in multiple settings, including rural communities, Indigenous communities, non-profit organizations (NPOs), and policy arenas. *The conclusion we reach is that context does matter and context-sensitive approaches and infrastructures are needed to support effective KT.*

For example, KT used by policy decision-makers typically relies on infrastructures that join researchers (or research-based knowledge) and research users through intermediaries who synthesize, translate, and transfer evidence-based knowledge (see the chapters written by Gough; Lenton; and McCabe). Alternatively, KT in NPOs, schools, and communities can benefit from a pre-research phase of exchanging relevant questions and answers. This can be facilitated by community-based research (CBR) approaches and sustained community – university collaborations (see chapters by Begoray & Banister; Benoit, Casey, Jansson, Phillips, & Burns; and Marshall & Guenette). Finally, KT in some Indigenous communities requires processes that can build iteratively from existing Indigenous knowledge and health practices to revised practices that may be inspired by but not identical to research-based knowledge produced outside of the community (see chapters by Moewaka Barnes, Henwood, Kerr, McManus, & McCreanor; and Smylie).

Each chapter in this book begins with the authors' efforts to coin nuanced language that is adequate to describe the processes of KT or making-what-we-know-more-widely-known in their own contexts. The diversity of approaches illustrates what the proliferating terminology also reflects: *How-what-is-known-becomes-more-widely-known is context dependent and context sensitive.* The chapters are organized into three sections reflecting the contexts of communities, policymakers, and Indigenous groups. Each highlights and responds to the question of how research-based knowledge can be effectively distributed and used. The KT processes revealed are characterized by context-relevant structures, needs, goals, timelines, modes of communication, access, research methods, and validity checks that determine how what is known comes to be known widely. Contrasts in KT that are related to contexts of communities, policymakers, and Indigenous groups are briefly summarized below.

Knowledge exchange and mobilization in community contexts offer opportunities to engage communities in identifying research questions and to build on their assets and interests to increase the likelihood that research knowledge will be used. The research methods guided by community-based or participatory action focus on problems identified by the community and draw on local community knowledge in addition to science-based findings (Lincoln, 2001). These research methods attempt to shift the traditional linear view of KT in which researcher-created results are pushed into communities that have the expertise to use it to one in which knowledge is co-generated and sometimes co-owned by both academic researchers and research users. Knowledge production is viewed as a collective activity. Ideally, the production and distribution of knowledge is a relatively seamless activity.

Knowledge translation relevant to policy decisions relies on timely access to research-based knowledge in the context of many competing sources of knowledge – persuasive anecdotes, constituent pressures, and the media (Shonkoff, 2000). Systematic reviews of research-based knowledge can and do support evidence-informed decision-making. However, opportunities for research-based knowledge to influence policy decisions rise and fall with changing governments and government agendas, priorities, and budgets. In this setting, knowledge-to-action mechanisms cannot be left to chance occurrences. To be effective, this process requires a stable infrastructure that has access to research-based knowledge as well as the capacity to make it rapidly accessible in useable formats. Hence, it is not surprising that using evidence-based knowledge to influence decision-making relies on knowledge brokers and organizations that work continuously across time. These infrastructures are needed to build receptive relationships with an often-changing slate of governing officials and to continuously produce usable syntheses, summaries, briefs, or testimonies of research-based knowledge on key social issues that are ready when needed (see chapter by Lenton).

Finally, in *Indigenous communities and settings*, KT strategies often require a starting point based on what is known and practised within a community, rather than what is science-based or endorsed by outside experts. Indigenous cultural knowledge and conceptual frameworks are central to these KT strategies and become the foundation for change. KT happens at a person-to-person level through exchanges that may include experiential demonstrations, personal endorsements, practical applications, storytelling, films, photography, et cetera. These practices may be prioritized over written instructions, expert advice, or demonstrations. From this perspective, efforts to bring new knowledge to influence health and social welfare problems are not achieved through raising awareness or providing information. Rather, effective

KT may require more active community engagement and participatory action. Science-based knowledge may stimulate or inspire processes of rethinking or reconstructing traditional ways of knowing in ways that improve health and social welfare, but considerable effort may be needed to reconfigure this knowledge into culturally and personally meaningful messages in these settings.

The chapters that follow detail the community, policy, and Indigenous approaches to KT through case study presentations that show the intersecting positions of knowledge producers and users and use within their own contextual settings.

Origins and Organization of the Book

The idea for this book was generated from an international workshop held in 2006 in Victoria, British Columbia, funded by the Canadian Institutes of Health Research (CIHR) and the British Columbia Child and Youth Health Research Network. The intent of the workshop was to gather a range of perspectives about KT and CBR from national and international researchers, policymakers, and practitioners. A second grant from the Social Sciences and Humanities Research Council of Canada (SSHRC) allowed KT researchers from across Canada, the United States, the United Kingdom, Australia, and New Zealand to come together to plan this book. The authors bring a variety of perspectives on KT that come from their positions as academic researchers, practitioners, research users, knowledge brokers, and policy specialists.

As noted, the three sections of the book represent community, policy, or Indigenous contexts of KT. In section one, Knowledge Translation in Community – University Contexts, authors discuss diverse mechanisms that enhance communities' use of research. In chapter 2, Benoit, Casey, Jansson, Phillips, and Burns report on their research on factors related to health and health care access of vulnerable populations. They show the need for support to establish long-term relationships and regular face-to-face exchanges between university and community partners. Sometimes it is necessary to blur the strict division between researcher and service provider. For example, NPO personnel were hired to participate in the research activities and to bridge institutional and cultural differences between academics and the NPOs. The hands-on knowledge these individuals had about vulnerable populations also helped to translate the research findings directly into practice and program innovations. In chapter 3, Marshall and Guenette employ a cross-cultural lens to describe how they shaped KT strategies to bridge the diverse stakeholder contexts of university colleagues, students, and community partners. This necessitated consultation and adaptation at each step of the research project, from conceptualization to dissemination activities. Using illustrations from their CBR projects focusing on youth health and work transitions, they argue that within-culture differences among academics or community partners can be equally, if not even more challenging than between-culture differences. They describe examples of power disparities and resource limitations that were resolved in the course of the study. In chapter 4, McKegg argues that ensuring community involvement in evaluative inquiry is important to the success of KT. Data and locally created knowledge can be incorporated into decision-making processes when researchers are sensitive to contexts and work alongside local leaders. For example, evaluative inquiry led to new knowledge for participants about the similarities and differences between Māori-medium and English-medium literacy. Enhanced interaction between researcher and research users was fundamental to the development of this new knowledge. In chapter 5, Wharf Higgins, Naylor, MacLeod Williams, and Sporer discuss their work with community representatives in designing a process evaluation toolkit for a provincial physical activity initiative called Active Communities. Ongoing, face-to-face contact with community representatives ensured that the toolkit was relevant to maximize use of the evaluation tool. The evaluation team worked closely with practitioners to package the toolkit in a user-friendly format.

In section two, Knowledge Translation in Policy Contexts, authors describe processes of KT that can lead to more informed decision-making by policymakers. In chapter 6, McCabe discusses how professional science organizations (e.g., Society for Research in Child Development [SRCD] in the U.S.) can serve as knowledge brokers or facilitators in effectively communicating scientific knowledge to policymakers. McCabe outlines some of the mechanisms by which research knowledge can be shared with a wide audience, ranging from scientists and administrators in federal agencies, to science and advocacy organizations, and policy journalists. She also describes how SRCD disseminates science-based knowledge through the popular media, how it fosters relationships with journalist colleagues who demonstrate skilled coverage of science, and how policymakers often learn of science through this mechanism. Likewise, Lenton, in chapter 7, describes KT measures that support the engagement of academic researchers in legislative change.

He draws on his experience in the translation of research findings into changes to cannabis law in the state of Western Australia. He argues that the capacity to influence policy and action can be greatly enhanced when researchers are invited into ongoing work with government personnel. He adds that researchers should prepare for policy change processes at legislative levels in order to act when opportunities arise. Policy advocates can help researchers access such windows of opportunity by bringing researchers and policymakers together. Gough, in chapter 8, argues that research users' access to and control of research agendas can enhance the relevance of KT for the wider community. He discusses how systematic reviews of research evidence provide opportunities for community participation in evidence-informed decision-making. He suggests a four-tiered communication strategy to create both a knowledge base and usable summaries. These tiers include the production of a web-based database of original raw data, a full technical report, a short, user-friendly main report, and a two-page summary.

In section three, Knowledge Translation in Indigenous Contexts, authors describe how research programs that engage Indigenous end-users in the research enhance the relevance of knowledge to Indigenous populations. Begoray and Banister, in chapter 9, describe a sexual health education program for Canadian Indigenous adolescents that featured the application of KT. They identify contextuality, collaboration, reciprocity, relationally, and reflexivity as primary dimensions of effective KT practice. For example, regarding contextuality, the community context demanded an experiential, active, and culturally appropriate program through which they could conduct their research. Gaining permission to access the community was facilitated by a local elder who cared about the maintenance of her culture by future generations and who believed that the education program could positively influence youth behaviour. In chapter 10 Moewaka Barnes, Henwood, Kerr, McManus, and McCreanor describe how engaging members of Indigenous New Zealand Māori communities in research helped to build research capacity and facilitate the use of data and findings. As Māori researchers, they were able to develop relationships with Māori communities and facilitate effective use of research knowledge. They describe how KT was enhanced using practices that interweave traditional, community, and academic expertise. Smylie, in chapter 11, discusses KT models used in partnering with Canadian Indigenous communities and shows that knowledge creation that is context-relevant contributes to enhancing Indigenous community health and well-being. For example, she describes how prenatal messaging about self-care delivered by an Inuit elder for an interactive CD-ROM helped translate current public health, evidence-based recommendations for prenatal and infant care.

In the final chapter, 'Concluding Thoughts,' we summarize what we learned from the chapters about the facilitators of and barriers to effective KT. We also offer suggestions for the next steps needed to advance KT processes and practices.

The international perspectives presented in the book highlight both commonalities and contextual differences in KT practices across countries and settings. These chapters demonstrate that KT is a multidirectional, dynamic process that expands and challenges our understanding of social and health concerns and their solutions.

Academic and community-based researchers and their partners in policy and practice settings will be the main audience. In addition to concrete examples of processes and infrastructure that facilitate effective KT, there are descriptions of adaptations and changes implemented to overcome barriers that can impede effective KT. The book may also help to develop the capacity of knowledge users as informed consumers of research-based social and health knowledge in order to transform service development and delivery. Indigenous communities and groups also will find descriptions of processes and procedures that are consistent with their values and worldviews. In addition, students in post-secondary (tertiary) programs will benefit from the developmental and practical orientation of the research projects described.

NOTE

1 *Knowledge transfer* is a reciprocal and mutual activity involving researchers and community-based service providers in the development, conduct, interpretation, and application of research and research-based knowledge (Landry, Amara, & Lamari, 2001). *Knowledge exchange* involves 'interaction between decision makers and researchers and results in mutual learning through the process of planning, disseminating, and applying existing or new research in decision-making' (Canadian Health Services Research Foundation [CHSRF], 2010. 5, paragraph 1). *Knowledge mobilization* is a bidirectional process between researchers and users for 'moving knowledge into active service for the broadest possible common good' (Social Sciences and Humanities Research Council of Canada, n.d., Objectives section, paragraph 3).

REFERENCES

Canadian Health Services Research Foundation (CHSRF) (2010). *Knowledge exchange.* Retrieved June 30, 2010, from http://www.chsrf.ca/knowledge_transfer/index_e.php

Davies, H.T.O., & Nutley, S.M. (2008). *Learning more about how research-based knowledge gets used: Guidance in the development of new empirical research.* New York: William T. Grant Foundation.

Gabbay, J., & le May, A. (2004). Evidence based guidelines or collectively constructed 'mindlines'? Ethnographic study of knowledge management in primary care. *British Medical Journal, 329*(7473), 1013–1016.

Graham, I.D., Logan, J., Harrison, M.B., Straus, S.E., Tetroe, J., Caswell, W., et al. (2006). Lost in knowledge translation: Time for a map? *Journal of Continuing Education in the Health Professions, 26*(1), 13–24.

Landry, R., Amara, N., & Lamari, M. (2001). Utilization of social science research knowledge in Canada. *Research Policy, 30*(2), 333–349.

Landry, R., Amara, N., Pablos-Mendez, A., Shademani, R., & Gold, I. (2006). The knowledge-value chain: A conceptual framework for knowledge translation in health. *Bulletin of the World Health Organization, 84*(8), 597–602.

Lavis, J.N., Robertson, D., Woodside, J.M., McLeod, C.B., Abelson, J., & The Knowledge Transfer Study Group. (2003). How can research organizations more effectively transfer research knowledge to decision makers? *The Milbank Quarterly, 81*(2), 221–248.

Lincoln, Y.S. (2001). Engaging sympathies: Relationships between action research and social constructivism. In P. Reason & H. Bradbury (Eds.), *The Sage handbook of action research: Participative inquiry and practice* (pp. 124–132). Thousand Oaks, CA: Sage.

Shonkoff, J.P. (2000). Science, policy, and practice: Three cultures in search of a shared mission. *Child Development, 71*(1), 181–187.

Straus, S.E., Tetroe, J., & Graham, I.D. (2009). Introduction. In S.E. Straus, J. Tetroe, & I.D. Graham (Eds.), *Knowledge translation in health care* (pp. 1–9). Retrieved June 30, 2010, from http://www3.interscience.wiley.com/cgi-bin/summary/122363217/SUMMARY

Tetroe, J. (2007). Knowledge translation at the Canadian Institutes of Health Research: A primer. *Focus* (Technical Brief No. 18). Retrieved June 30, 2010, from http://www.ncddr.org/kt/products/focus/focus18/Focus18

Walter I., Nutley, S.M., & Davies, H.T.O. (2005). What works to promote evidence-based practice? A cross-sector review. *Evidence & Policy, 1*(3), 335–364.

Weiss, C.H. (1979). The many meanings of research utilization. *Public Administration Review, 39*(5), 426–431.

PART ONE

Knowledge Translation in Community–University Contexts

2   Developing Knowledge Transfer with Non-profit Organizations Serving Vulnerable Populations*

CECILIA BENOIT, LAUREN CASEY, MIKAEL JANSSON,
RACHEL PHILLIPS, AND DAVID BURNS

It is widely recognized that there is a significant lag between the production of evidence-based knowledge and change in professional practice (Lavis, Robertson, Woodside, McLeod, & Abelson, 2003). While scholars continue to produce new results for enhancing health care and health care delivery, for example, only infrequently are they actually implemented at the clinic level (Estabrooks, Thompson, Lovely, & Hofmeyer, 2006). A similar problem occurs in the opposite direction – practitioners have gaps in their knowledge base, but these seldom translate into research questions that are investigated by health and social scientists.

Efforts are now underway to change this situation. Researchers are honing their tools to enhance the adoption of scientific results by various communities of practice, and clinicians are likewise looking for better ways to heighten the interest of scientists about questions emerging from practice. The assortment of terms currently in vogue – including knowledge transfer, diffusion, dissemination, interaction, utilization, mobilization, and exchange – is an indication of the increased attention to this matter. The term knowledge translation (KT) has recently gained attention because it highlights the iterative, reciprocal exchange that takes place between researchers and research-users when both are actively engaged in producing and applying knowledge (Choi, 2005). KT underscores the notion that different communities have different knowledge cultures and communication between them is neither assured nor automatic (Estabrooks et al., 2006).

Though growing agreement on the usage of the concept of KT is an important development, there nevertheless remains a paucity of research on how to 'bridge the gap between what is known and what gets done in practice' (Pablos-Mendez & Shademani, 2006, p. 81). Even health funding agencies are uncertain about the most effective KT strategies (Tetroe et al., 2008). This chapter offers some suggestions that arose from close partnerships with community-based, non-profit organizations (NPOs) participating in a research program studying the health and well-being of vulnerable populations. The individuals in these populations are vulnerable because many have diminished access to societal resources (e.g., income, education, social support, prestige) as well as fewer options to achieve better health and well-being when compared to other Canadians.

Collaboration between researchers and practitioners in the non-profit sector is particularly illuminating because the challenges faced by NPOs place them at a genuine disadvantage in comparison to large, public sector organizations with dedicated personnel available to participate in discussions regarding how to implement current research findings. Using NPOs as a case study is also informative because they have the advantage of being able to implement change relatively quickly. These organizations typically exhibit closer relationships between administrators and front-line service providers, and are accustomed to adapting to the changing imperatives of their varied funding sources.

Reflecting back on core research partnerships – some of which have been in place for over a decade – we report on two factors that were pivotal in developing authentic KT: strong multilevel partnerships and the use of skilled knowledge brokers. We provide a detailed examination of these two elements in the context of our particular research program; but we begin with a brief review of the relevant KT literature. Throughout it is important to remember that KT is a two-way process. While the transfer from *researcher* to *service provider* is explicitly the focus of some researchers, our definition of transfer explicitly includes the transfer of knowledge from *service provider* to *researcher*. This two-way process stems, at least in part, from our view of science as an iterative process.

The Snail's Pace of KT

It is now commonly accepted that findings from academic research need to be more accessible to practitioners in the formal health care system. There is also agreement that research quality and relevance are enhanced when practitioners have the opportunity to ask for further information and even pose new questions for future investigation (Davis et al., 2003; Lavis, Posada, Haines, & Osei, 2004; Pablos-Mendez & Shademani, 2006). Despite this shared understanding, most researchers would agree with Ian Graham and colleagues (2006) that the utilization of research evidence by different stakeholder groups remains 'slow and haphazard' (p. 13). According to one estimate, it takes approximately seventeen years to turn 14 per cent of funded research into benefits to patient care (Clancy, 2006). For example, the link between smoking and lung cancer was identified in 1957, but it was not until the early 1990s that significant changes to policy at the legislative level were accomplished (Lomas, 1997).

Martens and Roos (2005) compared the slow process of information sharing between academic researchers and health professionals to 'tectonic plates . . . moving slowly past each other' (p. 73). This lack of synergy results from an assortment of problems, including damaged communication, poor understanding about the generation of research results, and misconceptions about how organizational decisions are made. Other researchers have found that academic researchers and individuals in health service organizations exist largely independently of each other, with little concrete knowledge about each other's work worlds (Norman & Huerta, 2006).

Other barriers to research utilization by members of the non-academic community include the structural and symbolic constraints on the circulation, popularization, and subsequent enactment of new knowledge; this is the case even when there is adequate communication among researchers, policymakers, and practitioners. While academic researchers occupy a privileged and influential social position as expert knowledge creators, their research findings may be ignored if they are not circulated in a user-friendly, culturally sensitive manner, or if the target audience is not ready to accept new evidence. The same goes for retrieving questions that arise in everyday practice and translating them into questions for future scientific investigation. Questions that do not lend themselves to current research trends and funding opportunities are unlikely to make it into research proposals – or to be funded even if they are proposed.

To enhance sharing and mutual learning, funding and governance bodies in the health sector have begun to place greater emphasis on the complexity of community – academic linkages and to develop tools to ensure that evidence-based decision-making is more than a coincidence (Denner, Cooper, Lopez, & Dunbar, 1999; Small, 1996). One important impetus is that funders now frequently require academic teams to include representatives from the non-academic community and that community-based service initiatives include a research or evaluation component. This has resulted in renewed interest within the health research community in understanding when, how, and why results are used outside the academy. Written largely from the perspective of academic team members, an expanding literature has begun to document the achievements and challenges of such partnerships.

Many have found that collaborative research with specific KT aims is often lengthier and more resource-intensive than traditional models (LeGris et al., 2000). Given the sometimes slow pace of research, collaborators may have difficulty sustaining involvement over the course of a project as key contact persons leave or change positions and organizational priorities shift. An overall lack of resources and differing perspectives may mean that collaborations remain superficial and result in limited KT and uptake (Ebata, 1996). Institutional processes and priorities are additional barriers as well as university ethical guidelines that are seldom designed with community engagement in mind. Similarly, new knowledge may not be utilized if it cannot be readily applied to policy and practice imperatives or if it is released in the context of heated or incompatible political contexts (Boutilier, Badgley, Poland, & Tobin, 2001). Given these barriers, it is not surprising that researchers and policy and practice partners often become discouraged with the research partnership process and the meagre, evidence-based knowledge exchanged, realizing that the foreseeable rewards of such collaborations often do not match the effort expended.

Strategies to Pick Up the KT Pace

Fortunately, the existing literature takes us a long way in preparing for the difficulties noted above by offering a parallel set of KT best practices. As an initial educational activity as well as in preparation for subsequent research activities, researchers recommend synthesizing existing, high-quality research for policy and practice collaborators (Davis et al., 2003). The KT literature additionally recommends that teams engage in an exercise of critically appraising different kinds of available health data, including evidence emerging from research results, clinical experience, and information provided by patients

(Rycroft-Malone et al., 2002). Other recommendations include involving collaborators throughout the research cycle in order to improve their investment and help translate the results in a language that will be understood, considered relevant, and regarded as a decision-making resource (Martens & Roos, 2005). The concept of equal and engaged partners is also invoked in recommendations to invest in team-building strategies aimed at learning about different organizational needs and barriers, developing a shared language and culture, and identifying common priorities (Bowen, Martens, & The Need to Know Team, 2005; Greenhalgh, Robert, MacFarlane, Bate, & Kyriakidou, 2004; Lavis et al., 2005).

Resources are, however, typically unevenly distributed among research partners with respect to time, administrative support, and finances. Moreover, some research partners may be reluctant to state their opinions and may only minimally participate in the process, particularly when other team members hold knowledge that is deemed to be privileged by the dominant culture. Addressing these differing levels of power and variation in material and symbolic resources is especially important when working with the non-profit sector serving vulnerable populations. Among other things, these groups and their advocates often feel over-researched and are wary of tokenism when collaborating with researchers and policymakers. As Bowens et al. (2005) noted following a five-year research collaboration, it took over a year for community members to get familiar with the project and 'to build trust, develop a shared culture, identify common priorities, and undertake collaborative research' (p. 207). It can no doubt take a similar period for academic partners to become sufficiently acquainted with the interests, work culture, and organizational imperatives of their collaborators. Such observations underscore the importance of relationship-building as a precursor and pivotal building block for eventual KT.

Utilizing knowledge brokers – with the primary task of linking researchers, community agencies, and individual policy and practice experts – has also been noted as a core KT strategy (Lomas, 2007). Knowledge brokers occupy a unique in-between location; they are trusted by all parties and are familiar with the disparate sectors and priorities that may be brought together within a research team. These assets make it possible for knowledge brokers to (a) better understand the goals of various collaborating groups and their respective professional cultures and (b) use this information to forge new partnerships and promote the use of research-based evidence in decision-making.

Based on our experience conducting research in partnership with a select number of NPOs, the remainder of this chapter focuses on KT strategies in the context of research on vulnerable populations that are both hidden and highly stigmatized. Our reflections are based on the decade-long process of conducting three separate research projects on vulnerable populations residing in the Victoria Metropolitan Area of British Columbia. In the absence of highly reliable and valid indicators of the KT, we acknowledge that our strongest indicators of KT success are inter-organizational longevity in the context of major cutbacks to NPO funding as well as co-involvement in a variety of products, including workshops, conferences, and scholarly publications. Yet, it is also significant that engagement in these partnerships has changed all partners' previously held views of the target populations, the research endeavour, and the policy and practice implementation process. Below we highlight two crucial elements of KT success: strong inter-organizational partnerships and the use of knowledge brokers. We explore each in turn, but first we will describe the three interrelated projects in order to provide needed background.

The Three Studies

The Dispelling Myths Project involved close collaboration with an NPO: the Prostitutes Empowerment, Education, and Resource Society (PEERS). This front-line service organization is largely staffed by persons who formerly worked in the sex industry; it prides itself on its strong peer empowerment ethos. PEERS offers outreach services, public education, counselling, and job skills training to support adult women and men currently working in and those wishing to leave the sex industry; it has maintained a leadership role in educating the community about the sexual exploitation of youth.

PEERS opened its doors in 1995 and that year provided services to ninety-eight individuals. By 1999, the number had risen fivefold to 500, and the caseload has continued to grow at the same rate in subsequent years. Members of the PEERS Board of Directors concluded that research should assume a more central role in the organization's activities, given the expanding service need and paucity of reliable information on the working conditions and health status of persons working in the sex industry, especially those in off-street locations. This decision led to the Dispelling Myths Project. PEERS' chief aim in applying for research money was to collect data on adult persons working in the sex industry that would be useful to their outreach services and educational programs. It was also hoped that the research would draw recognition to the knowledge held by sex workers and simultaneously provide modest employment opportunities to a small number of peo- ple who had left the sex industry. These individuals were hoping to develop their mainstream job skills, and have some formal work expe- rience to record on their resumes.

After passing the letter-of-intent stage of a provincial health funding agency, PEERS sought the expertise of a non-profit management con- sultant and Cecilia Benoit (the first author of this chapter) to reshape the grant application into a collaborative research project that focused on the working conditions, health status, and exiting experiences of adult persons working in various venues (outdoor and indoor loca- tions) of the sex industry in the Victoria metropolitan region. The grant application was successful, and PEERS received research funds for the two-year project. An ad hoc advisory board was struck, including rep- resentatives from a number of government agencies, focused on health and legal issues of persons working in the sex industry as well as mem- bers of outreach organizations helping marginalized individuals.

In an attempt to better understand front-line service workers, we launched a longitudinal study called the Stigma Study funded by the Canadian Institutes for Health Research (CIHR) – Canada's premier funding agency for health research. This project focused on providing personal service work in non-unionized, gender-scripted, and low- prestige occupations (hairstyling, food and beverage service work, and sex work). A number of health care agencies and work groups gave input during the start-up stage; two NPOs have remained active par- ticipants over the three-year research cycle: PEERS and the Child and Family Counselling Association (CAFCA).

CAFCA is a front-line, community-based, counselling and sup- port organization largely funded by the provincial government of BC. Support counsellors from this NPO work in close contact with public sector social workers and probation officers to assist families, youth in government care and/or deemed to be at risk (street-involved or involved in criminal justice programs), and persons with disabili- ties. CAFCA provides assistance with employment, housing, income resource issues, family mediation, parental skill development, and access to recreational and other support resources. CAFCA has adopted a philosophy of continuous quality improvement and, as a result, has embraced the idea of partnering with researchers to ensure that organizational practice remains in step with current evidence regarding the services it delivers and the needs of its target client population. CAFCA also has a substantial amount of experience with research that emerges from questions raised in practice. Its involvement with both lower-income families and youth living on the street made CAFCA a suitable partner for the Stigma Study as well as our third study on vulnerable populations.

The third study, Risky Business, examines the impact of street life on the health and well-being of a purposive sample of female and male youth. This longitudinal panel study emerged from an earlier evaluation of a community program on sexually exploited youth conducted by two of this chapter's authors, Cecilia Benoit and Mikael Jansson. It was funded for the first five years by CIHR and received subsequent funding for three more years of data collection by the Social Sciences and Humanities Research Council of Canada (SSHRC). Risky Business has five community partner organizations, all of which have remained more or less active throughout the life of the project: PEERS, CAFCA, the Victoria Native Friendship Centre, the Victoria Youth Empowerment Society, and the Victoria Youth Clinic. Each of these organizations offers front-line services to street-involved youth, including crisis counselling, educational support, mentorship, and basic needs (e.g., nutritional and housing services).

A relatively large number of research assistants worked on this project, including former street-involved youth in their twenties who were willing to be trained in interviewing techniques. These individuals were identified by our community partners as promising researchers. Health and social service professionals and graduate students who indicated an interest in working part time on the study were also recruited as interviewers.

In the longitudinal research program, we made a concerted effort to (a) document barriers to participation for intersectoral team members and (b) cooperatively develop strategies to help address these barriers. The primary purposes were to have a democratic and consensual partnership – a goal identified as central to the development of successful collaboration among interdisciplinary and multidisciplinary professional teams (Henriksson, Wrede, & Burau, 2006; Wrede, Benoit, & Einarsdóttir, 2008). Some of the barriers identified related to variation in the amount of time and resources that the participating organizations were able to devote to the research program. These challenges were relatively easy to overcome if additional funds or personnel could be made available. However, more subtle barriers, such as those based in tensions regarding which kind of knowledge – academic or experiential – should be privileged, involved much more negotiation from all sides.

Not surprisingly, the intensity of collaboration among the research team members peaked at certain times, followed by periods of less contact. This can be especially true of longitudinal projects because of their multi-year duration. The opportunity to engage in various forms of KT and achieve success that informed each other's work was beneficial. However, we also had more difficult patches where collaboration did not reach its full potential. We will explore these experiences in more detail below, focusing on two strategies that we believe generated the most success.

Insights Derived from the Research Program

Drawing on the three interrelated studies described above, we now elaborate on two elements that were particularly useful in the KT between these two groups: inter-organizational partnership and knowledge brokers.

Inter-organizational Partnerships

As noted earlier, the majority of our long-term research partnerships have been with NPOs that serve vulnerable populations (e.g., persons working in the sex industry, street-involved youth and youth in government care, low-income workers, young families, and Aboriginal women). While representatives of provincial government service and policy teams have typically been involved at strategic points in the research cycle and often sit on advisory boards that govern the activities of affiliated interdisciplinary research networks, ongoing relationships have largely been between academics and NPOs.

In the last two decades, NPOs emerged in the local region to provide services to vulnerable individuals who, for various reasons, fall through the social safety net. They share a precarious funding base (i.e., their organizations struggle to balance their annual budgets with a mix of national and provincial government agency program funding, private donations, and local fundraising). Concurrently, funders are increasingly requiring NPOs to have a research component, which explains why NPOs have either invited academic researchers to lead a

line of research (Dispelling Myths Project) or have been open to joining academic research teams (Stigma and Risky Business Projects).
Considering their limited resources to conduct the research, evaluation, and knowledge-gathering activities to the extent that they would
like, NPOs have become increasingly open to collaboration with allies
in academic settings. We contend these long-term relationships with
non-profit, front-line organizations have contributed greatly to the success of academic researchers who have benefited from the transfer of
knowledge from NPOs.

Some key examples of using KT strategies include face-to-face meetings, proposal collaboration, research brief preparation, research presentations at NPO staff meetings, research roundtables and knowledge
translation workshops, and publication co-authorship. The strategies
that we had success with included engaging non-profit sector partners
in setting research objectives, posing research questions, collaboratively
designing studies, and communicating results through diverse channels. By engaging in these activities, we learned that NPOs typically do
not have time to consult with researchers due to the short time frame of
most proposals. Because we developed rapport and trust beforehand,
we often were able to find a volunteer from our research team to offer
assistance. The level of rapport and trust among research team members also made it easy to share research data on an ongoing basis.

Another achievement has been the opportunity to work out ethical
protocols. The requirements formalized by the University of Victoria
Human Research Ethics Board (HREB) are at times seen as paternalistic
and overly stringent by service providers who deal with multiple and
competing ethical issues on a daily basis. Negotiations around recruitment and informed consent, anonymity, and data management required
the most work. The HREB's requirements address the possibility that
participants may feel coerced to participate if recruited by front-line
personnel. At times, service providers found this requirement belittling
to their clients. Our three projects also required negotiations on how
to maintain the anonymity of participants (a core HREB requirement)
while attempting to contact them for their next interview. A successful strategy was to ask our NPO partners to help us with recruitment
since there was a high probability that participants' whereabouts were
known to these service-provider organizations. At the same time, we
had to ensure that participants would not be coerced into agreeing to
a follow-up interview or believe they would be cut off from services if
they did not participate.

Two data management issues – the separation of administrative and research data and access to the research data – were fundamental to guarantee the anonymity of our data; it required extensive negotiation among all collaborating partners. The research team members faced a temptation to mix data they collected with data collected by the regular administration of service programs when the latter were readily available. However, this temptation was tempered by the ethical problem of including administrative data on individuals without their explicit consent. Early in the research projects, there was discussion about who would have access to the collected research data because it was envisioned that the data would be useful for administrative or grant-writing purposes. Over time, we realized that there typically is little or no interest in accessing the data by anyone but immediate research team members. One advantage of this discovery was that research team members were able to produce reports on specialized topics using the data, such as the diversity of housing options needed by sex workers, upon request from front-line service groups.

Due to frequent staff turnover among front-line service workers, we learned that it is best to focus on developing enduring institutional partnerships that reach beyond specific individuals in either setting. Establishing institution-level partnerships allows collaboration over the long term and assures participating parties that institutional relationships will continue through periods of peak and slower research activity (LeGris et al., 2000).

To ensure stability, we learned that considerable time and resources must be set aside for engaging in face-to-face meetings in order to build and maintain mutual trust, continue negotiations of the parameters of the partnership, and keep participating parties engaged in each other's changing work environments and ever-challenging political landscapes. We also learned that establishing objectives, goals, and expectations about time investment at the outset of collaboration is extremely important.

An additional complication is that various non-profit organizations bring different values and philosophical orientations to the research process, which need to be openly communicated, negotiated, and duly honoured (Norman & Huerta, 2006). Failing to do so can result in limited investment on the part of NPOs, as representatives may conclude that their academic partners receive the bulk of the collaboration rewards. It is important, for example, to establish the degree of involvement that various partners wish to have in different aspects of the research process. Due to its limited administrative resources, CAFCA preferred to play a consultancy role in research design and translation at certain times and valued having research products prepared to meet its specific organizational needs. Yet, at other times, CAFCA staff and management played a greater role in guiding KT of research findings and identifying their practical implications. An example was an invitation to the academic researcher to present findings from the Risky Business study to CAFCA staff that were of direct relevance to recipients of CAFCA services. This resulted in a more general change in practice (i.e., to provide better evidence-based follow-up to clients). When involvement with research did not relate to real-life concerns, the results in terms of changes to practice at CAFCA were considerably diminished.

Another collaborating organization, PEERS, aimed for a very active role in research development, writing, and translation. This expectation rested on a philosophy of having experiential persons as the authors and developers of research that concerns them: 'nothing about us without us' (Boynton, 2002; Jürgens, 2005, p. 1). Over time, expectations for research engagement with PEERS have moved beyond simply participating in basic research design, helping recruit respondents, administering questionnaires, and obtaining honorariums for participants. PEERS' current desire is to engage more deeply in establishing research methods, data analysis and dissemination, along with equal involvement in presenting publications and research findings at academic conferences and co-writing for scholarly journals. Indeed, this chapter is one such collaborative effort.

We found it useful to establish annual research design and ethics workshops involving members of interested NPOs, researchers, graduate students, and HREB members. Such workshops served as a forum for fruitful dialogue about difficult research issues arising from the field and provided for co-learning about ethical procedures and protocols as they relate to hard-to-reach, vulnerable populations. We had the opportunity to organize one workshop and participate in another related to the Risky Business Project, both of which involved the active involvement of two community partners: CAFCA and the Victoria Youth Clinic. The results of one workshop formed a chapter in an edited book examining ethical challenges when researching vulnerable youth populations (Leadbeater et al., 2006). The other workshop resulted in the development of targeted health interventions for street-involved youth that are currently being implemented in the local area.

In summary, the academics and service providers involved in our research program independently realized that partnerships were not only advantageous to achieve their respective goals but also necessary in the current research and service-funding climate. Yet, the material and human resources required to maintain truly collaborative partnerships and to traverse the institutional, cultural, resource, and expectation differences between academic and NPO partners were considerable. We found over time that skilled knowledge brokers play a valuable role in maintaining partnerships.

Knowledge Brokers

Knowledge brokers are often paid research staff whose focus is linking community agencies with researchers and facilitating their interaction so that they are able to better understand each other's goals and professional cultures, influence each other's work, forge new partnerships, and promote the use of research-based evidence in decision-making (Lomas, 2007). Knowledge-brokering activities include finding the right players to influence research use in decision-making, bringing them together, creating and helping to sustain relationships among them, and assisting them to engage in collaborative problem solving (Lomas, 2007). Effective knowledge-brokering skills include having the capacity for networking, being trustworthy and credible, having concrete problem-solving and communication skills, and exhibiting proficiency in operating within and communicating about the cultures of both research and, in our case, non-profit community organizations. Knowledge brokers also participate in establishing research methodologies, particularly by helping the various partners understand each other's standards of rigour and negotiate shared research objectives, deliverables, and outcomes – including helping NPOs to conceptualize key research questions emerging from their practices that can be operationalized in research instruments (Lomas, 1997). Knowledge brokers assist partners to identify knowledge utilization and translation opportunities throughout the research process and also identify and assure that the research opportunities prioritized by community agencies are included as the research project develops and matures (Lomas, 2007).

We came to appreciate knowledge brokers as team members several years into our research program. We learned that academics and representatives of NPOs often have neither the time nor the expertise to carry out all the activities associated with a KT program. While the academic partners could readily identify the value of research findings and resources contained within compiled datasets, our NPO partner executive directors and their advisory board members were either unconvinced or had too little time to explore the research from a KT perspective. Academic partners had little policy and program practice expertise to guide them in effective KT. It was clear that our ongoing partnerships and KT goals required that we hire *bridge* individuals with specific skill sets dedicated to the task of KT. Knowledge brokers could attune our research to the needs of our hidden, marginalized, and highly transient research populations over the extensive duration of longitudinal research.

Individuals who have been employed as knowledge brokers on the above projects, two of whom are co-authors of this chapter (Casey and Burns), were recruited specifically because of their dual expertise in academic research and front-line service to marginalized persons. Knowledge brokers were well known to community partners and were familiar with the services delivered locally; they also had graduate-level training in research or a desire to pursue further education. Mentoring these individuals was a process that involved inclusion in various research roles over time (e.g., authorship of reports and grant applications, research instrument design, interviewing, and data analysis) as well as participation in numerous meetings and workshops where academic researchers and front-line service providers were brought together to talk about their common interests. In the case of the Stigma Study, a two-day pan-Canadian meeting of researchers and service providers to persons working in the sex industry was organized and provided both a strong base for understanding common research interests as well as exemplary networking opportunities for those involved.

Knowledge brokers on our research projects have found that successful KT depends on a number of principles and practices, which include establishing clear objectives and roles based on the perspectives of participating organizations. It is often beneficial to articulate roles, expectations, and objectives in an informal KT contract or statement of goals that knowledge brokers can then use as a tool to guide their work. This document can be revisited over the course of long-term research partnerships in order to assess progress and barriers. It can also be used as a basis for reorienting or increasing KT and collaboration activities, if required.

Given the institutional and cultural differences between academics and NPOs and the role of knowledge brokers in mediating these differences, it is essential that all partners are treated as equals and that they are able to conduct their work in an atmosphere of open communication and commitment to negotiation. In addition to having a diverse knowledge of research and service provision, knowledge brokers possess conflict mediation skills, the ability to focus on the larger goals of the partnership, and the vision to *stay the course* when conflicts or incompatibilities arise. In our experience, such conflicts ranged from differences in opinion over how to word questions or administer research tools, to debates regarding the risks affecting the vulnerable populations studied, and tensions over the degree to which the overall research objectives reflected academic or service provider knowledge frameworks. Having a strong footing in both worlds was fundamental for the knowledge brokers involved in the projects in facilitating the connection of differing cultural environments. Knowledge brokers familiar with the imperatives of both academic and NPO environments were essential because vulnerable and stigmatized populations (e.g., persons working in the sex industry, street youth, and the front-line service staff who serve them) are often cynical about research and have little time to devote to research concerns. During the studies we conducted, NPO staff serving these vulnerable populations stated that academic research was often too abstract to apply to their practice, that scholars had little appreciation for the constraints service providers face while carrying out their day-to-day activities, or that their staff did not have the academic training necessary to participate in research conversations. Thus, it was important that knowledge brokers not only were familiar to NPO staff but also that they had sufficient rapport, trust, and influence with the staff to overcome any existing aversion to research.

At the same time, while it might be tempting to recruit knowledge brokers employed by NPOs because of their potential influence within the organization, we have found that persons employed by NPOs in demanding positions often do not have to time to participate in KT activities to the fullest extent possible. In addition to promoting research on the front line, knowledge brokers also faced the challenging task of helping academic partners to align their research to the interests and current practices of NPOs so that the results would be regarded as practical in the NPO environment and, therefore, likely be integrated into the practice of front-line staff. Knowledge brokers must also have a solid knowledge of the imperatives that govern academic settings, including methodological rigour and ethical protocols, so that they can compatibly position NPO research interests within this framework (Lomas, 2007). Accustomed to orienting their research to the debates and standards within the existing scholarship of their discipline, academic researchers often find it difficult to merge their interests with the largely intuitive, experiential knowledge that influences the policy and practices of NPOs. The knowledge brokers for the three studies described above had to rely on their insider knowledge in order to negotiate these epistemological differences and other concerns, including bringing NPO staff and academic researchers together to discuss their respective concerns and to develop practical strategies to move forward when faced with an impasse.

While our knowledge brokers acknowledged the numerous rewards of such collaborative engagement, they noted that their roles were demanding and often difficult. It is important to have formal supports and sufficient resources available for knowledge brokers so that they can fulfil their responsibilities. Knowledge brokers also need time to become familiar with the operations of both the academic and non-profit worlds they must mediate. They need regular, face-to-face meetings with representatives of the research team in order to identify and assess progress on KT goals and activities. In addition, knowledge brokers should have opportunities to co-author conference or workshop presentations and research articles emerging from the projects. Finally, knowledge brokers should have the opportunity to participate in ongoing education opportunities that enhance their complex combination of networking, research, policy, and practice skills.

Discussion and Conclusions

Our experience working with an assortment of non-profit organizations across three projects investigating factors linked to the health and health care access of vulnerable populations has shown that to carry out KT in a meaningful way involves ongoing, resource-intensive, and strategic activities. These are best accomplished in the context of long-term institutional relationships, regular face-to-face exchanges, and a clearly negotiated, practical plan. While the KT literature is largely focused on research uptake by public sector policy and program experts in formal health care institutions and government bodies (Davis et al., 2003; Lavis et al., 2003; Pablos-Mendez & Shademani, 2006), we argue that organizations with limited resources located within the non-profit sector should also be included in the discussion. Their daily access to and hands-on knowledge of vulnerable populations, in addition to their unique capacity to translate findings directly into practice and program innovations are important reasons for inclusion.

Successes in research collaborations such as those described above include establishing an open and safe forum to share research activities and mutual support in drafting evidence-based funding proposals, assisting with policy development and staff education, and participating in educational and networking activities. They also include opportunities to co-present at academic conferences, co-organize workshops, collaborate on scholarly publications, and co-develop ethical protocols that deal with the potentially conflict-laden situation faced by front-line personnel.

Yet such collaborations are not seamless. We have encountered formidable challenges in carrying out KT work due to inadequate resources, having to find ways to negotiate the traditions of institutions with different values and cultures, and ensuring that rewards and sparse resources are equally distributed across all research partners. Employing knowledge brokers has taken us a long way in addressing these challenges, and we will continue to do this in the future. It has also been imperative for us to bring together representatives from academia and NPOs from the ranks of senior management and researchers as well as front-line providers and graduate students. In order to cement partnerships over the long haul, we have found that it is beneficial to have collaborators occupy different types of roles, ranging from advisory board member, paid research assistant or knowledge broker, and consultant to volunteer (for more on this strategy, see Jansson, Benoit, Casey, Phillips, & Burns, in press).

A few elements of this approach stand out for future development. The first element concerns the benefits and challenges of health research funding that involves two phases: a first phase of primary research, and a second phase of evaluating policy implications and program innovations. To date, research and program funding proposals between academics and NPOs have remained largely separate undertakings. Yet, one can envision the KT opportunities encompassed within a combined research and policy/program application enterprise. While this would, no doubt, raise new and complex challenges, combining research, policy/program, and evaluation activities would bring added focus to the KT agenda and compel partners to learn even more about each other's work and where it does and does not intersect. In addition, it would likely result in greater joint investment in the collaboration process from the beginning.

A second element requiring further development concerns how knowledge brokers develop their competence and how to best facilitate their important work. How do knowledge brokers amass their specialized and diverse skill sets; can this education be incorporated into academic and community-based settings to further enhance the capacity of those interested in applied research, health policy, and KT more generally? Lomas (2007) and others have begun this work; much more needs to be done, especially for collaborative partnerships involving the non-profit sector.

Finally, there is a need to achieve agreement among all parties involved as to how to measure the effectiveness of KT. This would put us in a position of evaluating the impact of alternative strategies of KT with the ultimate goal, at least in our case, of improving the health of the population.

REFERENCES

Boutilier, M.A., Badgley, R.F., Poland, B.D., & Tobin, S. (2001). Playing on shifting sand: Reflections on the impact of political shifts on community action and public health [Commentary]. *Canadian Journal of Public Health, 92*(2), 87–89.

Bowen, S., Martens, P.J., & The Need to Know Team. (2005). Demystifying knowledge translation: Learning from the community. *Journal of Health Services Research & Policy, 10*(4), 203–211.

Boynton, P.M. (2002). Life on the streets: The experiences of community researchers in a study of prostitution. *Journal of Community & Applied Social Psychology, 12*(1), 1–12.

Choi, B.C.K. (2005). Understanding the basic principles of knowledge translation [Speaker's Corner]. *Journal of Epidemiology and Community Health, 59*(2), 93.

Clancy, C. (2006). Closing the knowledge translation gap will help to improve health service delivery. *Bulletin of the World Health Organization, 84*(8), 662–663.

Davis, D., Evans, M., Jadad, A., Perrier, L., Rath, D., Ryan, D., et al. (2003). The case for knowledge translation: Shortening the journey from evidence to effect. *British Medical Journal, 327*(7405), 33–35.

Denner, J., Cooper, C.R., Lopez, E.M., & Dunbar, N. (1999). Beyond 'giving science away': How university – community partnerships inform youth programs, research, and policy. *Social Policy Report, 13*(1), 1–17.

Ebata, A.T. (1996). Making university – community collaborations work: Challenges for institutions and individuals. *Journal of Research on Adolescence, 6*(1), 71–79.

Estabrooks, C.A., Thompson, D.S., Lovely, J.J.E., & Hofmeyer, A. (2006). A
   guide to knowledge translation theory. *Journal of Continuing Education in the
   Health Professions, 26*(1), 25–36.
Graham, I.D., Logan, J., Harrison, M.B., Straus, S.E., Tetroe, J., Caswell, W.,
   et al. (2006). Lost in knowledge translation: Time for a map? *Journal of
   Continuing Education in the Health Professions, 26*(1), 13–24.
Greenhalgh, T., Robert, G., MacFarlane, F., Bate, P., & Kyriakidou, O. (2004).
   Diffusion of innovations in service organizations: Systematic review and
   recommendations. *Milbank Quarterly, 82*(4), 581–629.
Henriksson, L., Wrede, S., & Burau, V. (2006). Understanding professional
   projects in welfare service work: Revival of old professionalism? *Gender,
   Work, & Organization, 13*(2), 174–192.
Jansson, M., Benoit, C., Casey, L., Phillips, R., & Burns, D. (in press). In for the
   long haul: Knowledge translation between academic and non-profit organizations. *Qualitative Health Research.*
Jürgens, R. (2005). *'Nothing about us without us' – Greater, meaningful involvement of people who use illegal drugs: A public health, ethical, and human rights
   imperative.* Toronto, ON: Canadian HIV/AIDS Legal Network. Retrieved
   June 20, 2008, from, http://www.aidslaw.ca/publications/publicationsdo
   cEN.php?ref=85
Lavis, J.N., Davies, H., Oxman, A., Denis, J.-L., Golden-Biddle, K., & Ferlie, E.
   (2005). Towards systematic reviews that inform health care management
   and policy-making. *Journal of Health Services & Research Policy, 10*(Suppl. 1),
   35–48.
Lavis, J.N., Posada, F.B., Haines, A., & Osei, E. (2004). Use of research to inform public policymaking. *Lancet, 364*(9445), 1615–1621.
Lavis, J.N., Robertson, D., Woodside, J.M., McLeod, C.B., & Abelson, J. (2003).
   How can research organizations more effectively transfer research knowledge to decision-makers? *Milbank Quarterly, 81*(2), 221–248.
Leadbeater, B., Banister, E.M., Benoit, C., Jansson, M., Marshall, E.A., &
   Riecken, T. (Eds.). (2006). *Ethical issues in community-based research with chil-
   dren and youth.* Toronto, ON: University of Toronto Press.
LeGris, J., Weir, R., Browne, G., Gafni, A., Stewart, L., & Easton, S. (2000).
   Developing a model of collaborative research: The complexities and chal-
   lenges of implementation. *International Journal of Nursing Studies, 37*(1), 65–79.
Lomas, J. (1997). *Improving research dissemination and uptake in the health sec-
   tor: Beyond the sound of one hand clapping.* (C97-1). Hamilton, ON: McMaster
   University Centre for Health Economics and Policy Analysis.
Lomas, J. (2007). The in-between world of knowledge brokering. *British
   Medical Journal, 334*(7585), 129–132.

Martens, P.J., & Roos, N.P. (2005). When health services researchers and policy makers interact: Tales from the tectonic plates. *Healthcare Policy/ Politiques de Santé, 1*(1), 72–84.

Norman, C., & Huerta, T. (2006). Knowledge transfer & exchange through social networks: Building foundations for a community of practice within tobacco control. *Implementation Science, 1*(1), 20.

Pablos-Mendez, A., & Shademani, R. (2006). Knowledge translation in global health. *Journal of Continuing Education in the Health Professions, 26*(1), 81–86.

Rycroft-Malone, J., Kitson, A., Harvey, G., McCormack, B., Seers, K., Titchen, A., et al. (2002). Ingredients for change: Revisiting a conceptual framework. *Quality and Safety in Health Care, 11*(2), 174–180.

Small, S.A. (1996). Collaborative, community-based research on adolescents: Using research for community change. *Journal of Research on Adolescence, 6*(1), 9–22.

Tetroe, J.M., Graham, I.D., Foy, R., Robinson, N., Eccles, M.P., Wensing, M., et al. (2008). Health research funding agencies' support and promotion of knowledge translation: An international study. *Milbank Quarterly, 86*(1), 125–155.

Wrede, S., Benoit, C., & Einarsdòttir, T. (2008). Equity and dignity in maternity care provision in Canada, Finland, and Iceland. *Canadian Journal of Public Health, 99*(Suppl. 2), 16–21.

3 Cross-Cultural Journeys: Transferring and Exchanging Knowledge among Researchers and Community Partners

E. ANNE MARSHALL AND FRANCIS GUENETTE

Supports and barriers to developing and sustaining knowledge translation (KT) have been identified by several authors (Estabrooks, Thompson, Lovely, & Hofmeyer, 2006; Landry, Amara, & Lamari, 2001; Lavis, Robertson, Woodside, McLeod, & Abelson, 2003). One barrier is the diversity of players or stakeholders, especially in community-oriented projects. Describing the challenge of this diversity, Ginsburg and Gorostiaga (2001) proposed a *two-culture* thesis – that university and community are two different cultures that need to be bridged. Shonkoff (2000) identified three cultures: university researchers, community practitioners, and policymakers. University researchers, community-based practitioners, and policymakers have been characterized as being in different camps; competing priorities, assumptions, and divergent norms lead to difficulties and communication gaps among the groups. Although a number of authors have described these gaps and have recommended specific strategies to improve communication among the players (Landry et al.; Lavis et al.; Shonkoff), we believe that the underlying contextual or *cultural* issues that contribute to and maintain the gaps are not often acknowledged.

We would argue that *multiple* cultures, not simply two or three, are involved in community-based research (CBR) projects, and that differences among these multiple cultures must be addressed in order to transfer and exchange knowledge successfully. In this chapter, we draw from our experiences in university – community research projects to address this issue. We will begin with a discussion and clarification of terms. We then describe our particular research culture, including our team context and two of our multidisciplinary projects. This is followed by a discussion of principles and practices of knowledge translation and exchange in our cross-cultural research journeys with colleagues, students, and community partners. Examples from our CBR projects illustrate these processes. We also discuss lessons learned and implications for CBR. The chapter concludes with a summary of what we have found to be effective for knowledge exchange and uptake, particularly for multidisciplinary research projects.

Our cross-cultural analysis is guided by Chambers' (2000) broad and inclusive definition of culture as 'those understandings and ways of understanding that are judged to be characteristic of a discernable group' (p. 852). Culture is nuanced and complex; it encompasses evolving values, norms, language, perceived power, role expectations, priorities, and practices that shape members' behaviours and ways of understanding (Pedersen, 1991).

We have adopted a cross-cultural lens in our CBR with youth and families on topics related to life, health, and work transitions. Shonkoff (2000) maintains that challenges to establishing effective knowledge exchange processes in research reflect the value differences embedded in different cultural world views. Thus, building and sustaining cross-cultural research relationships requires that we identify shared values and assumptions, demonstrate mutual respect, accommodate differences, practise open communication, learn each other's language, and anticipate potential problems. Moreover, consistent with Sue and Sue's (2007) assertion that there is as much if not more diversity within a culture as between cultures, we have found that projects involving multidisciplinary university research teams demand translation processes *within* the team as well as *between* or *among* other stakeholders, such as community partners and policymakers. Groups and cultures outside the academy are even more diverse. As Baskin (2007) points out, the universal terms *Aboriginal* or *Indigenous* can be problematic because there are many differences among these peoples with regard to cultural practices, lifestyles, languages, beliefs, and opinions. Community agencies, government bodies, non-government organizations (NGOs), and other non-academic groups represent considerable variations in size, formality of operations, financial resources, personnel, and priorities. These differences affect all aspects of research and are particularly critical to consider when transferring and exchanging knowledge.

Knowledge Translation Terminology

Despite the growing literature on KT and its processes and mechanisms, little consensus exists with respect to terminology across disciplines.

A plethora of terms have been used to describe the movement of knowledge between people and organizations, including knowledge translation, knowledge transfer, knowledge transmission, knowledge transformation, knowledge utilization, knowledge uptake, knowledge exchange, and knowledge application (Estabrooks et al., 2006; Landry et al., 2001). Some terms appear to have generally accepted meanings; knowledge transmission, for example, tends to refer to a one-way process of moving research knowledge from researchers to practitioners or from practitioners to policymakers, whereas knowledge exchange suggests a reciprocal process.

In our team's CBR context, we prefer the term knowledge transfer and exchange (KTE), as described by Kiefer et al. (2005): the interactive exchange of knowledge between research users and research producers. We believe that the phrase *transfer and exchange* illustrates the diverse and developing nature of communication about research. Sometimes there is a direct *transfer* of knowledge, such as giving information or explaining a procedure; at other times, there is a two-way *exchange* of knowledge, such as a joint discussion of data implications. This approach to collaborative sharing of knowledge among researchers, community partners, and decision-makers promotes mutual learning and effective research partnerships (Graham et al., 2006; Mitton et al., 2007).

Our Research Team Culture

In this section, we will describe our research team, projects, and partners in order to provide background relating to the priorities and parameters that shaped our processes and decisions. Our team is situated within a Faculty of Education at a medium-sized university in Western Canada; our disciplinary affiliation is counselling psychology. Our disciplinary culture emphasizes knowledge and professional skill development in mental health settings. The particular research we conduct focuses on life, health, and work transitions for young people and families in urban and rural contexts, including several Aboriginal communities. Anne Marshall (the first author) is a university faculty member and the research team leader; Francis Guenette (the second author) is a doctoral candidate who coordinates the operation of several research projects. Other team members include master's and doctoral graduate students, undergraduate and graduate research assistants, community partners, and faculty collaborators in our own and other academic departments and institutions. Several subsets of team members work together at any given time; these groups evolve and often re-form for subsequent research projects. Two of our multidisciplinary CBR projects are described below; the KTE illustrative examples used in this chapter are drawn from our experiences in these projects.

The Healthy Youth Study

The Healthy Youth (HY) study focused on the health priorities and decision-making processes among urban youth in the context of social and economic restructuring. This project was one of seven linked together in an interdisciplinary Community Alliance for Health Research project (Leadbeater et al., 2006). Our study concentrated on adolescents' experiences of physical and mental health risks, stress, health decisions, and coping skills. Focus groups, key informants, and individual interviews were our main data sources (Marshall & Shepard, 2006). At the outset, our community partners were three non-profit community-service agency partners: two youth employment agencies and one sexualized violence prevention and education program. Unfortunately, two agencies closed within two years of the project's initiation, due to budget cuts and social services restructuring. Lack of funding is a serious challenge for many youth-focused non-profit organizations. Closure of these agencies mid-project created KT challenges due to changes in personnel and procedures. As a result, we had to adjust our initial research schedule and make sure that new team members had opportunities to contribute to project planning.

Coasts Under Stress Study

Coasts Under Stress (CUS) was a large interdisciplinary research project that investigated the impact of social, economic, and environmental restructuring on the health of individuals and communities. In this project, *restructuring* was defined as small to large-scale societal shifts that resulted in significant changes to, for example, forestry and fishing practices, work availability, social supports, and community cohesion. The entire CUS team included over fifty faculty co-investigators from the East and West Coasts of Canada representing social sciences, natural sciences, and humanities, plus a host of postdoctoral fellows, research associates, community partners, graduate students, research assistants, and staff (Ommer & The Coasts Under Stress Research Project Team, 2007).

Our team's particular study within the larger CUS project focused on supports and barriers facing Aboriginal and non-Aboriginal youth aged sixteen to twenty-five in rural and small coastal communities during school-to-work transitions (Marshall, 2002). Community partners included two rural school districts, three secondary schools, three First Nations bands, a community development agency, and a non-profit environmental education society. Data were obtained from a rural youth survey (Harrison, 2005) and from individual and focus group interviews with youth, teachers, parents, and community residents (see Marshall; Ommer & Team; Rawdah, Guenette, & Marshall, 2007). One key finding was the need for information and support from adults to help young people translate their skills, experiences, and goals from their school environments to the larger contexts of work and community participation. For example, parents could provide information about local employment patterns and community business people could offer advice about the training needed for specific jobs. A common barrier experienced in these small and often remote communities was access to a range of post-secondary and work training opportunities. Teachers and other adults assisted young people to identify transferable knowledge and skills and to discern multiple potential outcomes.

Knowledge Transfer and Exchange within the Research Team

As Wu, Hsu, and Yeh (2007) observed, there has been minimal investigation of KT at the team level. Within our particular research team culture, we have observed an increasing integration of KTE processes over time. Our involvement in CBR has sensitized us to the importance and variety of cultural influences that shape research teams and projects. We developed an approach that socializes graduate students and undergraduate research assistants (RAs) to the team research culture and prepares them for work in the field. Prior to their fieldwork, new members are briefed about our research objectives, methodologies, team culture, and individual goals. A binder of information, forms, policies, and procedures was available to everyone; new and experienced team members were encouraged to add their suggestions. We have adopted a *cascading model* of mentorship where doctoral students mentor master's students and they, in turn, mentor undergraduate RAs. Graduate students and RAs work with a more experienced team member and gradually assume more responsibilities and independence. To promote maximum learning exchange, every graduate student and

RA participates in all research activities, including literature searches, preparing bibliographies, proposal writing, interviewing, transcribing, creating posters, writing scholarly papers, and presenting findings. This approach facilitates KTE among team members, regardless of their level of experience, and enables graduate students and RAs to enter a field-based research experience or a scholarly conference presentation with confidence.

The team is constantly evolving as projects end and students complete their degrees and move on. New members are socialized to the team culture and then change that culture as they contribute their own knowledge and experience. Our developmental process is guided by Johnson and Johnson's (2005) model of *task* (instrumental) and *maintenance* (relationship) functions; maintaining a balance between task achievement and relationship-building promotes optimal team productivity. This balancing approach is mirrored in our relationships with research colleagues across various teams as well as with our community partners; we have learned that when outcome goals are not achieved, maintenance has usually been neglected and needs attention. Within the team, we practise the same KTE principles and strategies that we utilize with academic colleagues and community partners in the field. In other words, we negotiate particular roles and responsibilities and provide support and mentoring. To demonstrate their learning, individual team members maintain a research portfolio that provides evidence of how they met knowledge and skill-learning goals. The portfolio serves as a record of research skill acquisition and becomes part of our team's research culture history that is shared with new team members.

Knowledge Transfer and Exchange with Academic Research Colleagues

The increasing emphasis on collaborative interdisciplinary research within and across academic institutions emphasizes the importance of KTE processes. Faculty and disciplinary cultures have certain scholarly traditions, expectations, power structures, and reward systems. Within our Faculty of Education, for example, we have department-specific tenure and promotion requirements that influence how faculty members conduct research and the types of dissemination products that are valued. Within our counselling discipline, there are differing theoretical frameworks that shape research design and procedures (Ginsburg & Gorostiaga, 2001). Our research colleagues from disciplines in other faculties have their particular cultural lenses through which they view research methods, processes, and outcomes. It is imperative that we find common ground and negotiate differences in order to maximize our ability to collaborate and facilitate KTE among interdisciplinary research team members.

In our experience, there has been insufficient attention given to illuminating the differences among team members' assumptions and strongly held values and how these impact research decision-making and problem-solving processes (Shonkoff, 2000). For example, in the CUS project, economists, fish biologists, educators, geographers, and ethnobotanists each proposed different approaches to the issue of how to measure community health. Frank discussion and consideration of several methodological alternatives enabled us to reach agreement on varied and complementary data collection methods. Sharing research documents such as consent forms and memoranda of understanding led to templates and examples that all team members could access through a common website. Accompanying colleagues on a field trip or demonstrating a community interview technique promoted appreciation for the benefits of collaborative approaches among all team members.

Even within disciplines, methodological differences can serve as barriers to research collaboration. For instance, quantitative and qualitative researchers in counselling or educational psychology may privilege their own methodologies, and proponents of one approach may devalue the contributions of the other. Laboratory researchers and community-based researchers can have strong beliefs about the superiority of their particular methods. Without ongoing acknowledgement of these value differences, players can make assumptions leading to misunderstandings that impede progress. Establishing commonalities as well as areas of difference in a respectful manner is critical for success. On both the CUS and HY projects, we found that exchange of knowledge regarding how team members would operate together decreased the possibility of friction and unease that may not only have hindered our progress but also could have rippled out to community partners. In research meetings, graduate student seminars, and brown bag lunches, we literally and figuratively mapped out our plans and procedures together.

Knowledge Transfer and Exchange with Community Partners

Although differences among our disciplines needed to be addressed in our collaborative projects, there is nevertheless much shared culture among academics. However, conducting research with community partners presents further cultural challenges and a need for close attention to knowledge process differences. What is acceptable in one setting may not be in another. With publicly funded agencies, personnel and policy changes can occur frequently, in contrast to the usually slow pace of change in university settings. Researchers need to be vigilant and attentive to potential variations that may affect the research process. It is imperative that they avoid making assumptions based on previous knowledge or experiences with other groups that might appear to be similar.

·For example, our team carried out numerous group and individual interviews to investigate career aspirations of secondary school students in partnership with several secondary schools (Guenette, Marshall, & Morley, 2007; Marshall, 2002). However, the ways we set up and conducted interviews with an honours biology class in an urban school was different from our approach in a small, rural school with a sizeable Aboriginal population. These two groups of students had unique experiences and knowledge to impart, and we needed a high degree of community and cultural awareness to know how to best facilitate their participation. In another instance, there were several staff changes at one community partner agency. Each new staff person had somewhat different experiences and priorities with respect to the ongoing research that necessitated additional meetings and renegotiation of data-gathering and dissemination procedures. In these two examples, our community partner contacts provided invaluable information about the culture of the setting so that we were informed beforehand of the people, processes, and politics that may have affected our project.

Attention to cultural protocol and practices is essential when partnering with Aboriginal communities (see chapter 10 by Moewaka Barnes, Henwood, Kerr, McManus, & McCreanor, and chapter 11 by Smylie in this volume). A number of scholars have called attention to issues such as exploitation, community damage, inaccurate results, and ethical divergence related to research studies focused on Indigenous populations and communities (Brant Castellano, 1986; Hoare, Levy, & Robinson, 1993; Kirkness & Barnhardt, 1991; McCormick, 1998). Understandably, the history of these difficulties has resulted in research being viewed with mistrust and suspicion by Aboriginal peoples. Because of this, we embarked on a learning and consultation process in the early research planning stages. The assistance from people referred to by one partner as *community champions* was instrumental in supporting the partnerships. They offered contextual and cultural information and helped us connect with band councils and local community agencies. We included Aboriginal and non-Aboriginal graduate students and RAs on our research teams. In our experience, trust-building and negotiating agreements with our Aboriginal community partners required more time and more meetings than with our non-Aboriginal partners.

Sometimes, *researcher overlap* occurs, where different researchers or teams may be working with the same community partner on different research questions. On the CUS project, for example, one school district was partnered with three different university researchers: one interviewing teachers about their changing work demands, one working with elders and elementary school students about traditional plant knowledge, and one (our team) investigating future life and work plans of secondary students. In this situation, the three researchers had to coordinate requests for meetings with school district personnel for initial permission, data collection, and dissemination to strike a balance between efficiency and project integrity. The three of us were not always able to travel to the district at the same time, so each of us conveyed messages and documents for one another on a regular basis. Two of us shared a graduate student RA who lived in the district, which helped facilitate coordination and save some travel costs. This overlap had several benefits, but it demanded that the researchers keep each other informed of progress and developments. An omission or misstep on the part of one team or one RA could affect the other. Again, this emphasizes the need for effective communication in order to facilitate smooth working relationships and knowledge exchange with both research colleagues and community partners.

Cultural Field Trips

When starting with a new community partner or faculty collaborator, we schedule a field trip to their territory. With one community partner, a youth employment service agency, we arranged a meeting at its offices at the beginning of the project. Before the meeting, the university team members discussed potential roles, procedures, and outcomes, and also generated a list of questions and proposed activities. We looked at their website and reviewed some of their informational documents. At the meeting, we toured the facility, read some of their literature, spoke briefly with staff, and observed general client interactions. We then met with key staff members to share impressions, ask questions, explore the research aims, discuss goals, set priorities, and agree upon a rough timeline for the project. A few digital photographs provided a visual record of the visit and were used in a research newsletter and on a dissemination poster. This visit served as a concrete demonstration of our commitment to understanding and involving the partner agency from the beginning. In addition, we had a clearer picture of their setting, clientele, priorities, and services. After the visit, we sent a note of thanks along with a summary of the discussion and agreed-upon next steps.

Regular, face-to-face meetings resulted in several advantages for researchers and for our community partners. Partners saw a tangible commitment to community research, experienced the willingness of university researchers to leave their institution, and had an opportunity to show us important aspects of their culture – their setting, activities, and services. We in turn observed our partners in their daily work environment, gained some understanding of their clientele, ascertained their capacity related to the project, and built trust. After such meetings, we would send a brief summary that accomplished multiple purposes: it confirmed the research partnership, furnished a record of the research process, provided an opportunity to correct inaccuracies or highlight missing elements, served as a draft for a partnership contract or memorandum of understanding, and could be used in later reports or publications. One summary on the CUS project included topics covered, action steps, unresolved issues, data ownership principles, and future meeting dates. Recording these elements encouraged dialogue and follow-up; this contributed to the success of our research partnership and to the project overall.

Visits to community partner settings also provided opportunities to observe and address *within* culture differences. Within an agency, for instance, an administrator who authorized our research collaboration had somewhat different priorities than the service provider, who was our primary contact for the project. We had to make sure that both priorities were incorporated into our research plan. Within our Aboriginal partner communities, band council members and residents often had divergent views on issues such as education and health care delivery. Teachers in the same school had varying interests and capacities related to research projects. Real and perceived power differences operated in all settings, and these needed to be acknowledged for potential project impact. Successful partnerships require sensitivity to within-setting diversity and a willingness to work with a variety of goals and outcomes.

Field trips provided important learning experiences for graduate students and RAs. Opportunities to participate in the research process promoted KTE. In addition, since many of our team members were aspiring professionals, community contacts were essential for goodwill and visibility. Anne Marshall was a community practitioner before entering the academy; her experience has been an asset in undertaking CBR involving mental health service provider partners. For the CUS follow-up project, Francis Guenette was gathering data in three coastal communities in which she had lived and worked. Her local knowledge helped to develop and sustain our community partner relationships.

Lessons Learned from Cross-Cultural Knowledge Transfer and Exchange

Our experiences with complex interdisciplinary projects suggest several key practices that can help researchers navigate partnerships with academic colleagues and community partners. These include building and maintaining relationships, addressing power differences, reciprocating, communicating purposefully, and avoiding assumptions.

Building and Maintaining Relationships

The quality of researcher and partner relationships is a critical element of successful KTE (Bringle & Hatcher, 2002; Gowdy, 2006; Landry et al., 2001; Lasker, Weiss, & Miller, 2001; Mitton et al., 2007). Adopting a cross-cultural orientation helps researchers and community partners focus on the need for continual negotiation of understandings and procedures throughout the research process. In many instances, there are multiple cultural aspects at play. For example, as researchers and research assistants from an urban university setting, we may have assumed that we understood the culture of an urban-based, funded, mental health agency serving adolescents. However, only through ongoing mutual exchanges did we come to know whether our expectations regarding priorities, resources, and clientele were accurate. Similarly, when partnering with a rural, lay counselling, volunteer agency that provided service for young to early adult populations through the CUS project, we had many factors to consider. Their broad service mandate coupled with very limited resources necessitated flexibility and practical limitations with respect to research goals and plans, both of which had to accommodate their fluctuating finances and constant personnel changes.

In Aboriginal research contexts, relationship-building was extremely important, given the long and difficult history of colonization and appropriation of traditional knowledge. On the CUS project, for example, careful attention to protocol was essential; we first obtained an introduction to the community through a professional, social, or familial contact. The next step was either an exchange of documents, such as proposals, instruments, and interview questions, or a meeting with anywhere from one to fifty community members. Travel to the community for discussion of research objectives and procedures demonstrated respect for Indigenous knowledge and social systems; face-to-face meetings were often preferred. These processes often involved considerable time and expense; however, as McCormick (1998) contends, without this commitment to an active demonstration of cultural respect, non-Aboriginal researchers will be perpetuating the colonial and unethical practice of knowledge appropriation. When collaborating with Aboriginal communities, we also recognized the cultural importance of bringing gifts and sharing food – these practices had to be built into our research design and budgets.

When forming new research relationships, we found that the identification of shared values and differences among the participants (Graham et al., 2006) is important at the outset. On the interdisciplinary CUS project, our overarching question was: What are the health risks and benefits associated with social and economic restructuring in coastal communities? We had to learn each other's disciplinary language and research methodologies in order to reach consensus on what was to be studied and how. This transfer and exchange carried through to dissemination of results and writing joint publications. Building these relationships led to later collaborations on new research projects and partnerships.

Addressing Power Differences

Power is a central aspect of cross-cultural relationships (Gaventa & Cornwall, 2001; Marshall & Batten, 2004). In KTE contexts, this includes power differences within and between academic researchers and community groups. Although university academics are often seen as powerful and well-resourced, politics, power dynamics, and reward systems within the academy, along with government policymakers and national research granting councils present substantial challenges, especially for new and untenured faculty (Martin, 1998). Competition for research grants, publication, recognition, and resources is increasing; this situation is not conducive to collegial cooperation.

Perceived or actual power differences among academic researchers related to discipline, seniority, tenure status, or administrative position present real barriers to collaborative relationships. For example, our team had a relatively minor role within a natural science disciplinary team study on the CUS research project. Although our contribution was acknowledged verbally as being important, it appeared that our social science disciplinary background was not viewed as being as rigorous as natural science training. Members of the other team listened politely; however, we felt that our participation in the project was merely a form of tokenism. Our team tended to be forgotten with regard to team meeting planning, publication drafts, and decision processes. In cross-disciplinary settings, it is important that inclusive practices be followed by all co-investigators so that the participation of all those who are involved is acknowledged and respected (Marshall, Shepard, & Leadbeater, 2006).

Students and RAs can be disempowered due to their dependency on faculty and supervisor support for program completion and funding. Although these power differentials are largely structural, clear and respectful communication of shared goals and expectations helps to avoid the pitfalls of relationships where power distribution is unequal. We believe that it is the responsibility of those with more power to initiate open dialogue early in team relationships related to expectations, responsibilities, and division of roles (Marshall & Batten, 2004). With respect to KTE, our team atmosphere of trust and willingness to work towards common goals benefited from early and ongoing discussions related to dissemination roles and authorship credit (Gaventa & Cornwall, 2001). For example, the Healthy Youth project co-investigators initiated a discussion that led to authorship guidelines explicitly describing our agreed-upon policies and processes for determining authorship and for resolving conflicts (University of Victoria Centre for Youth & Society, n.d.).

University researchers entering a community are often seen as experts who possess knowledge and power (Martin, 1998). This perceived power could be a barrier to establishing trust and reciprocal working relationships in CBR contexts. Communicating to community partners that we see them as experts regarding their own community's needs and resources has helped us to establish more equitable research relationships. Attending to power and protocols is particularly important in Aboriginal communities (Brant Castellano, 1986; Hudson & Taylor-Henley, 2001; Piquemal, 2001). Crigger, Holcomb, and Weiss (2001) suggest that the notion of power can be less problematic for a community when researchers join the community rather than enter as experts or interlopers. In view of this, our team members spent time interacting informally and socially at our community research sites. We attended community functions and frequented local businesses. Whenever possible, we hired local RAs to provide background information, facilitate meetings, and conduct interviews. On the other side, our perceived power at times benefitted our community partners. On both the Coasts Under Stress and Healthy Youth projects, our partnership agreements were used to leverage additional funding for partners' community programs. We have also been asked to make presentations of our research results to municipal councils, Aboriginal bands, and other community groups in support of local programs and services for youth.

Reciprocating

The notion of reciprocity is integral to knowledge exchange in CBR (Hudson & Taylor-Henley, 2001; Lasker et al., 2001). Among academic partners, shared publications and student training are often part of research collaborations (Marshall et al., 2006). Typically, we negotiated in-kind contributions or services to give to our community partners rather than making cash contributions. Not-for-profit agencies and NGOs often have meagre budgets and limited time to write proposals for funding. Therefore, we assisted one of our HY partners with writing a grant application, which was a mutually beneficial opportunity for knowledge exchange; it provided an opportunity for both parties to learn more about each other's goals and procedures, which in turn led to methodological refinements to our shared research project.

In another illustration, our team negotiated an exchange of knowledge with a youth group that was planning a community engagement and action event. We adapted one of our Possible Selves group data-gathering exercises that had originally been developed for career planning and decision-making (Marshall & Guenette, 2008). In this adaptation, we created a visioning activity in which the youth explored their hopes, fears, and expectations about the upcoming event. They recorded their goals and intended outcomes on paper and through digital photographs. Through this exercise, we as researchers gained insight about the goals and needs of youth in this community, provided a skill-building experience for them, and were able to pilot test a new data-gathering tool. In turn, our young community partners learned a novel approach to decision-making, generated ideas for their presentation, and went on to stage a very successful community event. We sought such opportunities for reciprocity and capacity-building with community partners when in the field for data collection or dissemination. These mutual KTE experiences inevitably strengthened our working relationships.

Communicating Purposefully

It is well accepted that communication is a key factor in successful KTE relationships (Ginsburg & Gorostiaga, 2001; Graham et al., 2006; Landry et al., 2001). We have found, however, little discussion of how the cultural contexts of our research colleagues and partners affect decisions regarding when, what, and how to communicate. As Kiefer et al. (2005) suggest, the specifics of the communication process need to be worked out among team members. We typically drew up a joint plan for communicating in the early stages of a project. Most of our community partners were from the non-profit sector and seldom had time for detailed replies or prolonged discussion; however, it was essential to keep everyone in the communication loop. Some team members were more active in certain phases of the research than in others. Our graduate and undergraduate students took an active role in maintaining open and regular communication. We also found it expeditious to have a primary contact person at the agency or partner site and a similar primary contact person on the research team. These two individuals had frequent contact and served as knowledge brokers for the project team members; their role was salient for coordinating the steps of the research work plan.

Use of technology also supported the communication process. For example, we established a *Moodle* website that allowed research team members to share information, questions, and research outputs in a timely, creative fashion. Managed by the research team coordinator (Francis Guenette), the *Moodle* site provided a secure location for photos, documents, data analysis, presentations, and publication drafts that all the team members could easily access. Membership to the site was adapted as team composition changed.

Among academic collaborators, scholarly books and journals are familiar and expected sources of information and targets for dissemination.

With community partners, however, we found that we needed a wider variety of knowledge sources in order to promote culturally relevant KTE. These sources included community newspapers, local radio and television broadcasts, newsletters, websites, community directories, brochures, and town hall meetings. Gathering artefacts and attending local events yielded information about community structure, decision processes, and local (cultural) norms. In addition, such cross-cultural information-gathering helped identify potential key informants for research purposes. For dissemination in community locations, our community partners strongly favoured posters, pamphlets, short articles, and community workshops over peer-reviewed journal publications.

Avoiding Assumptions

In cross-cultural relationships, unstated assumptions can frequently lead to difficulties (Diller, 2007; Pedersen, 1991; Sue & Sue, 2007). In research collaborations, the enthusiasm of a new partnership or idea, or the ever-present press of time, can lead to mistaken assumptions about shared knowledge or agreement on procedures. Such misunderstandings can be particularly problematic with community partners (Bringle & Hatcher, 2002). The following two examples serve to illustrate how assumptions of understanding on our part as researchers led to knowledge breakdown.

In the first instance, we corresponded via email with a community member some distance away to arrange a partnership agreement that would include a group interview in the community, a joint conference presentation, and a journal article submission. We soon realized the limitations of using email as our sole method of communication. When we arrived for the group interview, it became obvious that the expectations of several group participants were different from what we thought were our agreed-upon objectives for the research interview. They believed that we were meeting to help them finance a community recreation site. In the email correspondence, we had failed to explain the purpose and process of a research interview in sufficient detail. In addition, our community partner thought that the upcoming conference was a fundraising opportunity for his community group. We had not clarified the meaning of an academic conference presentation, and it obviously meant something quite different to him. We resolved the misunderstandings through discussion and negotiation and then proceeded to a mutually successfully partnership; however, our differing expectations and needs could have had serious repercussions on our ability to have an effective exchange of knowledge. From this experience, we learned about the need to clarify mutual understanding of terms and procedures as early as possible. The use of multiple communication formats (such as phone, fax, and email) can help facilitate this process.

Another example involved a partnership with a secondary school teacher. A colleague on the larger project team had previously secured the research participation agreement. When we began our phase of the data collection, however, it became apparent that we had made some assumptions about potential research outcomes. Our expectations as researchers focused on data-gathering, analysis, and the dissemination of results in scholarly and community settings. The teacher had additional priorities, including establishing internship placement opportunities for her students, finding a sustainable site for future student placements, and obtaining photos for program fundraising and promotional activities. Once we moved beyond our initial assumptions to clarify and expand the potential outcomes from the research partnership, we developed a more effective knowledge exchange and a mutually satisfying research partnership.

Concluding Thoughts

Berwick (2003) maintains that innovation usually comes from outside a system, whereas implementation of that innovation comes from the inside. Knowledge transfer and exchange with academic colleagues, community research partners, policymakers, and other stakeholders can provide the impetus for change within the academy. We believe that bringing a cultural lens to KTE is a good example of such an opportunity. As Fisher and colleagues (2002) suggest, this necessitates consulting broadly throughout a research project, from conceptualization to dissemination. In health research contexts, it means intentionally applying a cultural perspective to the evaluation of research risks and benefits, developing respectful informed consent procedures, creating culturally appropriate guidelines relating to confidentiality, addressing equity and power differences, and incorporating diverse forms of knowledge. All of these practices must be negotiated together *with* research colleagues, students, community partners, service providers, policymakers, and end-user groups.

Adopting a cross-cultural lens has had a profound impact on our research team. We have been welcomed into research and community settings where we have gained a first-hand appreciation of how multiple cultural perspectives can be, and indeed, must be incorporated into research design and processes. Colleagues and community partners have been patient with us as we went through the learning process. Moreover, we have found that this perspective has transformed our work in other spheres of clinical and teaching practice. Respectful and reciprocal practices in CBR can help to break down institutional silos of knowledge so that the richness, potential, and diversity of knowledge can be shared across participating groups. We can maximize effective communication and uptake of research results if we work with, rather than against, the diversity within a team, between teams, and among researchers, community partners, and policymakers. Using a cultural lens sensitizes all groups to seek common ground and to value differences as we strive to share knowledge for societal health and well-being. The outcomes are well worth the effort.

REFERENCES

Baskin, C. (2007). Working together in the circle: Challenges and possibilities within mental health ethics. *Journal of Ethics in Mental Health, 2*(2), 1–4.

Berwick, D.M. (2003). Disseminating innovations in health care. *Journal of the American Medical Association, 289*(15), 1969–1975.

Brant Castellano, M. (1986). Collective wisdom: Participatory research and Canada's native people. *IDRC Reports, 15*(3), 24–25.

Bringle, R.G., & Hatcher, J.A. (2002). Campus–community partnerships: The terms of engagement. *Journal of Social Issues, 58*(3), 503–516.

Chambers, E. (2000). Applied ethnography. In N.K. Denzin & Y.S. Lincoln (Eds.), *The Sage handbook of qualitative research* (2nd ed., pp. 851–869). Thousand Oaks, CA: Sage.

Crigger, N.J., Holcomb, L., & Weiss, J. (2001). Fundamentalism, multiculturalism, and problems of conducting research with populations in developing nations. *Nursing Ethics, 8*(5), 459–468.

Diller, J.V. (2007). *Cultural diversity: A primer for the human services* (3rd ed.). Belmont, CA: Wadsworth.

Estabrooks, C.A., Thompson, D.S., Lovely, J.J.E., & Hofmeyer, A. (2006). A guide to knowledge translation theory. *Journal of Continuing Education in the Health Professions, 26*(1), 25–36.

Fisher, C.B., Hoagwood, K., Boyde, C., Duster, T., Frank, D.A., Grisso, T., et al. (2002). Research ethics for mental health science involving ethnic minority children and youths. *American Psychologist, 57*(12), 1034–1040.

Gaventa, J., & Cornwall, A. (2001). Power and knowledge. In P.W. Reason & H. Bradbury (Eds.), *The Sage handbook of action research* (pp. 70–80). London: Sage.

Ginsburg, M.B., & Gorostiaga, J.M. (2001). Relationships between theorists/ researchers and policy makers/practitioners: Rethinking the two-cultures thesis and the possibility of dialogue. *Comparative Education Review, 45*(2), 173–196.

Gowdy, E.A. (2006). *Knowledge transfer and health networks literature review.* Calgary, AB: Southern Alberta Child & Youth Health Network. Retrieved July 12, 2008, from http://sacyhn.ca/pdfs/knowledge_transfer_health_networks_ literature_review.pdf

Graham, I.D., Logan, J., Harrison, M. B., Straus, S. E., Tetroe, J., Caswell, W., et al. (2006). Lost in knowledge translation: Time for a map? *Journal of Continuing Education in the Health Professions, 26*(1), 13–24.

Guenette, F., Marshall, E. A., & Morley, T. (2007). Career experiences and choice processes for secondary science students. In T. Pelton, G. Reis, & K. Moore (Eds.), *Connections 2007 Proceedings* (pp. 77–84). Victoria, BC: University of Victoria Faculty of Education.

Harrison, K. (2005). *Changing youth, changing communities, changing dreams: A survey.* Unpublished master's thesis, University of Victoria, Victoria, British Columbia, Canada.

Hoare, T., Levy, C., & Robinson, M.P. (1993). Participatory action research in Native communities: Cultural opportunities and legal implications. *Canadian Journal of Native Studies, 8(1),* 43–68.

Hudson, P., & Taylor-Henley, S. (2001). Beyond the rhetoric: Implementing a culturally appropriate research project in First Nation communities. *American Indian Culture and Research Journal, 25*(2), 93–105.

Johnson, D R., & Johnson, F.P. (2005). *Joining together: Group theory and group skills* (8th ed.). Boston: Allyn & Bacon.

Kiefer, L., Frank, J., Di Ruggiero, E., Dobbins, M., Manuel, D., Gully, P.R., et al. (2005). Fostering evidence-based decision-making in Canada: Examining the need for a Canadian population and public health evidence centre and research network. *Canadian Journal of Public Health, 96*(3), 111–119.

Kirkness, V.J., & Barnhardt, R. (1991). First Nations and higher education: The four Rs – respect, relevance, reciprocity, responsibility. *Journal of American Indian Education, 30*(3), 1–15.

Landry, R., Amara, N., & Lamari, M. (2001). Utilization of social science research knowledge in Canada. *Research Policy, 30*(2), 333–349.

Lasker, R.D., Weiss, E.S., & Miller, R. (2001). Partnership synergy: A practical framework for studying and strengthening collaborative advantage. *Milbank Quarterly, 79*(2), 179–205.

Lavis, J.N., Robertson, D., Woodside, J.M., McLeod, C.B., & Abelson, J. (2003). How can research organizations more effectively transfer research knowledge to decision makers? *Milbank Quarterly, 81*(2), 221–248.

Leadbeater, B., Banister, E.M., Benoit, C., Jansson, M., Marshall, E.A., & Riecken, T. (Eds.). (2006). *Ethical issues in community-based research with children and youth.* Toronto, ON: University of Toronto Press.

Marshall, E.A. (2002). Life-career counselling issues for youth in coastal and rural communities. The impact of economic, social, and environmental restructuring. *International Journal for the Advancement of Counselling, 24*(1), 69–87.

Marshall, E.A., & Batten, S. (2004). Researching across cultures: Issues of ethics and power. *Forum Qualitative Sozialforschung / Forum: Qualitative Social Research, 5*(3). Retrieved July 13, 2008, from http://www.qualitative-research.net/index.php/fqs/article/view/572/1241

Marshall, E.A., & Guenette, F. (2008, October). Mapping participant experiences. Techniques to facilitate engagement in qualitative inquiry. Paper presented at the 14th Annual Advances in Qualitative Methods Conference, Banff, AB.

Marshall, E.A., & Shepard, B. (2006). Youth on the margins: Qualitative research with adolescent groups. In B. Leadbeater, E. Banister, C. Benoit, M. Jansson, E.A. Marshall, & T. Riecken (Eds.), *Ethical issues in community-based research with children and youth* (pp. 139–156). Toronto, ON: University of Toronto Press.

Marshall, E.A., Shepard, B., & Leadbeater, B. (2006). Interdisciplinary research: Charting new directions collaboratively. *International Journal of the Humanities, 2*(2), 953–960.

Martin, B. (1998). Academics. In *Tied knowledge: Power in higher education* (chap. 2). Retrieved October 17, 2008, from http://www.uow.edu.au/~bmartin/pubs/98tk/tk02.html

McCormick, R.M. (1998). Ethical considerations in First Nations counselling and research. *Canadian Journal of Counselling, 32*(4), 284–297.

Mitton, C., Adair, C.E., McKenzie, E., Patten, S.B., & Waye Perry, B. (2007). Knowledge transfer and exchange: Review and synthesis of the literature. *Milbank Quarterly, 85*(4), 729–768.

Ommer, R.E., & The Coasts Under Stress Research Project Team. (2007). *Coasts under stress: Restructuring and social-ecological health.* Montreal, QC: McGill-Queen's University Press.

Pedersen, P.B. (1991). Multiculturalism as a generic approach to counseling. *Journal of Counseling & Development, 70*(1), 6–12.

Piquemal, N. (2001). Free and informed consent in research involving Native American communities. *American Indian Culture and Research Journal, 25*(1), 65–79.

Rawdah, N., Guenette, F., & Marshall, E. A. (2007). Adolescent reports of family and health factors: A comparison of two samples. In T. Pelton, G. Reis, & K. Moore (Eds.), *Connections 2007 Proceedings* (pp. 141–147). Victoria, BC: University of Victoria Faculty of Education.

Shonkoff, J.P. (2000). Science, policy, and practice: Three cultures in search of a shared mission. *Child Development, 71*(1), 181–187.

Sue, D.W., & Sue, D. (2007). *Counseling the culturally diverse: Theory and practice* (5th ed.). New York: Wiley.

University of Victoria Centre for Youth & Society. (n.d.). *Authorship guidelines for the Canadian Alliance for Health Research (CAHR) project publications.* Retrieved August 4, 2008, from http://www.youth.society.uvic.ca/sites/default/files/images/Authorship%20Guidelines%2C%20CAHR.pdf

Wu, W.L., Hsu, B.F., & Yeh, R.S. (2007). Fostering the determinants of knowledge transfer: A team-level analysis. *Journal of Information Science, 33*(3), 326–339.

4 Using Evaluative Inquiry to Generate Knowledge about the Quality and Value of Community Initiatives

KATE MCKEGG

In communities all over the world, people are striving to improve their lives and meet the needs of their families and communities. They care passionately about making a difference and about achieving outcomes of significance for those around them. However, caring passionately does not necessarily translate into improved outcomes or realize people's hopes and expectations about making a difference (Friedman, 2005). Good intentions are not sufficient for meeting the needs of communities or for achieving the results and outcomes wanted and needed (Foege, Daulaire, Black, & Pearson, 2005).

Many of the conditions, factors, capacities, skills, resources, and actions that are likely to make a difference to the provision of health services – from the delivery of housing to those in need, to the education of children and adults, to the choices made by young people – have been extensively researched, reported, published, and synthesized. In spite of evidence that this information can have significant benefits and pay-off in terms of improvements in outcomes (Schryer-Roy, 2005), the vast pool of research-based knowledge is largely underused by service providers and practitioners in communities (Landry, Amara, Pablos-Mendez, Shademani, & Gold, 2006).

Bridging the gap between what is more formally and explicitly known about improving the effectiveness of programs, policies, and services in community contexts, and individuals working within communities, has received the focus of considerable attention from academics as well as global and national organizations and institutions (Walter, Nutley, & Davies, 2005). Knowledge translation (KT) is one term among many used to describe this effort (Levesque, 2008). KT is also situated within a much wider, evidence-based movement (Culyer &

Lomas, 2006) that aims to increase the uptake of research-based evidence into policy development and the delivery of services (Walter, Nutley, & Davies, 2005).

The central promise of KT is that if the wealth of research information is suitably tailored for audiences then it will contribute meaningfully to the decisions made and the actions taken about policies, programs, projects, and operations (Landry et al., 2006). A key assumption underpinning much KT effort is that it will result in learning, insight, and subsequently practitioner behaviour change. In turn, KT is expected to lead to improvements in the lives of the people in our communities.

However, the promise of KT has been sadly under-realized. Many community organizations, workers, and practitioners do not notice or use research information and evidence. Previous bad experiences with research can also result in some communities quite actively rejecting information or advice from *expert* outsiders. Other communities are suspicious and wary of external researchers – many with good reason – following years of exploitation and marginalization by imperialist and colonizing regimes (Cram, 1997; Tuhiwai Smith, 2005).

Nevertheless, growing efforts, research, and literature are addressing ways in which KT's effectiveness can be improved in community settings, and particularly in community health settings. There is a mounting impetus to redefine KT, not as a technical push-or-pull dissemination strategy but as a learning approach that builds, creates, leverages, and mobilizes knowledge within communities (Pablos-Mendez & Shademani, 2006). This reconceptualization of KT challenges the dualism and separation of knowledge and practice, also known as the know-do gap (Landry et al., 2006, p. 1). Knowledge and action are unified in the redefinition; knowledge is understood as something that occurs in action, not separate from it (Elkjaer, 2003; Schwandt, 2008). In particular, key factors that contribute to more successful and more effective KT include opportunities for communities to own, participate in, and lead research processes; collaborative exchanges between researchers and communities where relationships of trust are built over time; and the connections that are made with wider community and research networks (Hemsley-Brown, 2004). In other words, knowledge mobilization and transfer is enhanced through participation, action, and human exchange.

Exactly which strategies effectively promote the learning orientation of KT, the knowledge-building and mobilization aims, and the improved outcomes in communities, are not entirely clear. However, evaluative inquiry is one strategy that has an explicit learning and action orientation, uses a highly participative approach, and is quite deliberately focused on quality, value, and performance (Preskill & Torres, 1999). Certainly within the evaluation community, there is growing interest in evaluative inquiry as a trigger for learning and for improved decision-making and action (Cousins, Goh, & Clark, 2006).

Evaluative Inquiry

Evaluative inquiry has been described by several key evaluation theorists (Cousins et al., 2006; Cousins, Goh, Clark, & Lee, 2004; Owen & Lambert, 1998; Preskill & Torres, 1999). For example, Preskill and Torres (1999) described evaluative inquiry as 'an ongoing process for investigating and understanding critical organizational issues. It is an approach to learning that is fully integrated with an organization's work practices' (p. 1). Cousins et al. (2006) described it as 'the systematic gathering and analysis of data for organizational problem solving and decision making ... suggested to have high potential as a trigger for organizational learning capacity' (p. 156). A key aspect that distinguishes evaluative inquiry from other forms of inquiry is its focus on quality, value, and importance.

Like traditional evaluation, the vision and focus of evaluative inquiry is on goodness, advanced well-being, and social betterment. It is also intentional about the systematic use of data in sense-making, learning, and judgment about quality, value, and importance. As used here, the term data does not imply a valuing of scientific data only; it also refers to practitioner knowledge, traditional knowledge forms and practices, and the 'wisdom born of everyday experiences' (Greene, 2005, p. 10). However, evaluative inquiry is not the same as evaluation. Evaluation is usually applied to a program, policy, or initiative, and tends to have a discrete beginning, middle, and end. In contrast, evaluative inquiry is a process that is ongoing and focused on day-to-day problem-solving and decision-making within an organization or community setting.

Evaluative inquiry can help clarify what we do and why we do it; how we define and measure progress and success; what feedback, data, and information we do – and do not – need to inform decision-making; what information we consider valid and usable, and what is not; and how we might continuously generate feedback into our practice to improve decision-making (Bickel, Nelson, & Millett, 2002).

Evaluative inquiry is developmental. It aims to enable a process of ongoing questioning and systematic feedback to communities and initiatives that can inform context-specific decision-making and action (Patton, 1997). The inquiry is an internal function of the community that is integrated into its everyday action (Westley, Zimmerman, & Patton, 2006).

Fundamentally, evaluative inquiry is a practice that positions communities at the centre of evaluative judgment, where they hold primary agency to develop the criteria upon which judgments of goodness will be made, and make meaning of their experience and take appropriate action. Evaluative inquiry also positions the evaluative inquiry facilitator or evaluator as an integral part of the context in which evaluative judgments are made, rather than an independent observer of it.

I argue that evaluative inquiry is not a concept that has a precise meaning; rather, it is a sensitizing concept. Patton (2007) reminded us that Herbert Blumer (1954) was originally credited with the idea of a 'sensitizing concept' (Patton, p. 102). Sensitizing concepts provide direction to a study and orient action. Their meaning is shaped in different contexts and situations through the ongoing movement of the observer between the concept and the lived social experience. Examples of sensitizing concepts are notions such as the learning organization, middle age, youth, and so forth. As a sensitizing concept, evaluative inquiry has broad patterns and themes, but these will always differ according to the time, place, culture, and circumstances in which it is applied.

Many aspects of evaluative inquiry (e.g., questioning, systematic data collection, investigation, dialogue, participation, facilitation, collaboration, reflection, knowledge co-creation, learning, and so on) have been described by previous theorists and are more or less present in different contexts. However, the concept focuses our attention on what is happening, how, to whom, in what ways, and under what conditions. At the heart of evaluative inquiry is a human process of interaction and dialogue that includes inquiry, questioning, investigation, engagement, reflection, and the creation and interpretation of information. The subsequent co-creation of knowledge and learning is explicitly framed by questions about the quality, value, or importance of something in order to take future action.

Evaluative Inquiry, Learning, and KT

Evaluative inquiry is grounded in constructivist theories of learning that have their roots in the work of Vygotsky (1978), the tradition of cultural-historical activity theory (Elkjaer, 2003), and the more recent work of Lave and Wenger (1991). Learning is understood to be much more than a cognitive activity where an individual acquires data or has knowledge delivered from somewhere external. Knowledge is not something that is out there, waiting to be acquired or transferred to another individual or learner (Elkjaer, 2003). Rather, learning and KT are understood to take place within human processes of interaction, dialogue, and participation. 'Dialogue is what facilitates the evaluative inquiry learning processes of reflection, asking questions ... Through dialogue, individuals make connections with each other and communicate personal and social understandings that guide subsequent behaviours' (Preskill & Torres, 1999, p. 53). The process of becoming a knower requires opportunities to participate in shared activity. Knowing is an active process involving human dialogue and sense-making, noticing, processing, encoding, and organizing new information and experiences (Spillane, Reiser, & Reimer, 2002). Knowledge is something people develop, create, and share through individual and shared sense-making, experience, and action (McElroy, 2003).

Evaluative inquiry is a collaborative and participative process. It entails a way of thinking and reflection that is orientated towards the use of data and other research information as well as questions about its quality, improvement, and value in order to take action. Conceptual and theoretical links established between evaluative inquiry and organizational learning (Cousins, Goh, & Elliott, 2007) suggest it is a promising strategy to use to create the conditions for learning and KT.

Conditions Necessary for Effective Evaluative Inquiry

As a human process, the success of evaluative inquiry is highly dependent on the ability of those involved to be situationally responsive, in particular, to be paying attention to the dynamics of human relationships amid real-life situations. Effective evaluative inquiry, therefore, requires some intentionality on the part of those involved. The following discussion introduces a range of conditions emerging from the literature and recent empirical work that show promise for those using evaluative inquiry as an intentional KT strategy.

Responsiveness: Context, Culture, and History Matter

To carry out effective evaluative inquiry, paying attention to context in all its historical and cultural richness and diversity is to be responsive

(Greene, 2005). To engage both meaningfully and effectively in inquiry with any individual, group, or organization requires sensitivity and appreciation of the context in which the inquiry is being undertaken. The meanings of quality and value are embedded in our historical, political, institutional, and cultural contexts. How we and others respond to questions about quality, importance, or value is enmeshed in this context. It is in our nature to default to what we know and what we are comfortable with. So, for KT, which is fundamentally about social betterment and change, an understanding of context is critical. As Spillane et al. (2002) stated, 'our usual approach to processing new knowledge is a conserving process, preserving existing frames rather than radically transforming them' (p. 398).

What we understand about a new message or process depends on the knowledge and experience we already have. We construct our understandings in terms of what we already know and believe. We are also biased towards interpretations consistent with our prior beliefs and values. Therefore, concrete and familiar examples from our own experience often carry more weight in judgment and decision-making than abstract ideas or information (Spillane et al., 2002). 'Despite one[']s best intentions, it's the recipient who ultimately decides what constitutes responsiveness' (New Zealand Ministry of Social Development, 2007, p. 18).

Leadership

One of the key elements repeatedly found in literature on the conditions for learning and knowledge-sharing in organizations is about leadership or, at the very least, influential people (Davidson, 2003; Hemsley-Brown, 2004; Walter et al., 2005). The leadership of a community, initiative, or organization influences the culture and the value that are placed on learning, reflection, inquiry, et cetera. Recent empirical work in schools by Cousins et al. (2006) found that leadership was pivotal to the effectiveness, acceptability, and sustainability of evaluative inquiry; that is, a leader's motivation and inclination to value inquiry as well as to model use of data has a 'potent effect' (p. 172).

Long-Term Commitment and Engagement

As previously discussed, learning occurs through a process of creating and recreating meaning, and through interpreting and understanding our experiences in relationship to both others and the environment around us. For deeper learning to occur, a sustained engagement with a series of problematic ideas with an explicit goal of making sense of them for a particular purpose is usually required (Spillane et al., 2002). The development of long-term partnerships and engagement among evaluators, initiatives, and organizations facilitates a climate where evaluators can easily challenge or question and where communities can test new ideas and practices (Patton, 1997; Walter et al., 2005). Patton described the evaluator's role within these long-term relationships as one of holding a community's feet to the 'fire of testing reality' (p. 104).

As Nutley, Walter, and Davies (2003) noted, 'However, a striking feature of the literature on RU/EBP [research utilization/evidence-based practice] implementation is that much of it concludes by endorsing the development of partnerships between researchers and practitioners as the way forward' (p. 138). This was also found in a New Zealand study (McKegg, 2005) of evaluative inquiry and utilization. One of the preconditions for evaluative inquiry that had positive and meaningful impacts on programming was a long-term commitment and engagement among key stakeholders. As one respondent indicated,

> We had strong stakeholder involvement . . . a 'hands on' role to facilitate the process . . . lots of detailed involvement and engagement . . . None of us on our own could have done what's been achieved, on our own . . . We all need to have connection . . . the evaluation and the policy and project have been totally interwoven. (McKegg, p. 11)

Trust, Integrity, and Reciprocity

In order for collaboration, meaningful dialogue, critical questioning, and courageous action to take place, there needs to be a climate where people trust each other, where the people and the processes have integrity and relevance to those involved, and where there is a balanced exchange of resources, time, and effort that recognizes and values diverse contributions (New Zealand Ministry of Social Development, 2007). Preskill and Torres (1999) argued that evaluative inquiry is all about taking risk. Trust is a vital ingredient if people are going to demonstrate risk-taking and vulnerability with others. Developing such trust takes time; it results from engaging in mutual practices where integrity and reciprocity have been evident.

The following vignette from an evaluator working alongside a community project in New Zealand illustrates a form of reciprocity that highlights the mutual exchange of knowledge and expertise:

> As a formative evaluator working primarily with community action projects, I experience reciprocity in what I think is a unique way. While I am not 'invited' but rather 'assigned,' it is my responsibility to establish the relationships required for me to work effectively with project staff. It is my privilege to work with people who are endeavouring to support and lift their communities. I am in a position to make a contribution to the processes, as they are being developed and implemented. The reciprocity is in the project staff accepting me and the skills I am offering; and the process whereby I am providing services, knowledge and expertise in a way that is meaningful and valuable. We are learning, therefore we are building our capacity simultaneously. The value of this process is in the sustainability of the initiatives that are developed. (New Zealand Ministry of Social Development, 2007, p. 15)

Motivation

An environment where there is interest in and openness to inquiry is an important condition for effective evaluative inquiry. This is supported by the findings of the New Zealand study. McKegg (2005) found that a desire to engage in evaluation and a willingness to question policy and practice were important enablers of effective evaluative inquiry. Having a champion who will nurture the process of evaluative inquiry – or at the very least, having people who care and are motivated to participate – is vital to the success of evaluative inquiry. Patton (1997) calls this personal factor 'the presence of an identifiable individual or group of people who personally care about the evaluation and the findings it generates' (p. 44). As King (2007) suggested, sustaining motivation is something that really needs to be intentional, not left to chance.

Facilitation and Support

A cross-sector review of research into the mechanisms underlying evidence-based policy and practice found that support and facilitation are necessary in assisting people to learn new skills and to maintain momentum using data and research in everyday settings (Walter et al., 2005). In the New Zealand study, McKegg (2005) found that having support in the form of facilitated expertise was considered an important enabler of effective evaluative inquiry by many study participants. This finding is supported by Preskill, Zuckerman, and Matthews (2003) and King (2007), who all viewed active facilitation as a necessary feature of effective evaluative inquiry.

Benefits and Consequences of Evaluative Inquiry

Examples from two studies illustrate some of the benefits and consequences of evaluative inquiry. One study was conducted by Cousins, Goh, and Clark (2006) in Canada, and the other was conducted in New Zealand (McKegg, 2005).

The first study was qualitative and part of a wider research program investigating the relationship between evaluative inquiry and organizational learning capacity. Based on the results of a survey of forty-one Manitoba schools (Goh, Cousins, & Elliott, 2006), four schools that scored the highest on four key variables (organizational learning capacity, evaluative inquiry, organizational readiness for evaluation, organizational support systems) were selected to participate in the study. The study was designed to examine the nature and benefits of evaluative inquiry and to understand forces that either enhance or impede schools' propensity to embrace evaluative inquiry for decision-making (Cousins et al., 2006).

The second study based in Wellington, New Zealand, was also qualitative, and was part of a wider work program to develop an evaluation strategy for a government educational agency. In this study, a range of participants drawn from nine completed evaluations were interviewed to gain insight and explore the different ways evaluation affects, shapes, changes, and influences people and programs in the organization. The study organizer also wanted to examine the structures and systems that support or hinder evaluative inquiry and evaluation use.

Program Adaption, Change, and Adjustment

A consistent finding from both studies was that involvement in evaluative inquiry leads to people's involvement in programs, where they adapt and fine-tune what they do. Cousins et al. (2006) found that schools engaging in evaluative inquiry were likely to use data to fine-tune and adjust existing programs. For example, in one school, ongoing evaluative inquiry helped educators stay focused on the needs of learners and avoid actions that were not important. Similarly, McKegg (2005) found that being involved in evaluative inquiry led respondents to make changes to their programs, that is, 'being part of the evaluation changed our focus for the program' (p. 26). In one program for parents of young children with autistic spectrum disorders, evaluative inquiry led the program developers and implementers to reconsider access and uptake issues for Māori and Pacific families, and to adopt a broader, parent-education focus than what had been previously considered.

Direct Impact on Strategic and Structural Decisions

In some cases, evaluative inquiry influences strategic or structural decisions and changes in programs. For example, Cousins et al. (2006) found that evaluative inquiry led to schools using research to engage in deeper, systemic analysis and to make structural decisions about their organization. In one school, they found that evaluative inquiry enabled a systematic analysis of issues concerning a school timetable system, revealing that assumed benefits from the existing system were not being realized. Subsequently, structural changes were made to the timetable system of the school. In another school, a structural decision to adopt a semester system was made because of evaluative inquiry.

Similarly, McKegg (2005) found examples of evaluative inquiry having a direct impact on strategic decision-making as well as facilitating quite fundamental changes to a program. As two respondents indicated, 'The evaluation had a direct and specific influence on the next phase of policy ... [The] new design of the project was informed by the evaluation process' (p. 26). For example, in a professional development program developed for the implementation of the arts curriculum for schools, a respondent indicated that evaluative inquiry led to policy changes in the arts curriculum as well as substantial changes for the professional development program. In a digital opportunities program designed to assist schools to be experimental with new technology, evaluative inquiry led to policy changes, in particular to the focus and purpose of the project. The program now has a specific focus on removing barriers to achievement, something that it did not have before.

New Insights

Another benefit of being involved in evaluative inquiry that Cousins et al. (2006) and McKegg (2005) observed was that people developed new insights and knowledge about complex social connections, program issues, relationships, and so forth. In the New Zealand study, the manager of the digital opportunities program in schools indicated that evaluative inquiry helped him understand that connections between a program's implementation and learning outcomes for students were more complex and indirect than he had previously considered. 'It helped us realise that we can't isolate specific learning outcomes ... the whole thing is a complex set of relationships' (McKegg, 2005, p. 28). In a literacy program for Māori-medium schools, a respondent indicated that evaluative inquiry had resulted in new knowledge for the organization about the similarities and differences between Māori-medium and English-medium literacy: '[Evaluative inquiry] contributed to my understanding of the relationship between Māori medium literacy and English literacy ... it highlighted the similarities and the links ... perhaps the differences have been overemphasised over the similarities' (ibid., p. 28).

As these examples illustrate, the insights generated from evaluative inquiry can be quite wide-ranging in scope. One of the key findings from recent studies is that being involved in evaluative inquiry can lead to a greater appreciation and valuing of inquiry, data, and research. Cousins et al. (2006) found that 'data use leads to data valuing' (p. 172). In other words, by actually experiencing how data and locally created knowledge can be incorporated into the decision-making process, people come to understand the potential benefits of evaluative inquiry. This finding was supported by McKegg's (2005) study, where respondents were involved in evaluative inquiry in a number of ways, including design, in the development of contracting processes for external providers, in analysis and reporting, and even in the field, in some cases. Respondents indicated they had learned a great deal about the conduct of evaluative inquiry. The process also increased their motivation and belief in the value of inquiry itself:

> It's been a learning experience ... a practical experience in how to go about evaluation. My own knowledge is much more [expansive] ... I learned heaps about methods and approaches too. It has been useful in exploring ways ... to find indicators, how to measure impact. [It] reinforced for me that evaluation should be part of the developmental and planning process. (McKegg, 2005, p. 27)

This finding aligns with recent literature on learning and KT: that knowledge is developed and created through participation, action, and human sense-making.

For the wider KT endeavour, this finding flips traditional social change theory (defined as the way to influence attitudes, values, and behaviour is by increasing awareness, knowledge, and information) on its head. This finding suggests that it is *meaningful involvement and participation* in inquiry that is crucial because it influences communities' attitudes towards and valuing of data and research. It strengthens the case for participative models of KT. Cousins et al. (2004) argued that organizations need to experience success in order to integrate evaluative inquiry as a cultural norm. Ensuring that involvement in inquiry is a meaningful and useful experience appears to be a vital step in the success of KT.

Discussion and Conclusion

Improving people's health, positively influencing social conditions, enabling people to lift themselves out of poverty, and achieving social justice and equity are some of the focus points of both KT and evaluative inquiry. Given this similarity in focus, evaluative inquiry has relevance for KT efforts. In the preceding pages, I have described evaluative inquiry and its key features as well as preconditions for its success and some of its benefits. It is my hope that I have presented sufficient evidence for evaluative inquiry as a promising strategy for achieving the aims of KT.

Working with communities and groups to build systematic data and evidence about the quality and value of what they do helps to develop their appreciation of inquiry, data, and research. A firm platform for KT can be created as communities and groups come to value inquiry and data as key parts of their everyday business and success.

In the very untidy realities of communities everywhere, seemingly intractable issues concerning the exchange of knowledge present genuine challenges to all of us who wish to make a difference. We are unable to ignore these issues, as they appear to overwhelm us at times. Being a change-maker is not easy for ordinary people; it is complex and full of forks in the road (Westley et al., 2006). Nevertheless, from this complexity come opportunities to make a difference and to become active participants in change. Simple, off-the-shelf remedies are unlikely; these opportunities will require us to be responsive to contexts, and to work with local leaders. This necessitates building long-term relationships of trust, demonstrating integrity and reciprocity in our actions, finding the courage to act, and sustaining our efforts in the face of all the challenges ahead. Evaluative inquiry is far from simple; there are no guarantees. But, as I have argued here, it can make a difference.

REFERENCES

Bickel, W.E., Nelson, C.A., & Millett, R. (2002). Challenges to the role of evaluation in supporting organizational learning in foundations [Feature: The civic mandate to learn]. *Foundation News & Commentary, 43*(2). Retrieved November 6, 2008, from http://www.foundationnews.org/CME/article.cfm?ID=1807

Blumer, H. (1954). What is wrong with social theory? *American Sociological Review, 19*(1), 3–10.

Cousins, J.B., Goh, S.C., & Clark, S. (2006). Data use leads to data valuing: Evaluative inquiry for school decision making. *Leadership and Policy in Schools, 5*(2), 155–176.

Cousins, J.B., Goh, S.C., Clark, S., & Lee, L.E. (2004). Integrating evaluative inquiry into the organizational culture: A review and synthesis of the knowledge base. *Canadian Journal of Program Evaluation, 19*(2), 99–141.

Cousins, J.B., Goh, S.C., & Elliott, C. (2007, November). *Integrating consequences of evaluation into evaluation capacity building inquiry.* Paper presented at the annual conference of the American Evaluation Association, Baltimore, MD.

Cram, F. (1997). Developing partnerships in research: Pākehā researchers and Māori research. *Sites, 35*, 44–63.

Culyer, A.J., & Lomas, J. (2006). Deliberative processes and evidence-informed decision making in healthcare: Do they work and how might we know? *Evidence & Policy, 2*(3), 357–371.

Davidson, E.J. (2003, April). *Applying evaluation-specific methodology to a specific case: Assessing organizational learning capacity.* Paper presented at the Arizona Evaluation Network, Phoenix, AZ.

Elkjaer, B. (2003). Social learning theory: Learning as participation in social processes. In M. Easterby-Smith & M.A. Lyles (Eds.), *The Blackwell handbook of organizational learning and knowledge management* (pp. 38–53). Malden, MA: Blackwell.

Foege, W.H., Daulaire, N., Black, R.A., & Pearson, C.E. (2005). *Global health leadership and management.* San Francisco, CA: Jossey-Bass.

Friedman, M. (2005). *Trying hard is not good enough.* Victoria, BC: Trafford Publishing.

Goh, S.C., Cousins, J.B., & Elliott, C. (2006). Organizational learning capacity, evaluative inquiry and readiness for change in schools: Views and perceptions for educators. *Journal of Educational Change, 7*(4), 289–318.

Greene, J.C. (2005). Evaluators as stewards of the public good. In S. Hood, R. Hopson, & H. Frierson (Eds.), *The role of culture and cultural context: A mandate for inclusion, the discovery of truth and understanding in evaluative theory and practice* (pp. 7–20). Greenwich, CT: Information Age Publishing.

Hemsley-Brown, J. (2004). Facilitating research utilisation: A cross-sector review of research evidence. *International Journal of Public Sector Management, 17*(6), 534–552.

King, J.A. (2007). Developing evaluation capacity through process use. *New Directions for Evaluation, Winter 2007*(116), 45–59.

Landry, R., Amara, N., Pablos-Mendez, A., Shademani, R., & Gold, I. (2006). The knowledge-value chain: A conceptual framework for knowledge translation in health. *Bulletin of the World Health Organization, 84*(8), 597–602.

Lave, J., & Wenger, E. (1991). *Situated learning: Legitimate peripheral participation.* Cambridge, UK: Cambridge University Press.

Levesque, P.N. (2008, June). *Connectable, connecting, connected: Improving the social life of what you know.* Paper presented at the National Institute for Early Childhood Professional Development & Research Symposium, New Orleans, LA.

McElroy, M.W. (2003). *The new knowledge management: Complexity, learning, and sustainable innovation.* Burlington, MA: Butterworth-Heinemann.

McKegg, K. (2005). *Evaluation strategy development – Utilisation study.* (Unpublished report). Wellington, New Zealand: Ministry of Education.

New Zealand Ministry of Social Development. (2007). *Report on the SPEaR Best Practice Māori Guidelines Hui 2007.* Retrieved November 5, 2008, from http://www.spear.govt.nz/documents/good-practice/spear-bpg-maori-final-report-anzea.pdf

Nutley, S.M., Walter, I., & Davies, H.T.O. (2003). From knowing to doing: A framework for understanding the evidence-into-practice agenda. *Evaluation, 9*(2), 125–148.

Owen, J.M., & Lambert, F.C. (1998). Evaluation and the information needs of organizational leaders. *American Journal of Evaluation, 19*(3), 355–365.

Pablos-Mendez, A., & Shademani, R. (2006). Knowledge translation in global health. *Journal of Continuing Education in the Health Professions, 26*(1), 81–86.

Patton, M.Q. (1997). *Utilization-focused evaluation: The new century text* (3rd ed.). Thousand Oaks, CA: Sage.

Patton, M.Q. (2007). Process use as a usefulism. *New Directions for Evaluation, Winter 2007*(116), 99–112.

Preskill, H.S., & Torres, R.T. (1999). *Evaluative inquiry for learning in organizations.* Thousand Oaks, CA: Sage.

Preskill, H.S., Zuckerman, B., & Matthews, B. (2003). An exploratory study of process use: Findings and implications for future research. *American Journal of Evaluation, 24*(4), 423–442.

Schryer-Roy, A.-M. (2005). *Knowledge translation: Basic theories, approaches and applications.* Retrieved November 5, 2008, from http://www.idrc.ca/uploads/user-S/11473620631Knowledge_Translation_-_Basic_Theories,_Approaches_and_Applications_-_May_2006.pdf

Schwandt, T.A. (2008). The relevance of practical knowledge traditions to evaluation practice. In N.L. Smith & P.R. Brandon (Eds.), *Fundamental issues in evaluation* (pp. 29–40). New York: Guilford Press.

Spillane, J.P., Reiser, B.J., & Reimer, T. (2002). Policy implementation and cognition: Reframing and refocusing implementation research. *Review of Educational Research, 72*(3), 387–431.

Tuhiwai Smith, L. (2005). On tricky ground: Researching the native in the age of uncertainty. In N.K. Denzin & Y. Lincoln (Eds.), *The Sage handbook of qualitative research* (3rd ed., pp. 85–107). Thousand Oaks, CA: Sage.

Vygotsky, L.S. (1978). *Mind in society: The development of higher psychological processes.* Cambridge, MA: Harvard University Press.

Walter, I., Nutley, S.M., & Davies, H.T.O. (2005). What works to promote evidence-based practice? A cross-sector review. *Evidence & Policy, 1*(3), 335–364.

Westley, F., Zimmerman, B., & Patton, M.Q. (2006). *Getting to maybe: How the world is changed.* Toronto, ON: Random House Canada.

5 Knowledge Translation Processes in Developing a Community-Based Evaluation Toolkit

JOAN WHARF HIGGINS, PATTI-JEAN NAYLOR, HEATHER MACLEOD WILLIAMS, AND TRINA SPORER

We live in an era in which chronic health issues are commonplace. These issues often appear to be the result of individual lifestyle behaviours, yet they are rooted in social, cultural, economic, and environmental contexts (Catford, 2007). Identifying coordinated solutions to address such complex issues that are valid, reliable, and transferable can be a daunting task for health promotion research; nevertheless, converting research knowledge into action is critical for advancing population health. To address this failing, the latest call from health promotion leaders reminds us that '[i]f we want more evidenced-based practice, then we need more practice-based evidence' (Green & Glasgow, 2006, p. 126).

In this chapter, we describe the development of a process evaluation resource with recreation and health practitioners for the Active Communities Initiative (ACI) that took place in British Columbia. We sought to provide ACI with an empirically driven evaluation toolkit that would be experientially meaningful and locally relevant. We discuss the key issues that the team faced, particularly related to knowledge translation (KT) challenges between two academics (Joan Wharf Higgins and Patti-Jean Naylor, the first two authors) and two recreation professionals (Heather MacLeod Williams and Trina Sporer, the last two authors), who were overseeing project implementation. We offer a brief introduction to KT literature and to ACI as well. Then we describe the experiences we had developing the process evaluation for the ACI and the KT issues we encountered. The chapter concludes with reflections on some lessons learned.

Health Promotion and Knowledge Translation

A disconnect exists between the evidence academia produces through research and how this knowledge is carried out in the practical world of health promotion (Gazmararian, Curran, Parker, Bernhardt, & DeBuono, 2005). It has been argued that, if the resources and time invested in academic research were effectively transferred to practical settings, significant benefits would be found in many disciplines (Dobbins, Rosenbaum, Plews, Law, & Fysh, 2007; Emmons, Viswanath, & Colditz, 2008). 'Stakeholders such as policy-makers and practitioners should consider the latest scientific research when making decisions in their daily settings,' noted Keown, Van Eerd, and Irvin (2008, p. 67), while acknowledging the time and resource difficulties associated with locating and understanding such evidence. Yet access and interpretation are just two problems facing practitioners when they put research-generated evidence into action. Since 'researchers and decision makers are normally separate groups with distinct cultures and perspectives on research and knowledge, with neither group fully appreciating the other's world' (Graham et al., 2006, p. 17), there is a need for increased communication, familiarity, and collaboration (Dobbins, DeCorby, & Twiddy, 2004; Jacobson, Butterill, & Goering, 2003).

Research also needs to be both situated in and relevant for the community (Dobbins et al., 2007). For example, examining how health promotion evidence was taken up and used by practitioners, Armstrong, Waters, Crockett, and Keleher (2007) found that issues of credibility, relevance, timeliness, applicability, and transferability were of primary concern. Confounding the situation were poor relationships between researchers and decision-makers. Both displayed little skill in evidence translation, nor did they understand how to bridge the know-do gap. As Lomas (2007) observed about this gap, '[R]esearcher to researcher communication about the next study ("more research is needed") is well organised and all too common; researcher to practitioner dialogue about implementing findings ("actionable messages") is poorly organised and all too rare' (p. 129).

Similarly, the credibility of such research is judged less by its rigour than by how it fits with professional or practice wisdom and experience (Nutley, Walter, & Davies, 2007). For example, in an ethnographic account of primary health care professionals' informed decisions, Gabbay and le May (2004) found that their collectively reinforced, internalized, and tacit guidelines drove their decision-making rather than research-informed evidence. The results, suggested the authors, were a socially constructed knowledge-in-practice. For Dobbins et al. (2004, 2007), it is critical for research-producing organizations to first identify and understand the intended users' needs, interests, resources, skills, and experiences to maximize the potential for evidence uptake. These are some of the concerns for effective KT.

Knowledge translation was defined by Straus, Graham, and Mazmanian (2006) as 'the scientific study of the methods for closing the knowledge-to-practice gap, and the analysis of barriers and facilitators inherent in this process' (p. 3). Collaborative problem-solving and interactive, mutual learning between decision-makers and researchers characterizes processes of KT (Jacobson et al., 2003), which result in applicable knowledge for both parties (Graham et al., 2006).

Knowledge brokers may serve to bridge the translation of research and enhance the uptake of the best practices. Knowledge brokers are individuals or agencies that connect research producers with users by filtering and disseminating findings through various strategies, which we will explain below (Nutley et al., 2007). From the outset, it is critical for the broker to establish partnerships and find a collaborative way of working between researchers and practitioners to understand the research objectives and needs of each group in a multidirectional information exchange. Using incentives or rewards can encourage positive attitudes towards research and its use among practitioners, as do local technical, financial, organizational, or emotional supports for increasing practitioners' skill and expertise. As well, researchers must improve the presentation and packaging of research findings with appropriate, tailored, user-friendly language and style, and they must also offer interpretations that are relevant to the practitioners.

Recreation and the Active Communities Initiative (ACI)

The field of recreation has a strong tradition in promoting health, preventing disease, and fostering community development. Recreation is viewed as a means to bridge social differences among people and to reduce inequities by creating civil, connected, and safer places to live, work, and play (Wharf Higgins & Rickert, 2005). Yet, to frame policy and advocate for more public funds, recreation professionals need evidenced-informed knowledge that is germane to their community context. Recreation professionals are often challenged to document the impact and outcomes of programs, yet their evaluation protocols frequently amount to little more than headcounts of participation/ registration numbers (C. Parker, personal communication, April 8, 2008). Consumed with being accountable for spending public funds in this way, practitioners often neglect to investigate what worked or what didn't, and why. Recognizing the limitations of a headcount approach, recreation professionals struggle to identify what indicators to measure and how to translate and apply findings to practice, particularly with restricted time, skills, and budgets to devote to evaluation.

The Active Communities Initiative (ACI) was a provincial program with the intent of increasing the proportion of the population who engage in moderate to vigorous physical activity during their leisure time by 20 per cent (British Columbia Recreation and Parks Association [BCRPA], n.d.). The initiative used a healthy communities or settings-based approach that is similar to health promotion and population-health initiatives related to physical activity (Wharf Higgins, Rickert, & Naylor, 2006). For example, the school-based program ActionSchools! BC seeks to improve the physical activity levels of elementary school-children by adopting a whole-school approach, with six zones that address multiple ecological layers relevant to children's physical activity (Naylor, Macdonald, Zebedee, Reed, & McKay, 2006).

ACI encouraged multi-sector, interdisciplinary, and citizen participation to create supportive environments designed to benefit physical activity opportunities for all British Columbians. The organization is part of a government initiative called ActNow BC that is under the leadership of the BCRPA, a not-for-profit professional association. For the purposes of ACI, communities were defined as a network of individuals with a common interest, not solely by geographical location; the term can refer to a school group, an Aboriginal band, or a municipality.

As of August 2009, 226 communities were registered in ACI. All registered communities were required to identify a leader and establish a team to develop a plan aimed at increasing physical activity levels. In return, the active communities (AC) were offered resources for planning and implementing their initiatives. These resources included a self-assessment checklist and planning guide, communication and marketing materials, regular updates and communiqués, resources for specific events (e.g., walking or workplace programs), access to grants and workshops, and web links to specific topics or resources (e.g., active-friendly environments, community development and capacity-building, physical activity and healthy living policy). ACI presented an opportunity for research teams to document its influence on the health of British Columbians (Petticrew et al., 2005). Recognizing that a process evaluation would be critical to the success of the ACI, in June 2006, BCRPA contracted an evaluation team (comprised of Joan Wharf Higgins, Patti-Jean Naylor, and Heather MacLeod Williams, the first three authors of this chapter, as well as three graduate students) at the University of Victoria to develop a process evaluation framework and toolkit that could be used by the registered communities.

The Process Evaluation Framework

Recently, the field of health promotion has moved beyond viewing physical activity and other health behaviours as an individual practice to include wider social and community contexts. A social-ecological model (Matson-Koffman, Brownstein, Neiner, & Greaney, 2005) is helpful here, as it acknowledges multiple levels of influence on behaviour that include intrapersonal factors (characteristics, knowledge, skills), interpersonal factors (social support/influences, quality and nature of human interactions, peers, family), and community factors (environmental/structural factors such as health policy, a community's ability to create health-promoting change) (Baker, Brennan, Brownson, & Houseman, 2000). Creating ecological, multilevel interventions can lead to significant change (for example, a 20 per cent increase in physical activity; Dooris et al., 2007), the cost-effectiveness of which is contingent on uptake (Chinn, White, Howel, Harland, & Drinkwater, 2006; Sallis et al., 2006). To date, most empirical evidence related to behaviour change is fraught with KT challenges, such as translating interventions demonstrated as successful when conducted in optimum experimental conditions to real-life contexts; such contexts are often under-resourced with overworked professionals delivering programs to citizens. For example, Brownson et al. (2007) found that the adoption of US national guidelines that distil the best practices for physical activity programming by health department staff was low, despite widespread awareness of the guidelines. Barriers to implementing the guidelines included a lack of financial and staff resources, and organizational policy support. Of those who utilized the guidelines, one-fifth modified them to accommodate their own setting and population.

As noted earlier, local context is an important consideration for practitioners' use of evidence. The organizational culture can create barriers where practitioners are overburdened by their workload, under-resourced to search out and interpret research, and unsupported in their efforts to do so. As a result, they become reluctant to use research in their practice (Nutley et al., 2007). Jacobson et al. (2003) suggested that to effectively understand the research utilization context, five domains must be considered: (1) characteristics of the user group and potential research users, their decision-making practices, and their organizational culture and structure; (2) policy relevance; (3) the nature of research and access to information; (4) the researcher – user relationship; and (5) dissemination strategies. Most notably, however, 'research conducted locally – within the context of its future use – stands more chance of being taken up' (Nutley et al., p. 70).

Barriers to effective uptake of physical activity initiatives are rarely reported in the literature (Rabin, Brownson, Kerner, & Glasgow, 2006). This exacerbates the difficulty of practitioners adopting best practices that do not meet community needs or oversimplify community realities (Dzewaltowski, Estabrooks, Klesges, Bull, & Glasgow, 2004; Glasgow, Vogt, & Boles, 1999). For example, one of the best practices for promoting physical activity is regularly cited as a community-based media awareness or education campaign (U.S. Centers for Disease Control and Prevention, 2001). Yet successful campaigns demand an infusion of large-scale resources, health communications expertise, and multiyear timelines – luxuries that few communities can afford without the support of external research monies and researchers. Such interventions, deemed efficacious under ideal, randomized research conditions (Communication Evaluation Expert Panel, Abbatangelo-Gray, Cole, & Kennedy, 2007), provide neither 'scalable efficiency' (Dearing, Maibach, & Buller, 2006, p. S11) for communities nor offer the possibility of sustainability.

Not surprisingly, there is ample evidence that fidelity to interventions is often lacking (Bergen & While, 2005). 'Street-level bureaucrats' (Lipsky, 1971, p. 391), or those responsible for the implementation of policy or programs, may make adaptations related to availability of resources and compatibility with organizational and professional expertise and values rather than comply with best practice. Undoubtedly, such issues are integral to KT when researchers and decision-makers fail to understand 'the constraints and realities of each other's practice' (Gagliardi, Fraser, Wright, Lemieux-Charles, & Davis, 2008, p. 60) – constraints such as organizational disinterest in research, lack of understanding of the nature of research, time commitments and competing demands, and the language each group uses in their work.

Heeding advice from KT and physical activity literature, our team recognized from the outset the importance of engaging recreation and health promotion colleagues in the design of the evaluation framework. To satisfy the needs of the funding agency for the development of a standardized tool as well as those of the intended practitioner audience, the ACI process evaluation framework needed to be rigorous and context-sensitive. We selected the Reach, Efficacy, Adoption, Implementation, and Maintenance (RE-AIM) model (Dzewaltowski, Estabrooks, & Glasgow, 2004; Green & Glasgow, 2006) to frame the evaluation design, develop a toolkit, and report on the translation of ACI.

The architects of RE-AIM are critical of the classic randomized controlled trial and other experimental models because they fail to account for the complexities of real-world contexts, thereby leading to poor implementation and dissemination results. They suggest that the model be used to address KT challenges, including physical activity initiatives; for example, in Australia, the model guided the evaluation of a physician referral and counselling initiative, the 10,000 Steps Rockhampton project (Eakin, Brown, Marshall, Mummery, & Larsen, 2004). Integral to RE-AIM are participatory methods where professionals and academics work together to define the evaluation 'objects of interest' (Green & Kreuter, 2005, p. 138) and indicators, rather than relying on processes and standards imposed from outside sources (Judd, Frankish, & Moulton, 2001). Adopting a community-based research orientation to develop the toolkit would render it 'more understandable, responsive and pertinent to peoples' lives' (Flicker, Savan, Kolenda, & Mildenberger, 2008, p. 107). We valued the registered communities' involvement in applying the RE-AIM lens to their local ecology to enhance the translation of practice-based knowledge (Green & Glasgow, 2006; Kelly, Baker, Brownson, & Schootman, 2007; Sussman, Valente, Rohrback, Skara, & Pentz, 2006).

Our task was to create an evaluation framework and toolkit that would balance the state of science with the state of art as well as the workload for our evaluation team and the Active Communities. Cognizant of the barriers communities face in conducting evaluations (such as limited time, resources, and skills), we appreciated their practice-based insight (Dearing et al., 2006). As we were reminded by Flicker et al. (2008), 'having an outside academic facilitate and carry out research does not necessarily hinder a community from learning new skills nor perpetuate knowledge inequality if the knowledge is appropriately shared.

Finding an appropriate balance remains a constant tension in many CBR endeavours' (p. 112). From previous experience with community-based research (CBR) (Wharf Higgins, 1999), we decided to capitalize on existing opportunities where ACI representatives regularly gathered rather than expecting them to come to us.

Developing the Evaluation Toolkit

The team's approach for developing the evaluation framework and toolkit embraced the community-based participatory research and KT principles of engagement, interaction, and collaboration (Gagliardi et al., 2008; Leung, Yen, & Minkler, 2004). The evaluation team first identified process evaluation tools and strategies from the literature for gathering and utilizing data at the community level. In participation with fifteen purposefully sampled ACI-registered communities, we investigated the evaluation needs, resources, and capacities of communities, and engaged these communities in an action cycle (Graham et al., 2006) to pilot, critically analyse, revise, and finalize a process evaluation toolkit.

Participants

Eighty-eight communities registered as an Active Community by May 30, 2006, were recruited and incorporated into a sampling framework. The communities were stratified according to a number of factors that represented ACs throughout the province to help us adapt an evaluation process appropriate for their settings and circumstances (Patton, 1990). These factors included geographic region, physical activity levels (Statistics Canada, n.d.), and the lead partnering organization (recreation, school, public health, etc.). In addition, we assessed each AC's implementation readiness based on the extent of planning and achievements, history of collaboration, and breadth of partners engaged.

Based on the stratification, fifteen representative communities were purposely sampled to participate in the process evaluation. Lead persons in each AC were invited by email and telephone to participate; they were reminded that their information would remain confidential and that anonymity would be adhered to as much as possible. Ethical approval was granted from the University of Victoria's Human Research Ethics Board. Data collection strategies included telephone interviews, review of community documents, focus groups, and site visits.

Developing the Toolkit – Round 1

Data analysis revealed six evaluation requirements appropriate for ACs: (1) gather participant attendance and descriptive information at AC events and programs; (2) exchange information and success stories within and among communities; (3) track spin-off initiatives that may occur in schools or worksites; (4) document implementation processes, including in-kind contributions from partners and the community; (5) monitor awareness change and physical activity levels; and (6) obtain information related to sustainability and capacity-building of partnerships.

Echoing KT literature (e.g., Keown et al., 2008), the interviewees noted that the collection and interpretation of such data must be (a) easy to understand and use, and (b) unobtrusive regarding time, labour, and other resources. According to one AC leader, '[E]valuation [tools] need to come in packages that are easily "canned" and standardized.' Others wanted tools that could be adapted so that they were sensitive and responsive to local needs or, as one leader said, 'a basic tool that we have the freedom to modify.' Typical of others' challenges with engaging practitioners to use research (e.g., Brownson et al., 2007; Keown et al., 2008), participants identified the importance of evaluation to their work but felt paralysed when asked to measure progress beyond participation or budget expenditures. Representatives faced challenges such as lack of knowledge and autonomy to adopt evidence into practice, as described by two of our interviewees:

> I am very lost in what and how to do this [evaluation]. This includes the plan for what we are doing and how to measure it.
>
> . . .
>
> I would not even know how to start tracking information and what kind of information is possible [to collect].

The field of recreation is not alone in experiencing a disconnection between the evaluation of best practices and practice realities. In their study of how practitioners used evidence-based health resources in Australia, Armstrong et al. (2007) found that impractical resources – ones that were lengthy, too general, or not easily digested – made it difficult to use information for their own purposes, particularly in a time-sensitive manner. Adding to our participants' discomfort was their belief that evaluation meant measuring only physical activity levels as outcome evidence of their efforts to increase activity by the 20 per cent target set by the government. Communities that gathered evaluative data rarely could analyse or make sense of it for their ongoing planning. Participants identified examples of innovative practices, yet had little documentation that would inform communities about what initiatives had worked, for whom, and why.

Based on our findings, we revised select components of RE-AIM to accommodate the ACs' evaluation needs. For example, 'efficacy' was not relevant for process evaluation purposes, and to track communications, we substituted the phrase 'exchange of information'; 'maintenance of behaviour change' was replaced with 'maintenance of partnerships.' Crafting an evaluation toolkit was a highly iterative and reflective phase where we sought to balance concepts from the evaluation science literature with the voices of practitioners pleading for simplicity. In a process similar to that discussed by Keown et al. (2008), we engaged participants in a variety of ways (for example, in interviews, consultations, direct involvement in development/piloting) to maximize relevance and build capacity for using the evaluation tool. Over several months, our evaluation team formulated an evaluation process and selected tools, each time revisiting and often second-guessing our decisions.

Subsequently, we attended an ACI province-wide forum and conducted a focus group with representatives from our participating ACs to obtain feedback on the draft toolkit and process evaluation approach. Seven of the fifteen communities participated in the focus group; the remaining communities provided feedback via telephone and email.

The evaluation materials were not well received. They were perceived as too vague and cumbersome to adopt. One AC representative said, 'The toolkit needs to be prescriptive but with options. It is daunting if there is too much to choose from.' In our efforts to be user-friendly, we had watered down the explicitness and clarity of the evaluation tools while retaining their conceptual and measurement integrity so that they would be valid and reliable instruments. Comparable to the experience described by Keown et al. (2008), being flexible without 'compromising scientific rigour' (p. 70) was a difficult task to achieve.

A main recommendation from participants was that we align the process evaluation tools with the AC self-assessment checklist and planning guide and with existing resources. The toolkit would minimize communities' duplication of planning and evaluation efforts and narrow the range of materials offered. Another recommendation was that the tools be concrete, accessible, and easy to use. Communities wanted to know how their initiatives were faring in provincial and local contexts. This meant providing standardized evaluation tools to produce results that could be compared within and across communities.

Humbled by the focus group feedback, the evaluation team returned to the drawing board and refined the process evaluation toolkit. During this time, we adopted the role of knowledge broker as described by Nutley et al. (2007). We made efforts to minimize barriers and create incentives to make evaluation easier for practitioners, and then we repackaged the toolkit in a user-friendly format. We collected and reviewed the available inventory of ACI resources to mirror what was already known and used. The team clarified the distinction between process and outcome evaluation (Green & Kreuter, 2005), instilling interest in ACs for gathering information that was not outcome-based, and addressing concerns over what ACs perceived to be a subjective evaluation process.

As we revised the evaluation tools and framework, the Tools and Resources for Active Communities Evaluation (TRACE) prototype evolved. Following the communities' recommendation, TRACE was built upon the AC self-assessment checklist and planning guide, which takes a community through a systematic process of planning and evaluation in one streamlined resource. The toolkit was designed so that ACs could utilize it for informing evaluation implementation and monitoring progress. The wording of RE-AIM was modified to be more practice-oriented rather than using, as one AC participant said, 'your language.' Paper and electronic copies of the toolkit and tools were prepared for piloting.

Ten core process evaluation tools accompanied the toolkit, each linked to the five RE-AIM dimensions. Opportunities for communities to use existing evaluation tools (e.g., Walking Program Resource Guide, Active Workplace Workbook, or instruments developed for community-specific events) were noted in the toolkit introduction. At the end of the document, each RE-AIM category score was summarized, providing an overall rating so that ACs could quantify their progress in each area, which satisfied their need for an objective look to the evaluation data. The toolkit concluded with four open-ended questions about AC achievements, lessons learned, and priorities to help ACs reflect on their experiences and further aid in planning. Communication strategies linked with specific tools to assist ACs in translating their evaluation data with their communities. Borrowing from health promotion experience, we developed templates to describe evaluation data when encountering the mayor in the elevator, the city planner at the water cooler, or the one-page success story to disseminate to media and partners (Lavinghouze, Webb Price, & Smith, 2007).

Developing the Toolkit – Round 2

Representatives from the evaluation team travelled to nine of the fifteen communities and consulted with five key community informants via telephone. One AC was unable to participate due to staff changes. The purpose of each visit was to (a) pilot TRACE using a hard copy and an abbreviated electronic prototype and (b) gather feedback about the evaluation design. The visits helped us to appreciate the context in which AC representatives worked, made decisions, and how and when evaluation processes would be completed in a 'deliberate effort [to create] co-learning processes that will benefit all involved parties' (Scharff & Mathews, 2008, pp. 94–95). The visits were approximately two hours in length and took place in each key informant's office. The telephone conversations were approximately one hour in length. Discussions were tape-recorded and documented with field notes. These recordings and notes were shared among team members two to three days following each visit. Team members analysed the notes and met over several weeks to identify key concepts and common themes.

Findings revealed that TRACE was well received by each of the fifteen communities, particularly because of its structured format, integration with existing resources, and electronic features. It appeared that we had successfully translated AC needs into a usable format. TRACE reflected an established scientific evaluation model embedded in a familiar planning resource, and provided structured but modifiable tools to capture the extent and diversity of community involvement, type, level of program implementation and adaptation, and inputs and outputs (figure 5.1 presents one page from the electronic version of TRACE). 'It will be helpful to keep us on track and keep motivated, and make it easier to report our accomplishments,' noted one AC leader. Key informants noted that the rating scale for interpreting data was neither labour- nor time-intensive. Moreover, the rating score helped communities track their progress relative to their own benchmarks and local activities rather than by a provincially determined standard; this helped level the playing field for the diverse stages of implementation occurring in the

ACIs. At the same time, ACs wishing to compare themselves to others could use the rating scale as a motivator or to challenge another community. Respondents offered suggestions for the practical terminology of the evaluation toolkit and application for communities. One participant said, 'We need real-life examples of what evaluation products look like; for example, specific questions from the tools that can be used for reports to share with the media, mayor/council, community partners, et cetera.'

There were two primary challenges identified by key informants concerning the use of the toolkit: time restraints in the face of competing priorities, and a lack of skills to organize, interpret, and utilize the evaluation data. These were similar reports about health promotion practitioners' barriers, where restricted resources and expertise curtailed the adoption of evidenced-informed strategies (Choi et al., 2005; Moseley &

Figure 5.1 Electronic prototype for TRACE

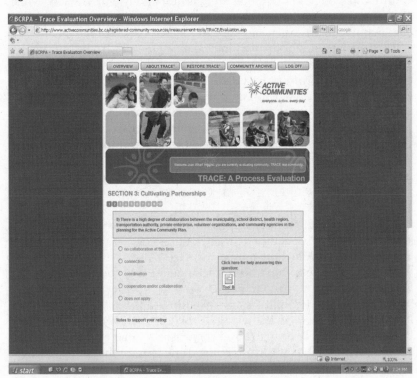

Tierney, 2005). One participant said, 'I would love to think that I would use it – I am worried about the time it will take.'

Discussion and Conclusion

Our experience with TRACE has been one of dual translation: developing a process by which ACs can capture their practice and turn it into evidence and, by doing so, understand and decode how we work and what we know. We concur with Bowen and colleagues (2005) who see knowledge transfer and exchange as a multidirectional process – one that is equitable and balanced in sharing information. As experienced and noted by others (Armstrong et al., 2007; Gagliardi et al., 2008; Innvaer, Vist, Trommald, & Oxman, 2002; Keown et al., 2008), the flow of information must go both ways; researchers can no longer expect to be only on the receiving end of data to answer research questions defined by them. Rather, we need to search out the interests of practitioners and return knowledge in ways that are relevant and useful to them. Nonetheless, even among those of us who call ourselves community-based researchers the process is not fail-safe.

Through our previous working relationships, a strong partnership had been established between the first two authors as researchers and the latter two as professionals, who in turn had collaborated with many of our AC leaders. We built on our mutual trust and respect to maximize the use of TRACE (Yancey, Ory, & Davis, 2006). Visiting communities to pilot TRACE face-to-face and gather their feedback helped key informants commit to the evaluation process and its utility for their own purposes. Enhancing adoption, ownership, and sustainability of an intervention is frequently cited as a benefit of community-based research methods (Scharff & Mathews, 2008); nonetheless, it is not always guaranteed. Even before TRACE was officially launched and distributed by BCRPA, key informants saw an immediate use for the tools and toolkit. 'Specifically, right away – coming up with ideas for marketing and asking how our partners feel. Also, we will use the event tracking tool – we haven't been tracking and it is good reminder that this is something we need to do.'

We had taken the road less travelled in academia, stumbling down Lomas' (2007) path of knowledge brokering where researchers and decision-makers connect 'to build consensus around a course of action' (p. 130). Without the time to understand and witness the context (Scharff & Mathews, 2008) within which the AC leaders were to evaluate their initiatives, our process evaluation toolkit would have been a wasteful exercise in academic elitism; it may have been scientific but it would have been blind to the realities of our clients for whom evaluation is only a small part of the mandate (Dooris et al., 2007). Practitioners reminded us that evaluation measures needed to fit with their core business: 'I [need] ready-made tools that are easy to use – that would be great. So I don't have to spend time developing tools, I can spend my time getting people active.'

When we asked how BCRPA could support the uptake of TRACE, key informants alluded to a knowledge-brokering model by suggesting that the process evaluation toolkit be widely marketed to inform others of its purpose and to persuade more ACs to adopt it. It will also demand an orientation for familiarizing ACs with the content and process of the toolkit and to address issues such as time, resources, and skill levels. It was suggested that orientation be accomplished through regular regional workshops or forums. To support ongoing use of the toolkit, key informants recommended providing access to technical assistance at a provincial level or funds to secure local evaluation resources to analyse, interpret, and disseminate findings.

Subsequent to its development, the implementation of TRACE from November 2007 through June 2008 included support from BCRPA that heeded key informants' advice and previous experience in the literature (e.g., Judd et al., 2001; Rabin et al., 2006). Akin to Armstrong et al.'s (2007) model of a knowledge broker who mediates among the producers of evidence to summarize, distil, and disseminate knowledge to the field, our team served as an evaluation broker to maximize the adoption of TRACE, providing 'the necessary human element of interaction, communication, mentoring, skills building and knowledge sharing required for effective evidence-based health promotion practice' (p. 259). As part of its implementation, the evaluation team will be conducting a process evaluation of TRACE in order to gauge its effectiveness for community use (Dearing et al., 2006). AC representatives who attend training workshops or rely on technical assistance from the team will be surveyed regarding their attitudes, intentions, and use of the TRACE toolkit. We will also be closely scrutinizing the utility of the toolkit and tools to enhance its capacity to 'become embedded in routine life' (Dooris et al., 2007, p. 339).

The concern about KT to bridge the 'discovery to application' gap (Rabin et al., 2006, p. S32) is not new; it was previously known as the bridging theory or policy-to-practice gap. Closing this gap demands purposeful and intentional time spent with community partners to 'learn from and about [them] and use this information to guide the development of programs' (Scharff & Mathews, 2008, p. 95). Our attraction to the RE-AIM model was its promise to 're-aim our evaluation efforts' (Glasgow et al., 1999, p. 1325) by addressing the limitations of context-stripped, efficacy-based research where transferability is questionable when disseminated to public health settings. This meant engaging in a collaborative process to develop TRACE so that it would appeal to practitioners, familiarize them with the toolkit so that it would not be shelved, and present the evaluation resources in understandable ways (Sussman et al., 2006). Aligning AC's evaluation needs with user-friendly tools that matched the evaluation principles integral to RE-AIM was less science and more art, improving our respective skills in evidence translation and emphasizing the 'personal nature of the [knowledge translation] process' (Jacobson et al., 2003, p. 94). By adhering to the philosophy of the evaluation framework and staying true to community-based research and KT principles, we were able to recreate RE-AIM to reflect communities' and our academic ways of practice.

REFERENCES

Armstrong, R., Waters, E., Crockett, B., & Keleher, H. (2007). The nature of evidence resources and knowledge translation for health promotion practitioners. *Health Promotion International, 22*(3), 254–260.

Baker, E.A., Brennan, L.K., Brownson, R.C., & Houseman, R.A. (2000). Measuring the determinants of physical activity: Current and future directions. *Research Quarterly for Exercise and Sport, 71*(Suppl. 2), 146–158.

Bergen, A., & While, A. (2005). 'Implementation deficit' and 'street-level bureaucracy': Policy, practice and change in the development of community nursing issues. *Health & Social Care in the Community, 13*(1), 1–10.

Bowen, S., Martens, P., & The Need to Know Team. (2005). Demystifying knowledge translation: Learning from the community. *Journal of Health Services Research & Policy, 10*(4), 203–211.

British Columbia Recreation and Parks Association. (n.d.). *Active Communities homepage*. Retrieved March 1, 2006, from www.activecommunities.bc.ca

Brownson, R.C., Ballew, P., Dieffenderfer, B., Haire-Joshu, D., Heath, G.W., Kreuter, M.W., et al. (2007). Evidence-based interventions to promote physical activity: What contributes to dissemination by state health departments. *American Journal of Preventive Medicine, 33*(Suppl. 1), 66–78.

Catford, J. (2007). Chronic disease: Preventing the world's next tidal wave – The challenge for Canada 2007? *Health Promotion International, 22*(1), 1–4.

Chinn, D.J., White, M., Howel, D., Harland, J.O.E., & Drinkwater, C.K. (2006). Factors associated with non-participation in a physical activity promotion trial. *Public Health, 120*(4), 309–319.

Choi, B.C.K., Pang, T., Lin, V., Puska, P., Sherman, G., Goddard, M., et al. (2005). Can scientists and policy makers work together? *Journal of Epidemiology and Community Health, 59*(8), 632–637.

Communication Evaluation Expert Panel, Abbatangelo-Gray, J., Cole, G.E., & Kennedy, M.G. (2007). Guidance for evaluating mass communication health initiatives: Summary of an expert panel discussion sponsored by the centers for disease control and prevention. *Evaluation & the Health Professions, 30*(3), 229–253.

Dearing, J.W., Maibach, E.W., & Buller, D.B. (2006). A convergent diffusion and social marketing approach for disseminating proven approaches to physical activity promotion. *American Journal of Preventive Medicine, 31*(4, Suppl. 1), 11–23.

Dobbins, M., DeCorby, K., & Twiddy, T. (2004). A knowledge transfer strategy for public health decision makers. *Worldviews on Evidence-based Nursing, 1*(2), 120–128.

Dobbins, M., Rosenbaum, P., Plews, N., Law, M., & Fysh, A. (2007). Information transfer: What do decision makers want and need from researchers? *Implementation Science, 2*(July). Retrieved August 5, 2007, from http://www.implementationscience.com/content/2/1/20

Dooris, M., Poland, B., Kolbe, L., de Leeuw, E., McCall, D., & Wharf Higgins, J. (2007). Healthy settings: Building evidence for the effectiveness of whole system health promotion – challenges and future directions. In D.V. McQueen & C.M. Jones (Eds.), *Global perspectives on health promotion effectiveness* (pp. 327–352). New York: Springer.

Dzewaltowski, D.A., Estabrooks, P.A., & Glasgow, R.E. (2004). The future of physical activity behavior change research: What is needed to improve translation of research into health promotion practice? *Exercise & Sport Sciences Reviews, 32*(2), 57–63.

Dzewaltowski, D.A., Estabrooks, P.A., Klesges, L.M., Bull, S., & Glasgow, R.E. (2004). Behavior change intervention research in community settings: How generalizable are the results? *Health Promotion International, 19*(2), 235–245.

Eakin, E.G., Brown, W.J., Marshall, A.L., Mummery, K., & Larsen, E. (2004). Physical activity promotion in primary care: Bridging the gap between research and practice. *American Journal of Preventive Medicine, 27*(4), 297–303.

Emmons, K.M., Viswanath, K., & Colditz, G.A. (2008). The role of transdis-
    ciplinary collaboration in translating and disseminating health research:
    Lessons learned and exemplars of success. *American Journal of Preventive
    Medicine, 35*(2, Suppl. 1), S204–S210.
Flicker, S., Savan, B., Kolenda, B., & Mildenberger, M. (2008). A snapshot of
    community-based research in Canada: Who? What? Why? How? *Health
    Education Research, 23*(1), 106–114.
Gabbay, J., & le May, A. (2004). Evidence based guidelines or collectively con-
    structed 'mindlines'? Ethnographic study of knowledge management in
    primary care. *British Medical Journal, 329*(7473), 1013–1016.
Gagliardi, A.R., Fraser, N., Wright, F.C., Lemieux-Charles, L., & Davis, D.
    (2008). Fostering knowledge exchange between researchers and decision-
    makers: Exploring the effectiveness of a mixed-methods approach. *Health
    Policy, 86*(1), 53–63.
Gazmararian, J.A., Curran, J.W., Parker, R.M., Bernhardt, J.M., & DeBuono,
    B.A. (2005). Public health literacy in America: An ethical imperative.
    American Journal of Preventive Medicine, 28(3), 317–322.
Glasgow, R.E., Vogt, T.M., & Boles, S.M. (1999). Evaluating the public health
    impact of health promotion interventions: The RE-AIM framework.
    American Journal of Public Health, 89(9), 1322–1327.
Graham, I.D., Logan, J., Harrison, M.B., Straus, S.E., Tetroe, J., Caswell, W.,
    et al. (2006). Lost in knowledge translation: Time for a map? *Journal of
    Continuing Education in the Health Professions, 26*(1), 13–24.
Green, L.W., & Glasgow, R.E. (2006). Evaluating the relevance, generalization,
    and applicability of research: Issues in external validation and translation
    methodology. *Evaluation & the Health Professions, 29*(1), 126–153.
Green, L.W., & Kreuter, M.W. (2005). *Health program planning: An educational
    and ecological approach* (4th ed.). New York: McGraw-Hill.
Innvaer, S., Vist, G., Trommald, M., & Oxman, A. (2002). Health policy-
    makers' perceptions of their ruse of evidence: A systematic review. *Journal
    of Health Services Research & Policy, 7*(4), 239–244.
Jacobson, N., Butterill, D., & Goering, P. (2003). Development of a framework
    for knowledge translation: Understanding user context. *Journal of Health
    Services Research & Policy, 8*(2), 94–99.
Judd, J., Frankish, C.J., & Moulton, G. (2001). Setting standards in the evalua-
    tion of community-based health promotion programmes – a unifying ap-
    proach. *Health Promotion International, 16*(4), 367–380.
Kelly, C.M., Baker, E.A., Brownson, R.C., & Schootman, M. (2007). Translating
    research into practice: Using concept mapping to determine locally rel-
    evant intervention strategies to increase physical activity. *Evaluation and
    Program Planning, 30*(3), 282–293.

Keown, K., Van Eerd, D., & Irvin, E. (2008). Stakeholder engagement opportunities in systematic reviews: Knowledge transfer for policy and practice.
Journal of Continuing Education in the Health Professions, 28(2), 67–72.

Lavinghouze, R., Webb Price, A., & Smith, K.-A. (2007). The program success
story: A valuable tool for program evaluation. *Health Promotion Practice, 8*(4),
323–331.

Leung, M.W., Yen, I.H., & Minkler, M. (2004). Community based participatory
research: A promising approach for increasing epidemiology's relevance in
the 21st century. *International Journal of Epidemiology, 33*(3), 499–506.

Lipsky, M. (1971). Street-level bureaucracy and the analysis of urban reform.
Urban Affairs Review, 6(4), 391–409.

Lomas, J. (2007). The in-between world of knowledge brokering. *British
Medical Journal, 334*(7585), 129–132.

Matson-Koffman, D., Brownstein, J., Neiner, J., & Greaney, M. (2005). A site-
specific literature review of policy and environmental interventions that
promote physical activity and nutrition for cardiovascular health: What
works? *American Journal of Health Promotion, 19*(3), 167–193.

Moseley, A., & Tierney, S. (2005). Evidence-based practice in the real world.
Evidence & Policy, 1(1), 113–120.

Naylor, P.-J., Macdonald, H.M., Zebedee, J.A., Reed, K.E., & McKay, H.A.
(2006). Lessons learned from Action Schools! ΒC – an 'active school' model
to promote physical activity in elementary schools. *Journal of Science and
Medicine in Sport, 9*(5), 413–423.

Nutley, S.M., Walter, I., & Davies, H.T.O. (2007). *Using evidence: How research
can inform public services.* Bristol, UK: Policy Press.

Patton, M.Q. (1990). *Qualitative evaluation and research methods* (2nd ed.).
Newbury Park, CA: Sage.

Petticrew, M., Cummins, S., Ferrell, C., Findlay, A., Higgins, C., Hoy, C., et al.
(2005). Natural experiments: An underused tool for public health? *Public
Health, 119*(9), 751–757.

Rabin, B.A., Brownson, R.C., Kerner, J.F., & Glasgow, R.E. (2006). Methodologic
challenges in disseminating evidence-based interventions to promote physical activity. *American Journal of Preventive Medicine, 31*(4, Suppl. 1), 24–34.

Sallis, J.F., Cervero, R.B., Ascher, W., Henderson, K.A., Kraft, M.K., & Kerr,
J. (2006). An ecological approach to creating active living communities.
Annual Review of Public Health, 27(1), 297–322.

Scharff, D.P., & Mathews, K. (2008). Working with communities to translate
research into practice. *Journal of Public Health Management & Practice, 14*(2), 94–98.

Statistics Canada. (n.d.). *Your community, your health: Findings from the Canadian
community health survey (CCHS).* Retrieved June 6, 2006, from http://dsp-psd.
pwgsc.gc.ca/Collection/Statcan/82-621-XIE/82-621-XIE.html

Straus, S.E., Graham, I.D., & Mazmanian, P.E. (2006). Knowledge translation: Resolving the confusion. *Journal of Continuing Education in the Health Professions, 26*(1), 3–4.

Sussman, S., Valente, T.W., Rohrbach, L.A., Skara, S., & Pentz, M.A. (2006). Translation in the health professions: Converting science into action. *Evaluation & the Health Professions, 29*(1), 7–32.

United States Centers for Disease Control and Prevention. (2001, October 26). *Increasing physical activity: A report on recommendations of the task force on community preventive services* [Morbidity and Mortality Weekly Report: Recommendations and Reports, 50(RR18), 1–16]. Retrieved March 12, 2006, from http://www.cdc.gov/mmwr/preview/mmwrhtml/rr5018a1.htm

Wharf Higgins, J. (1999). Closer to home: The case for experiential participation in health reform. *Canadian Journal of Public Health, 90*(1), 30–34.

Wharf Higgins, J., & Rickert, T. (2005). A taste of healthy living: A recreational opportunity for people at risk of developing type 2 diabetes. *Leisure Sciences, 27*(5), 439–458.

Wharf Higgins, J., Rickert, T., & Naylor, P.-J. (2006). The determinants of physical activity – why are some people active and others not? In C.P. Saylor (Ed.), *Weight loss, exercise and health research* (pp. 99–152). New York: Nova Science Publishers.

Yancey, A.K., Ory, M.G., & Davis, S.M. (2006). Dissemination of physical activity promotion interventions in underserved populations. *American Journal of Preventive Medicine, 31*(4, Suppl. 1), 82–91.

PART TWO

Knowledge Translation in Policy Contexts

6 Sharing Knowledge for Policy: The Role of Science Organizations as Knowledge Brokers

MARY ANN MCCABE

Research is increasingly important for guiding public decision-making, and policymakers are placing greater emphasis on the need for evidence-based programs and policies to increase the likelihood of favourable results from their public sector investments. Researchers and universities are also under pressure to increase the utilization of research. But there are wide gaps between the production of science-based knowledge and its utilization by policymakers.

This chapter summarizes the scholarly literature on both obstacles and solutions to problems of knowledge translation (KT) as it relates to policy development. I highlight some of the reasons knowledge brokers are needed to create sustained connections between knowledge production and knowledge use by policymakers. Using the example of one professional organization that is committed to this work – the Society for Research in Child Development (SRCD), I illustrate how professional science organizations (i.e., associations that represent member scientists) can serve as effective knowledge brokers. SRCD is an interdisciplinary organization of developmental scientists from many countries. Its mandate includes sharing research with policy decision-makers to improve the lives of children and families.

The literature on knowledge translation summarized here came to life in both my daily work and long-term planning as director of SRCD's Office for Policy and Communications. I needed to become an effective knowledge broker – to help bridge the worlds of researchers and policymakers. It was critical that I understand this role in order to promote activities for sharing research that might effectively inform policy. I needed to find ways to collaborate with researchers in the dissemination and translation of research and to create an appetite for research information in policymakers.

The challenges of sharing research for policy were brought to life for me on a regular basis: research does not always provide the answers that policymakers need, nor are they always ready to use the information that researchers provide. It was important for me to remember that the goal was to gradually inform policymakers' thinking with ideas born from empirical research. In turn, one key responsibility of a knowledge broker is to educate researchers about the policy questions at hand, so as to help them set realistic expectations for the role of research in the policymaking process.

In this chapter, I argue for the need to invest in formal organizations that can broker KT between scientists and policymakers. I begin with an outline of the challenges involved in bridging science and policy. Next, the potential uses of science in enhancing policymaking are described. This is followed by a discussion of successful mechanisms for sharing science with policy audiences and the specific work of knowledge brokers. The final section describes the role of science organizations as knowledge brokers, using the work of the SRCD as an example.

Throughout the chapter I rely on a *process* view of KT that emphasizes, 'factors explaining the utilization of scientific and technical knowledge by decision-makers' (Landry, Amara, & Lamari, 2001, p. 396). The term *policymaker* is used to encompass legislators and those who enact laws and regulations or oversee government research. The policy audience refers to federal, state/provincial, and local decision-makers. This chapter also refers to both *science policy* (i.e., decisions about funding or prioritizing scientific inquiry) and *social policy* (i.e., decisions that govern public programs). These two fields are often interconnected. Policymakers prioritize an area of social policy as needing increased scientific inquiry and funding (e.g., obesity), thus directing science policy. Scientific knowledge is useful for science policy by guiding priorities for future research and for social policy by suggesting potential solutions to societal problems.

Challenges in Bridging Science and Policy

Though not specific to the policy user, Landry et al. (2001) emphasized that research on successful knowledge utilization is still in its infancy. They argued that research utilization is best described as a *process* composed of several stages rather than as a *product* arriving at the final stage of decision-making. Using a modification of Knott and Wildavsky's (1980) six progressive stages of knowledge utilization (transmission, cognition, reference, effort, influence, and application), Landry et al. (2001) described several barriers to moving up this KT ladder that can be located on each side of the research and policy systems. Weiss and Bucuvalas (1980) described the interaction between social science and policymaking in terms of three loosely joined systems: producers of research, policymakers (or users) of research, and the linkage systems between these two groups (that is, the institutions and people who disseminate information to and from the users of research). These linkage systems are referred to as knowledge brokers (see chapters by Benoit et al. and Lenton). The need for formal linkage systems or knowledge brokers can be gleaned from a growing list of obstacles to KT.

The lack of connection between the production of scientific evidence and its use for policy has been widely acknowledged. Scientists and policymakers employ different frames of reference to judge the validity and credibility of various knowledge sources (Weiss & Bucuvalas, 1980). These two groups are immersed in different cultures that use evidence in dissimilar ways and may hold divergent ideologies and values (Shonkoff 2000). The scientists' goal is to advance knowledge, whereas policymakers strive to use information to address a public concern or agenda. The amount of time during which scientists concern themselves with a body of knowledge may encompass many years, but that time may be short for policymakers who must deal with the changing contexts of political and socio-economic forces. Therefore, policy windows that open on an area of research interest may be short-lived and are often too narrow for the time needed for research results to be made available for consideration.

Research has traditionally been limited in influencing policy for several reasons: information generated from research may be used for *negotiation* among competing interests rather than for the decision itself; research is never comprehensive or convincing enough to provide *the* answer or cover all the issues that decision-makers need to consider; many decisions seem to happen without a formal decision-making process, with research information not getting much or any attention; and, finally, even with clear-cut decisions, people do not always know what information they need and fall back on what they know.

To overcome these obstacles, I argue that the gaps between research and policy cultures can be bridged through the sustained effort and expertise of individuals known as knowledge brokers aligned with professional organizations. Individuals who are familiar with the workings of both cultures and who are dedicated to promoting knowledge utilization can make a difference. I will first provide an elaboration on the uses of science by policymakers that will illustrate how important the roles of knowledge brokers are.

Uses of Scientific Knowledge in Policy Decisions

Despite cultural differences and challenges, research can and does find its way into the policymaking process. Many policymakers believe that their case is stronger when they can cite research evidence. Three distinct roles for research in the policymaking process have been identified: instrumental uses (directly acting on research in specific ways), conceptual uses (indirectly influencing policy through ideas), and symbolic uses (either justifying a position that has already been taken for other reasons, or justifying inaction) (Landry et al., 2001; Lavis, Robertson, Woodside, McLeod, & Abelson, 2003).

From a *conceptual* standpoint, research can be used to define a problem and create an appetite for scientific knowledge about it (Huston, 2008). Research can also be used to warn that something is going wrong, provide direction for improving programs and policies, or suggest new approaches for viewing existing programs and policies (Weiss, 1988). From a *strategic* standpoint, research can be used to mobilize support, either from allies or opponents (Weiss). Finally, from a *legislative* stand-point, research can be used to create legislation, regulations, or government-funded programs. It can help determine how legislators vote on legislation that creates programs, reauthorizes programs, or appropriates money.

The impact of academic research on public policy is perhaps best envisioned as *informing* policymaking and analysis. Cohn (2006) argued that policymakers are influenced not so much by the specific work of individual scholars as they are by schools of thought. As policymakers become aware of widely held academic schools of thought related to an issue, they incorporate this body of research into their own outlook in order to better understand or narrow the range of potential solutions. Beyond specific research findings, policy audiences need theory, concepts, and a general fund of background knowledge (Bogenschneider & Gross, 2004).

Ideas that stem from research typically only help to shape the development of policy gradually. These come into currency with both policymakers and interest groups through diffuse processes, but these processes can be slow and indirect; greater expertise in framing science for policy use is needed.

Research Characteristics That Promote Policy Use

Given policymakers' need for access to broad, research-informed knowledge or schools of thought, the ideal research for the policy audience may be specific, policy-oriented analyses of scientific research. Distinguished from the broader category of applied research, Huston (2005) defined the essential conditions in policy research as framing policy-relevant research questions, using rigorous and multiple research methods, producing information in a form that is accessible to policymakers, including considerations of costs versus benefits, and being cautious in interpretations that are strictly linked to data. For research to be usable for policy, it typically needs to include information about causal variables, thresholds for good or bad outcomes, and the significance of the effect size.

Legislators and their staff may need more education in understanding basic aspects of science. Huston (2005, 2008) recommended that scholars play a role in educating policymakers, informing them about what to expect from science, how to evaluate scientific findings, and emphasizing its value. Similarly, McCall and Green (2004) suggested that researchers take responsibility to educate users about the relative merits and limitations of different methodological approaches for particular research questions and to clarify that multiple methods are typically needed to provide a full understanding of the effectiveness of social policies and programs.

Mechanisms for Sharing Scientific Knowledge for Policy

Research filters through to policymakers in many ways, including information transmitted from their staff, reports from expert groups, and media coverage, along with information provided by networks of people, advocates from special interest groups, and knowledge brokers. The optimal utilization of scientific knowledge relies on ongoing, reciprocal exchanges between researchers and policymakers.

One robust, multi-method approach for sharing research with policymakers is used by the Family Impact Seminars in the U.S. (Bogenschneider, Olson, Linney, & Mills, 2000). The ongoing activities of this organization include seminars, briefing reports, and follow-up activities aimed to translate research concerning families into relevant policies. The activity topics are determined, in part, by the express needs of the policymakers. Scholars seek feedback from participating policymakers to gather information about the usefulness of their research compared to information from constituents and special interest groups.

Knowledge of what works when translating scientific research into meaningful information for policymakers is frequently beyond the scope of both scholars and policymakers, creating the need for bridging organizations and systems. McCall and his colleagues (McCall & Green, 2004; McCall & Groark, 2000) provided a range of activities knowledge translators should engage in: knowing current or impending policy issues, informing legislators that information exists on a topic when it becomes a priority, knowing how to access that information, knowing how to select information that is relevant for policy, knowing how to disseminate information to policymakers in a useable form, and knowing how to follow-up with policymakers.

McCall, Groark, and Nelkin (2004) described the unique kinds of expertise needed for effective liaison with the policy audience, including political experience for effective relationships with policymakers, scholarly knowledge to filter scientific information, communication skills to translate the information effectively, awareness of the topics of interest to policymakers, and relationships with academic experts in those topics. The essential role of knowledge brokers, given their targeted investment, special expertise, and greater availability relative to scholars is evident.

Expertise in the communication industry is also needed to broker the gaps between knowledge production and its use by policymakers. The media plays a critical role in sharing science and in determining and prioritizing issues for society. Research can be translated through the media in order to influence public policy; however, scholars often lack the time and skills to effectively collaborate with journalism colleagues in developing science coverage.

The Internet and social media also provide mechanisms for providing research information to the public, the media, and policymakers (Rothbaum, Martland, & Bishop-Josef, 2007). Yet Internet-based information is rapidly proliferating, wildly competitive, and typically lacking a peer-review system to guide users on its scientific merit. Huston (2008) argued that this explosion of information increases the need for knowledge brokers to assess the quality of knowledge translated to policymakers. As one example, Rothbaum and his colleagues at Tufts University have attempted to meet this need for assisting users with judging the quality of information on the Internet. First developed in 2001, the Child and Family Webguide searches the Web for sites that include research-based resources and information, provides a systematic evaluation of a site's trustworthiness (e.g., citations), and shows the evaluative information along with the site (see http://www.cfw. tufts.edu/). This pioneering initiative harnesses information that can be disseminated via the Internet, distinguishes it from non-scientific information, and provides the user with specific tools with which to judge the credibility of the source. The site is a knowledge broker in electronic form.

What Can Knowledge Brokers Do?

Clearly, knowledge brokers can create sustained linkages between decision-makers and scholars, and their role is growing in importance. They can also work to identify policy concerns and disseminate these analyses in a timely way to advise decision-makers. Knowledge brokers can search for and summarize ideas or schools of thoughts developed by scholars that can be useful to decision-makers when policy windows open. Referring to the stages of knowledge utilization (Landry et al., 2001) described earlier in this chapter, the gulf between research and policymakers is bridged by the ongoing interaction between researchers and knowledge brokers, and between knowledge brokers and decision-makers. Thus, the work of the knowledge broker is as important to the transmission and adoption of schools of thought as the scholarly research itself.

Moreover, knowledge brokers can address obstacles to knowledge utilization on both sides of the knowledge production and use equation. Researchers can be perceived as biased sources of information and might lose public credibility if they promote their own research with the policy audience. However, when scholars make their research findings accessible to knowledge brokers, they improve their chances of influencing public policy (Cohn, 2006).

Landry et al. (2001) argued for the cost-effectiveness of knowledge brokers by highlighting the costs to individual scholars for acquiring the necessary funding, time, and skills, and then the effort it takes adapting their materials to share research with users. For example, to adapt a scholarly journal article for the policy audience requires creating a report that is short, appealing, readable, and easily understood by a layperson, with specific conclusions and operational recommendations. The cost of these activities can be large relative to the demand for any particular area of research. Knowledge brokers can prioritize and prepare to disseminate a range of research that is or could become relevant for policy.

Cohn (2006) described the operation of *advocacy coalitions*, in which individuals and organizations work collaboratively over an extended period and acquire political influence. These coalitions can identify academic ideas and evidence that could uniquely foster the reconciliation of views that might not find common ground otherwise. In turn, advocacy coalitions can affect the context of decision-makers, creating a favourable climate for views advanced by academic researchers. Knowledge brokers can sometimes protect individual researchers from the risks they could face by becoming involved in advocacy efforts on their own (Cohn, 2006). This is because advocacy is often identified as being tied to a specific policy agenda.

In contrast to individual scientists, scientific organizations are often perceived as particularly trustworthy sources or knowledge brokers – provided that they remain bipartisan and objective – because they represent a body of research or scientific discipline rather than a specific policy agenda. Professional organizations may be uniquely well-positioned to help the public and policymakers identify reliable, high-quality research findings (Huston, 2005). In conclusion, I describe the policy-relevant work of a professional organization that brokers research in child development to enhance the scientific basis of policy that aims to promote the well-being of children and youth.

Case Illustration of a Knowledge Broker: SRCD

The Society for Research in Child Development (SRCD) membership includes both interdisciplinary and international scholars. The U.S. National Research Council founded SRCD in 1933 to advance interdisciplinary research in child development and to encourage the application of research findings to improve the lives of children and families. SRCD policy activities focus on bringing science to the policy process. The organization does not engage in advocacy activities related to social issues and avoids political partisanship. Owing to its origins, political neutrality, exercise of restraint in politically laden activities, professional relationships and networks, and the depth of scholarship in its membership, SRCD is afforded considerable credibility with a range of social policy audiences. These perceptions of trustworthiness are the result of, and the foundation for, its success in bringing science to policy. SRCD's Office of Communication and Policy engages in activities that support research funding (science policy) and interprets science for policymakers and the public (and thereby influences social policy).

One of SRCD's most important policy missions is to ensure adequate federal funding for child development research. To be effective in this pursuit, SRCD participates in a number of coalitions with other behavioural, social, biomedical, and physical science organizations. When an event or issue comes to the forefront and provides a critical policy window, SRCD is prepared to highlight the importance of enhanced funding for research that can improve the lives of children and families.

SRCD also works to keep its members informed of current issues in science and social policy, enabling those member scholars who are interested in engaging in policy activities to remain poised to do so. In supporting social policy, SRCD serves as a resource to legislative staff by providing scientific expertise, individual experts (e.g., for information, personal testimony, or briefings), and bodies of research on specific topics. Events and issues that capture the attention of policymakers provide windows of opportunity to highlight specific areas of developmental research. SRCD routinely generates products that provide the policy audience with syntheses of research on topics related to social policies concerning children and families. Its peer-reviewed quarterly publication, *Social Policy Report* (*SPR*), contains non-technical reviews of research on a variety of topics, with commentaries by other scholars and policy practitioners. Current legislative agendas, as well as critical events, help to determine the topics covered in the *SPR*. The *SPR* is routinely shared with a wide audience, ranging from scientists and administrators in federal agencies to science and advocacy organizations, and policy journalists. More recently, a *Social Policy Report Brief* was developed to present material from the longer report in an appealing, concise, readable format that highlights policy recommendations (see www.srcd.org). The *SPR Brief* is distributed to the federal, state, and local policy audiences as well as to SRCD member scientists in order to enhance their skills in research translation.

Another critical dimension of SRCD activities is its policy fellowship programs. The Congressional Fellowship program, begun in 1978, is currently co-supported by the William T. Grant Foundation. The Executive Branch Fellowship program, begun in 1991, is funded through contracts with the agencies in which fellows are placed. Early- and mid-career fellows serve as resident scholars in both congressional offices and federal agencies and work as ambassadors for developmental (and behavioural/social) science. As Huston (2005) stated, 'Probably the best way to filter respect for science, data, and good research into policymaking is for people trained in research to participate in the process' (p. 13). The fellowships build capacity by producing a growing pool of scholars who have acquired the expertise, enthusiasm, and professional networks for improving the policy relevance of their research and for translation to and from the policy audience.

A final area where SRCD more indirectly shares knowledge for policy is in disseminating science through popular media. Drawing upon the specialized skills of a science writer and media consultant, SRCD routinely produces press releases on its leading journal, *Child Development*, and fosters relationships with journalism colleagues who demonstrate skilled coverage of science. Policymakers frequently learn of scientific findings through this mechanism. Moreover, strong media coverage can enhance public understanding of the benefits of science. A new SRCD journal, *Child Development Perspectives*, is also well suited to reach a wider audience (including policymakers), with short, non-technical summaries on topics of current interest.

These varied SRCD activities and products for bridging research and policy illustrate many points highlighted in this chapter about effective KT. They rest upon the credibility and availability of SRCD as a trusted knowledge broker for policymakers. Many of these same features can be found in other science organizations that aim to share research knowledge to inform the policymaking process.

Conclusion

In this chapter I have provided an overview of theory, concepts, and research related to transferring research knowledge to policy. This overview lays a foundation for understanding the challenges involved, the many uses of research for policy development, and mechanisms by which research knowledge can be shared with the policy audience. I have highlighted the role of knowledge brokers as intermediaries in this process. In particular, I argue that professional science organizations can play a key role in sharing research knowledge with policy audiences. Their availability, credibility, neutrality, skills, and resources for translating science, and their direct contact with both scientists and policymakers enhance their success in KT processes. Science organizations also need to collaborate with researchers and with funding agencies in the evaluation of the effectiveness of these KT efforts.

REFERENCES

Bogenschneider, K., & Gross, E. (2004). From ivory tower to state house: How youth theory can inform youth policy making. *Family Relations, 53*(1), 19–25.

Bogenschneider, K., Olson, J.R., Linney, K.D., & Mills, J. (2000). Connecting research and policymaking: Implications for theory and practice from the family impact seminars. *Family Relations, 49*(3), 327–339.

Cohn, D. (2006). Jumping into the political fray: Academics and policy-making. *Institute for Research on Public Policy (IRPP) Matters, 7*(3), 8–36. Retrieved July 7, 2010, from http://www.irpp.org/pm/index.htm

Huston, A.C. (2005). Connecting the science of child development to public policy. *Social Policy Report, 19*(4), 3–18.

Huston, A.C. (2008). From research to policy and back. *Child Development, 79*(1), 1–12.

Knott, J., & Wildavsky, A. (1980). If dissemination is the solution, what is the problem? *Knowledge: Creation, Diffusion, Utilization, 1*(4), 527–528.

Landry, R., Amara, N., & Lamari, M. (2001). Climbing the ladder of research utilization: Evidence from social science research. *Science Communication, 22*(4), 396–422.

Lavis, J.N., Robertson, D., Woodside, J.M., McLeod, C.B., & Abelson, J. (2003). How can research organizations more effectively transfer research knowledge to decision makers? *Milbank Quarterly, 81*(2), 221–248.

McCall, R.B., & Green, B.L. (2004). Beyond the methodological gold standards of behavioral research: Considerations for practice and policy. *Social Policy Report, 18*(2), 3–19.

McCall, R.B., & Groark, C.J. (2000). The future of applied child development research and public policy. *Child Development, 71*(1), 197–204.

McCall, R.B., Groark, C.J., & Nelkin, R.P. (2004). Integrating developmental scholarship and society: From dissemination and accountability to evidence-based programming and policies. *Merrill-Palmer Quarterly, 50*(3), 326–340.

Rothbaum, F., Martland, N.F., & Bishop-Josef, S.J. (2007). Using the Web to disseminate research and affect public policy. In J.L. Aber, S.J. Bishop-Josef, S.M. Jones, K.T. McLearn, & D.A. Philips (Eds.), *Child development and social policy: Knowledge for action* (pp. 265–280). Washington, DC: American Psychological Association.

Shonkoff, J.P. (2000). Science, policy, and practice: Three cultures in search of a shared mission. *Child Development, 71*(1), 181–187.

Weiss, C.H. (1988). Evaluation for decisions: Is anybody there? Does anybody care? *Evaluation Practice, 9*(1), 5–19.

Weiss, C.H., & Bucuvalas, M.J. (1980). *Social science research and decision-making.* New York: Columbia University Press.

7 Knowledge Translation at the Political Level: Bridging the Policy Research to Policy Practice Gap

SIMON LENTON

This chapter[1] is concerned with the translation of public policy-relevant research into policy practice, specifically legislative change. I describe my experience as a drug policy researcher involved in the translation of research findings into changes to cannabis law in one Australian state, Western Australia (WA). This involved the conduct of research, research reviews, knowledge translation, and collaboration with policymakers and legislators in the introduction of a system of *prohibition with civil penalties* for minor cannabis offences. Often termed decriminalization, this entails legal changes that alter the status of a cannabis offence from a *crime* to that of a *civil* offence. The changes maintain the illegality of the act (in this case, the possession, use, and cultivation of small amounts of cannabis) but allow for civil penalties (fines and infringement notices) rather than more serious criminal penalties (a criminal record or the possibility of a custodial sentence).

Having a framework of the policy change process can be helpful in understanding and guiding the knowledge translation (KT) process involved in government policy and legislative change. I provide an overview of Kingdon's (1984, 1995) well-cited model. The example of WA's cannabis law changes demonstrates a number of challenges for translating research into public policy; the chapter addresses a number of issues regarding KT at this level. The need for having a lengthy time frame and using a range of strategies for disseminating research findings, along with the importance of establishing and maintaining long-standing relationships in KT are discussed. Although mass media is only one of the vehicles for research dissemination when trying to affect change in government policy and legislation, it is a very useful tool in bringing research findings to the attention of policymakers. At its best, research can be a means of giving voice to the unheard in the community. Nevertheless, researchers must face the dilemma of whether to stay outside or work within government structures, and whether they should take on the role of advocate or seek others to disseminate research findings. Considering one's audience is central to all KT and is particularly salient when trying to inform politicians, senior bureaucrats, and other policymakers. However, some researchers may believe that KT is not a legitimate academic activity. I argue that academic researchers should be engaged in KT and provide examples of measures that can support this activity within universities.

To provide some background, the federal government in Australia controls customs, importation, and border interdiction, but most laws concerning drug possession, use, manufacture, growing, and supply are the jurisdiction of the eight states and territories. I work as a senior researcher in drug policy at the National Drug Research Institute (NDRI) at the Curtin University of Technology in Perth, WA. NDRI is one of three national research centres funded by the Australian government through its Department of Health and Ageing under the National Drug Strategy. With additional research funding from both inside Australia and the international community, NDRI conducts research on minimizing harm from alcohol and other drug use, which informs interventions in legislative, fiscal, regulatory, and educational arenas.

The Challenge of Translating Research Findings into Public Policy

Many academics concerned with generating research evidence become frustrated when senior administrators, public servants, and legislators involved in public policymaking and implementation overlook their findings or recommendations. For example, commenting on attempts to improve evidence synthesis in the policy area, Sheldon (2005) made the following statement:

> There has been disappointment at the lack of progress in promoting evidence-based policy and management compared with the relative success of evidence-based medicine ... the consumers of policy and management research have not found the outputs sufficiently relevant and useful, and

researchers have become frustrated by the lack of uptake of the results of such systematic reviews by policymakers and managers. (p. 1)

Black (2001) noted that 'many researchers are politically naive. They have a poor understanding of how policy is made and have unrealistic expectations about what research can achieve' (p. 277). Whereas treatment practitioners often actively seek out research to guide their practice, those with a responsibility to implement drug policy (policymakers, bureaucrats or civil servants, legislators, politicians and their advisers or staffers) are often harder to reach and less likely to be active consumers of drug policy research (Lenton, 2004; Lenton & Allsop, 2010).

Few researchers understand that policymakers are often confronted by competing policy alternatives, all of which are supported by evidence, or else they are forced to make choices among policy options where there is little or no evidence. As a result, researchers may fail to understand that the evidence generated by research efforts will only be one small factor of many influencing policymaking, policy implementation, and legislative change. Among other things, politicians must consider the policies and views of their party, the views of party supporters and other stakeholders, and public perceptions. Also important are the number of seats the various parties hold in the legislature, other deals and obligations, and past policy history (Lavis, Robertson, Woodside, McLeod, & Abelson, 2003). While research is important, senior politicians from each side of the political spectrum during the WA cannabis law debate argued that politics is about perceptions (Lenton, 2004; Lenton & Allsop, 2010). For those involved in drug policy research, at best such research will be used by politicians to support their arguments when findings are consistent with them, or it will be ignored when findings suggest a contrary policy position (Lenton, 2004). While academe is about evidence and argument, politics is about perceptions and bargaining (Kingdon, 1984, 1995).

A Useful Model

A number of theoretical models aim to account for or inform the process of policy change (e.g., Baumgartner & Jones, 1993; Berry & Berry, 1999; Kingdon, 1984, 1995; Lindblom, 1959; Sabatier, 1988; Weiss, 1977). Each model offers an explanation of KT at the level of government policy and legislative change. Kingdon's theory provides a good description of my experience undertaking KT. A schematic representation of the policy change process, largely based on Kingdon's model, is presented in figure 7.1 (see also Lenton & Allsop, 2010).

As noted elsewhere (Lenton & Allsop, 2010), Kingdon (1995) points out that 'policy windows[or] ... opportunities for action on given initiatives' (p. 166) open and close and, when they close, they often stay closed for a long time. However, the list of subjects that government officials attend to is not randomly generated but is built by the joining, or 'coupling' (p. 172), of three streams of processes: problems, policy alternatives, and politics (see figure 7.1). This includes visible and less visible participants. 'Visible participants [are] those who receive considerable press and public attention' (p. 199): politicians, media commentators, political parties, and campaigners. The less visible, or 'hidden cluster includes academic specialists, career bureaucrats, and [government advisers and] staffers' (p. 199). Typically, the visible participants affect the agenda and the hidden cluster affects the alternatives (Kingdon, 1984, 1995).

Kingdon (1984, 1995) noted that in the problem stream, some problems occupy the attention of government officials more than others do. Problem recognition is crucial to agenda-setting, but conditions and problems are different. We put up with many conditions every day, such as bad weather and unavoidable, untreatable illnesses. A problem is a condition that has been defined as unacceptable. When an issue is framed as a problem and thus something that government must address, it has a better chance of rising on the political agenda. 'Policy entrepreneurs invest considerable resources bringing their conception of problems to officials' attention, and trying to convince them to see problems their way' (Kingdon, 1995, p. 198).

In the policy stream, alternatives emerge from what Kingdon (1995) called the 'policy primeval soup' (p. 116) through a process akin to natural selection. Policies that survive are usually technically feasible, congruent with community values, achievable within budgetary and other constraints, acceptable to the public, and politicians are receptive to them. Kingdon stated:

> Policy entrepreneurs do not leave consideration of their pet proposals to accident. Instead, they push for consideration in many ways and in many forums. In ... policy development, recombination (the coupling of already-familiar elements) is more important than mutation (the appearance of

Figure 7.1 A schematic representation of the policy change process

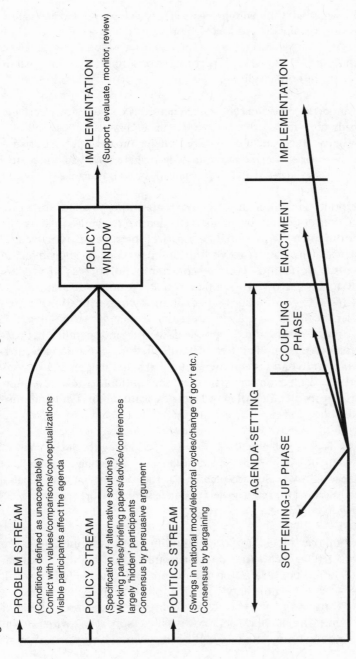

PROBLEM STREAM

(Conditions defined as unacceptable)
Conflict with values/comparisons/conceptualizations
Visible participants affect the agenda

POLICY STREAM

(Specification of alternative solutions)
Working parties/briefing papers/advice/conferences
largely 'hidden' participants
Consensus by persuasive argument

POLITICS STREAM

(Swings in national mood/electoral cycles/change of gov't etc.)
Consensus by bargaining

POLICY
WINDOW

IMPLEMENTATION
(Support, evaluate, monitor, review)

AGENDA-SETTING

SOFTENING-UP PHASE   COUPLING PHASE   ENACTMENT   IMPLEMENTATION

POLICY ENTREPRENEUR

This schematic (also published in Lenton & Allsop, 2010) is largely based on Kingdon's model (1984, 1995). Note: The author's schematic is an overview of Kingdon's model and includes issues of implementation that occur beyond the agenda-setting and opening of policy windows.

wholly new forms). Thus, entrepreneurs who broker people and ideas are often more important than policy inventors. (p. 201)

As seen in figure 7.1, there is a long process of softening up the system, which is critical to policy change:

Policy windows ... pass quickly and are missed if policy proposals have not already gone through the long gestation process before the [policy] window opens. The work of floating and refining proposals is not wasted if it does not bear fruit in the short run. Indeed, it is critically important if the proposal is to be heard at the right time. (Kingdon, 1995, p. 201)

However, policy entrepreneurs do more than simply push for their proposals and conceptions of problems to be heard. 'They also lie in wait – for a window to open ... [then, like a surfer] they are ready to paddle and their readiness, combined with their sense of riding the wave and using forces beyond their control, contributes to success' (Kingdon, 1995, p. 181). This narrowing of possible policy responses to a shorter list from which choices are made is called 'alternative specification' (p. 200) by Kingdon.

In Kingdon's (1995) model, the political stream is independent of problem recognition or the policy stream. 'Political events flow along according to their own dynamics and own rules. Participants perceive swings in national mood, elections bring new administrations to power ... interest groups ... press ... their demands on government' (p. 198), and ministerial portfolios change. As he noted:

Consensus is built in the political stream by bargaining [trading concessions for support], more than by persuasion ... [or] meeting logical tests such as feasibility or value acceptability ... The combination of national mood and elections is a more powerful agenda setter than organized interests. (Kingdon, 1995, p. 199)

Interest groups can block, support, or modify proposals, but they rarely set agendas on their own. When interest groups 'conflict with ... national mood and elected politicians, the latter combination is likely to prevail, at least as far as setting the agenda' (Kingdon, 1995, p. 199).

Reading Kingdon's (1995) book after being involved in research and KT concerning cannabis law changes was like someone switching on a light in a dark room where I had been groping around. Although

Kingdon says little about policy implementation, the following sections draw on this experience to describe areas to consider when contemplating KT at the levels of government policy and legislative change.

A Long Time Frame

As noted by Baumgartner and Jones (1993), policy changes are rare punctuations in long periods of equilibrium where little happens. As such, researchers committed to evidence-based policy need to operate with a long-term perspective. They cannot be concerned by a short-term lack of political support for research findings. For example, in the case of the research leading to the new cannabis laws in Western Australia, more than ten years passed between the publication of my first research paper on cannabis law and the enactment of those laws (Lenton, 2004). Rather than be discouraged by the process, policy researchers need to recognize that opportunities for policy change come and go. They also must be ready to feed research findings into the policy process, both directly and indirectly through the media (Lenton). Researchers need to keep watch on the political stream (the electoral cycle, changes of ministers, public statements by politicians, and information from contacts within the bureaucracy) and the problem stream (stories of rising or falling incidents of drug use and problems, drug crises), which may indicate impending opportunities for influencing policy (Kingdon, 1995).

Disseminating Research Findings When Policy Windows Are Closed

When policy windows are shut, it is still important to place research findings in public view. Contributing to the public debate – even when it appears that no one in government is taking notice (the softening-up phase seen in figure 7.1) – can serve an 'enlightenment function' (Weiss, 1977, p. 531) by providing background information and by influencing how people orient their own views to the issue. There may not be a discernable impact in the short term, but profound policy impacts may occur over the long term (Weiss, 1977). For example, from 1993 to 2000, I published eight refereed journal articles and ten reports with colleagues on cannabis and the law that were disseminated through six media releases, resulting in seventy-five stories in the print and electronic media (Lenton & Allsop, 2010). This research, along with studies conducted by colleagues in Australia, including some that were a part of the *Research into the Social Impacts of the Cannabis Expiation Notice System of South Australia* (Ali, 2000), composed a substantial body of evidence concerning the suitability of criminal or civil penalties for minor cannabis offences (see figure 7.2). Nevertheless, the Western Australia conservative government that was in power until February 2001 continued to respond to the research findings supporting the introduction of a civil penalty scheme by saying they would not decriminalize cannabis (e.g., Martin, 1999; Reed & Barnes, 2000). The important point in this example is that, although the conservative government was not willing to contemplate change, others were listening, and, as described below, some went on to positions of power where they were able to implement policy changes.

Figure 7.2 Summary of the main research findings on cannabis law, 1993–2000

Summary of the Main Research Findings on Cannabis Law 1993–2000

- In Australia, there were high levels (72–75 per cent) of public support for applying prohibition with civil penalties for minor cannabis offences but not for legalization (37–55 per cent) (Bowman & Sanson-Fisher, 1994; Lenton & Ovenden, 1996).
- Public support for prohibition with civil penalties schemes in Western Australia existed across the political spectrum (Lenton & Ovenden, 1996).
- Most West Australians who received a criminal conviction for a minor cannabis offence were, apart from their cannabis use, a non-criminal section of the community (Lenton, Ferrante, & Loh, 1996).
- A cannabis conviction can have significant adverse impacts on employment, further involvement with the criminal justice system, relationships, and accommodation. However, conviction fails to deter future cannabis use by many of those apprehended (Erickson, 1980; Erickson & Murray, 1986; Lenton & Heale, 2000).
- The social costs of a cannabis conviction are far greater than those under a civil penalties system where infringement penalties apply, but it appears that a criminal rather than a civil penalty may be

more likely to erode offenders' attitudes towards police (Lenton, Heale, Humeniuk, & Christie, 2000).

- Neither criminal nor civil penalties had much impact on the cannabis use of the vast majority of those apprehended (Lenton et al., 2000).
- The South Australian police and judiciary were supportive of civil penalties for minor cannabis offences (Sutton & McMillan, 2000).
- Research has failed to show that removing criminal penalties for personal use has led to an increase in the number of regular cannabis users in the general community (Donnelly, Hall, & Christie, 2000; Single, Christie, & Ali, 2000), among school students (Donnelly et al., 2000; Single et al., 2000), or university students (McGeorge & Aitken, 1997).
- However, prohibition with civil penalty schemes have been found to be far less expensive to the public purse than strict criminal penalty schemes in terms of criminal justice resources (Aldrich & Mikuriya, 1988; Brooks, Stothard, Moss, Christie, & Ali, 1999).
- The effectiveness of prohibition with civil penalties schemes depends largely on the details of how they are implemented. The South Australian scheme has been shown to have a low rate (45 per cent) of people paying their fines by the due date (Ali & Christie, 2000; Hunter, 2001), and there was reasonable evidence that organized crime had been syndicating cannabis cultivation under the expiable plant limit.

Source: Australian Bureau of Criminal Intelligence (1999); Sutton & McMillan (2000).

In 1998, with an existing track record of research on cannabis law in Australia, NDRI put together an international team of experts and won a tender to review the Australian and international literature on legislative options for cannabis. Based on the review, the team was to make recommendations for viable and appropriate options for one Australian state, Victoria. The report, entitled *The Regulation of Cannabis Possession, Use and Supply* (Lenton, Heale, Erickson et al., 2000), recommended a model of prohibition with civil penalties, which incorporated cautioning for first offenders. However, while the report was being considered, an election was called by the Liberal (conservative) Kennett government in Victoria so, for a number of reasons (see Lenton, 2004), the policy window in that state was effectively closed (Lenton & Allsop, 2010).

Although policy windows in Victoria seemed to be closing, policy windows in other states were opening. In 2000, the Western Australia (WA) branch of the Australian Labor Party (ALP), which was the opposition, was formulating its drug policy in preparation for an election the following year. In previous years, WA Labor figures had spoken in favour of cannabis law reform and attended public lectures by others and myself on the research evidence regarding cannabis law. Sensing a potential opportunity, I sent copies of the NDRI report to the WA Labor drugs spokesperson, and offered to consult with him on the issue. Labor then went to the 2001 election with a policy platform to hold a community drug summit and to decriminalize cannabis (Australian Labor Party Western Australia Branch, 2001). This incorporated many features of the cannabis model the NDRI report had proposed for the state of Victoria (Lenton & Allsop, 2010). Providing the research findings and recommended policy response directly to the politician drafting the ALP drugs policy was a tangible example of Kingdon's (1984, 1995) merging of the problem, policy, and political streams.

Despite a pre-election media campaign by the conservative government focusing on the ALP's cannabis law policy, the ALP won the February 2001 election. Subsequently, the new government's Community Drug Summit also supported the introduction of a prohibition with civil penalties scheme for cannabis (see Lenton, 2004; Lenton & Allsop, 2010). The government established a Working Group on Drug Law Reform (described below) to advise it on an appropriate legal model that was put before the WA Parliament and became law as the *Cannabis Control Act* of 2003.

Relationships, Trust, and Track Record

The importance of relationships and trust among individuals from the government bureaucracy, outside government, and the political sphere itself cannot be underestimated (Lenton & Allsop, 2010). These themes are frequently addressed in the KT literature (e.g., Golden-Biddle et al., 2003; Lavis et al., 2003). However, a recent report on Manitoba's *Need to Know* study suggested that 'there had been insufficient emphasis on personal factors in knowledge translation' (Bowen, Martens, & The Need to Know Team, 2005, p. 203). The study, which involved interviews with research and community partner stakeholders, found that quality of ongoing relationships and trust connected many forms of knowledge translation, with 'sustainability of relationships' (p. 209) emerging as a central issue.

In the cannabis law case described in this chapter, relationships built on trust enabled formal and informal channels to support KT. Doors may be opened by a trusted actor recommending someone to an influential third party as having something to offer. Having worked in the drug field for more than 20 years as a clinician, bureaucrat, and researcher, I had developed long-standing relationships with many key players inside and outside of government; these relationships helped bridge the gap between research and policy practice. For example, one long-standing work colleague, a senior bureaucrat, was unable, due to organizational protocols, to garner a meeting between his superior who was the government member responsible for drug policy and myself. However, I contacted a Greens Party parliamentarian with whom I had a good relationship who was able to arrange this meeting within days. The meeting proved crucial in supporting the legislative change because the government needed the political support of the Greens Party to get the Cannabis Bill through the Upper House of Parliament (Lenton & Allsop, 2010).

Western Australia, with a population of 2 million, is a small jurisdiction with a small drug policy community (Kingdon, 1995) and policy subsystem (Sabatier, 1988). This makes building relationships and reputation easier than in larger locations. Nevertheless, many of the relationships that proved important were not necessarily long standing but built on connections made while working in groups, committees, and other bodies that were often in parallel or tangential areas (e.g., the Planning Group for the WA Community Drug Summit and the Task Force on Drink, Drugs, and Driving). Although membership in some of these groups could be seen as time wasters or as not core researcher business in the short term, many bore fruit for KT in the end. Membership in forums like these can also help research to become decision-relevant and to help develop research-attuned decision-makers (Lavis et al., 2003). As such, these activities need to be supported by universities interested in improving KT at the level of government policy and legislative change. In the cannabis law case, my record of academic publications, clinical experience, and policy contributions, my media profile and my senior position at both a national research institute and a well-respected university, were all important credibility factors.

The Use of the Media

Drug policy is a polarized area of public debate. The media, which typically feeds on controversy, often actively seeks polarization in reporting drug policy issues. Unwittingly adding fuel to this is the major risk researchers take when disseminating research findings through the media. As described above, there are other ways of privately influencing policy through publication in academic journals, reports, submissions, briefings, and direct involvement in policy development and implementation. Yet using the media is an important part of KT for bringing research evidence to policymaking. There is little point in undertaking policy research if no one who can draft or implement policy is aware of it. All politicians and their advisers read newspapers; few read academic journal articles and reports. 'While many politicians will tend to ignore research that is not consistent with their own policy position, once research findings are in the media, they might be disputed or derided, but they are harder to ignore' (Lenton, 2004, p. 224). When one is on the outside of the political or policy process, the media is a way to achieve influence through communicating with the public (Kingdon, 1995). Thus, drug policy researchers interested in KT at the government policy level need to be media-savvy. This means understanding how the media works and getting media training as well as being prepared to communicate research outcomes clearly in a media-friendly fashion (Lenton, 2004).

At NDRI, there is a full-time media/communications officer position. With a background in media, public relations, and journalism, this individual provides support and training for academic staff in developing media strategies to disseminate research findings. This individual also monitors print and electronic media, consults with relevant research staff regarding media opportunities, and maintains ongoing relationships with individuals and organizations in the media industry. The communications officer is also a first contact point for media inquiries and contributes to corporate communications and website management. As a result, NDRI and its research staff have a high media profile. In 2008, NDRI was mentioned over 800 times in media stories, many of which disseminated or quoted the organization's research output.

Research as a Way for Grass-roots Community Members to be Heard

One important way the research contributed to the process of policy change described above involved collecting and documenting the opinions, knowledge, and experiences of those without a voice (especially cannabis users themselves) and of members of the general community. Cannabis and other illicit drug users are often marginalized, not least by the laws that proscribe drug use and make public self-identification as a drug user a potentially hazardous activity. A number of the studies (e.g., Ali et al., 1999; Lenton & Heale, 2000; Lenton, Heale, Humeniuk, & Christie, 2000) involved detailed qualitative and quantitative interviews with cannabis users, growers, and dealers. These studies explained participants' experiences of using the drug, their involvement in the cannabis market, and their contact with law enforcement. Some of the studies provided accounts, in the users' own words, of being apprehended and criminalized for simple cannabis possession and use. The ability to provide these anonymous verbatim reports to policymakers and politicians proved to be a powerful means of transferring community views.

Other studies involving anonymous telephone surveys of the general public allowed the attitudes and behaviours of a wider section of the community to be collated and reported (Bowman & Sanson-Fisher, 1994; Heale, Hawks, & Lenton, 2000; Lenton & Ovenden, 1996). By disseminating findings through expert advice to policymakers and via the media to the public and elected representatives, researchers can bring the experiences of those at the grass-roots level to those who may be able to make changes at the policy level. Such research can challenge stereotypes and misunderstandings held by some of those involved in policymaking. Such misunderstandings can serve as barriers to implementing effective policy. Thus, research can be particularly relevant when problems with existing policy and legal frameworks are being ignored, while the dominant understanding is one of individual deficit or behaviour (Lenton, 2005).

Inside vs. Outside – Public vs. Confidential

My experience in the Western Australian cannabis law reform process provides examples of the dilemmas that face researchers when they move from the outside to the inside of the policy process. Outside the power base of government, one can speak openly about research evidence but will often have little direct influence on policy. When invited into working parties with government, one's capacity to influence policy and action can be greatly enhanced, but this may require keeping discussions confidential. In order to bring about a desirable policy outcome, one may need to make compromises to maintain relationships with other players and stay in the game. This involves a constant weighing of the relative risks and benefits of options, the balance of which can change as the policy and implementation process unfolds. Sometimes the risks of not speaking out outweigh those of staying in the game (Lenton & Allsop, 2010). Yeates (2005) made the following statement to illustrate this point: 'Being on the inside of the policy process rather than external to it ... may require a high level of trust on the part of policy-makers and perhaps will involve a commitment to confidentiality that will be uncomfortable for both sides' (p. 56).

To illustrate these dilemmas, after their election win in December 2001, the Labor government established the Ministerial Working Party on Drug Law Reform to advise how the recommended reforms on cannabis and other drug laws could be implemented. The eight-member group was chaired by a law society representative and included members of the police service, a justice official, a medical practitioner, a representative from the new Drug and Alcohol Office, and myself. From the commencement of our deliberations, and even after vigorous and reasoned argument, there was no unanimous position but compromise was required to reach consensus (Lenton & Allsop, 2010). For example, the first issue was group membership. Some members, including myself, strongly believed that a representative of a drug user group should be included. Evidence from the drug field indicated that involving members of the affected communities was a cornerstone of negotiating successful government responses in contentious areas. However, the minister who had put the group together rejected the idea. For me, this raised the question of whether I should take a principled stand and risk being removed from the Working Party or compromise and find other ways to attempt to get the drug user perspective reflected in the deliberations. Given the risks of exclusion and a very public stumble at the group's inception, I decided on the latter. The possibility that the group could come up with a workable model supported by all at the table was the best chance for evidence-based cannabis law reform at any time in the past or foreseeable future. This was a position that could be justifiably criticized by drug user groups, members of the research community, and those who advocate a grass-roots, community-based approach to KT (Lenton & Allsop, 2010). Attempts were made to use the research evidence, including qualitative accounts from cannabis users, to bring their issues to the table. Nevertheless, the political reality meant the contribution of a cannabis user perspective was undoubtedly less than it could have been.

Researcher and Research Advocate

Building credibility as the KT messenger can be skill intensive and time consuming, 'but when researchers have the skills and experience to act as the principal messenger, their credibility will likely make them the ideal choice' (Lavis et al., 2003, p. 226). Yet there are risks in researchers taking an advocacy role. Not the least, researchers can be regarded as having lost their perceived objectivity – a criticism often made by those who hold a different policy position from that which the researcher is advocating. Avoiding statements that go beyond the evidence, taking a balanced approach, and using colleagues as peer evaluators on a regular basis can help reduce the damage this accusation can do. If other agencies or individuals are in a position to advocate for the research evidence successfully, this may be ideal. Yet, in the case of the cannabis law changes, I appeared to be the person best able to take on this role effectively.

Considering the Audience

Researchers need to consider their audience in undertaking KT. According to Black (2001), '[R]esearchers have tended to focus on enhancing the strength of the information available, with disappointing results. For research to have an impact it is necessary to target the values of the policymakers' (p. 277). Regarding report format, Lavis and colleagues (2005) suggested a 1-3-25 system: 1-page of take home messages, a 3-page executive summary, and a 25-page report backed up by a longer technical report, if necessary. In my experience, researchers often have difficulty mastering brevity – both in their KT with policymakers and through the media. Yet, like any skill, it comes with practice. Rehearsing sound bites may help to ensure the main message gets radio or television coverage. Writing letters to the editor of newspapers and magazines provides practice in honing one's message and can have an impact on policymakers directly.

Implications for What Counts as Legitimate Academic Activity

If we are interested in policy research having an impact, then we need to support researchers in this activity and demonstrate that research can influence policy. Canada is one country that is putting considerable effort and resources into raising the profile of KT. This includes research funding that supports the costs associated with push efforts to bridge the research – policy gap (Lavis, 2006).

For those of us in countries with less formal structures of KT, researchers' involvement can be supported by (a) including impacts on policy as a goal of research organizations and (b) providing appropriate resources and including strategies in duty statements and organizational plans. Senior research staff can model KT as an important, worthwhile activity. Having KT as a goal in institutional or organizational strategic plans, can provide a way to legitimize university-based researchers who undertake non-research activities that are necessary to facilitate KT. For example, one of the goals of NDRI is to '[c]onduct research that is valued by stakeholders as being of high quality, timely and relevant to public policy and practice' (National Drug Research Institute, 2004, p. 8). This is supported at an institutional level by Curtin University's value statement, which includes 'cultivation of responsive and responsible links with the wider community, emphasising service, practical relevance, social justice and ethical behaviour' (Curtin University of Technology, 2004, p. 2).

Implications for Institutional Support

This is an interesting time for issues of KT in Australia. The academic community had been preparing for the introduction of the Research Quality Framework (RQF), a new funding mechanism for university research based on similar schemes operating in the United Kingdom and New Zealand. Unfortunately, with the election of a new federal government in late 2007, the previous government's RQF model was abandoned. It is likely that the new government's initiative Excellence in Research in Australia (ERA) will have less emphasis on research impact than the previous government's model. However, over the last few years there has been considerable debate on the extent to which any such funding structure should be based on outputs (e.g., competitive research grants awarded, refereed journal publications, citations, journal impact factors) or impacts (e.g., social, economic, environmental and/or cultural outcomes) (Australian Department of Education, Science, and Training, 2005).

Evidence to demonstrate the former, more traditional indicators of academic excellence are easier to quantify, as there are academic metrics, software packages, and online bibliographic facilities that are set up to do just that. Demonstrating evidence for impact is more challenging.

The previously proposed RQF focused on a five-year window of enquiry to demonstrate academic excellence in terms of publications and citations. However, periods of a decade or more may be needed to gauge the impact of research on policy because knowledge has a cumulative effect on policymakers (Lindblom & Cohen, as cited in Sabatier, 1988). The softening-up phase may take considerable time. Furthermore, at least one cycle of formulation – implementation – reformulation may be required to get a realistic appraisal of its relative success or failure. Policy research has shown that programs appearing to have failed in their first few years may prove successful in the longer term, and vice versa (Sabatier, 1988).

Evidence Demonstrating KT at the Level of Government Policy and Legislation

Believing that one's research had an impact on policy or legislative change and being able to demonstrate it to a sceptical audience are two different things. Given the focus of the NDRI on contribution to policy and practice, a variety of evidence sources have been employed to support our claims of impact. These have been developed as practical responses to the need for workable performance indicators for the organization. The evidence sources for KT employed at NDRI include numbers and examples of citations of research publication in government reports, citation in Hansard (transcripts of parliamentary debates in the Westminster System), media statements by members of government, references in political party policy statements, official correspondence and invitations to join government working parties, written testimonials from Members of Parliament and other key stakeholders, and media articles and letters to the editor that demonstrate the impact and relevance of research. These materials support a case-study account of how an individual piece or a body of research has influenced the wider community.

Summary and Conclusions

Researchers need to understand that changing government policy and legislation is usually a slow process and windows of opportunity for such change come and go. When the window is closed, researchers can accumulate evidence, but they need to be prepared to step into the breach to contribute to the policy change process as opportunities emerge. Windows can open for a variety of reasons, but the process is not random, and it can be facilitated by policy advocates who bring together people and policy ideas. There is no point in conducting policy research if no one knows about the results of that research. While academic publications are important, providing confidential briefings and becoming members of government task forces and working parties allows researchers to influence directly the policy process. The importance of relationships and trust between researchers and policymakers cannot be underestimated, but there are risks for researchers in real and perceived integrity and independence. If invited to the policymaking table, researchers need to decide when to make compromises and when to hold their ground. Less directly, dissemination of research findings through the media can contribute to public debate and through this can influence policymakers. Few politicians read academic reports and journal articles, but they do read newspapers. Once research is in the public realm, it is harder for politicians to ignore it. Yet those presenting research in the media need to learn how to do this and must be prepared to be available to media outlets. The ability to be succinct is crucial.

At its best, research can give a voice to those at the grassroots who are often unheard and marginalized in public policy debates. Researchers wanting to improve KT at the political level and to bridge the gap between policy research and policy practice need to consider the risks and benefits of the researcher-advocate role and how to manage these risks. Researchers need to consider the extent to which they become involved as policy brokers or advocates, or whether to support others in undertaking this role.

NOTE

1 Some of the material presented in this chapter has recently been summarized elsewhere (Lenton & Allsop, 2010).

REFERENCES

Aldrich, M.R., & Mikuriya, T. (1988). Savings in California law enforcement costs attributable to the Moscone Act of 1976 – a summary. *Journal of Drug Issues, 20*(1), 75–81.

Ali, R. (2000). Introduction to special section: Cannabis expiation in South Australia. *Drug and Alcohol Review, 19*(3), 249.

Ali, R., & Christie, P. (2000). Offences under the cannabis expiation notice scheme in South Australia. *Drug and Alcohol Review, 19*(3), 251–256.

Ali, R., Christie, P., Lenton, S., Hawks, D., Sutton, A., Hall, W., et al. (1999). *The social impacts of the cannabis expiation notice scheme in South Australia – Summary report* (Monograph No. 34). Canberra, Australia: Publications Productions Unit, Commonwealth Department of Health and Aged Care.

Australian Bureau of Criminal Intelligence. (1999). *Australian illicit drug report 1997–98.* Canberra, Australia: Commonwealth of Australia.

Australian Department of Education, Science, and Training. (2005). *Research quality framework: Assessing the quality and impact of research in Australia* [Issues Paper]. Retrieved August 14, 2008, from http://www.dest.gov.au/NR/rdonlyres/E32ECC65-05C0-4041-A2B8-75ADEC69E159/4467/rqf_issuespaper.pdf

Australian Labor Party Western Australian Branch. (2001). *Drugs and crime – Breaking the cycle.* Perth, Australia: Author.

Baumgartner, F.R., & Jones, B.D. (1993). *Agendas and instability in American politics.* Chicago: University of Chicago Press.

Berry, F.S., & Berry, W.D. (1999). Innovation and diffusion models in policy research. In P.A. Sabatier (Ed.), *Theories of the policy process* (pp. 169–200). Boulder, CO: Westview Press.

Black, N. (2001). Evidence based policy: Proceed with care. *British Medical Journal, 323*(7307), 275–278.

Bowen, S., Martens, P., & The Need to Know Team. (2005). Demystifying knowledge translation: Learning from the community. *Journal of Health Services Research & Policy, 10*(4), 203–211.

Bowman, J., & Sanson-Fisher, R. (1994). *Public perceptions of cannabis legislation* (National Drug Strategy Monograph Series No. 28). Canberra, Australia: Australian Government Printing Service.

Brooks, A., Stothard, C., Moss, J., Christie, P., & Ali, R. (1999). *Costs associated with the operation of the cannabis expiation notice scheme in South Australia.* Adelaide, Australia: Drug and Alcohol Services Council.

Curtin University of Technology. (2004). *Curtin University of Technology annual report 2003.* Perth, Australia: Author. Retrieved August 15 2008, from http://about.curtin.edu.au/local/docs/ar2003/curtin_annual_report_03_full.pdf

Donnelly, N., Hall, W., & Christie, P. (2000). The effects of the cannabis expiation notice system on the prevalence of cannabis use in South Australia: Evidence from the national drug strategy household surveys 1985–95. *Drug and Alcohol Review, 19*(3), 265–269.

Erickson, P.G. (1980). *Cannabis criminals: The social effects of punishment on drug users.* Toronto, ON: Addiction Research Foundation Books.

Erickson, P.G., & Murray, G.F. (1986). Cannabis criminals revisited. *British Journal of Addiction, 81*(1), 81–85.

Golden-Biddle, K., Reay, T., Petz, S., Witt, C., Casebeer, A., Pablo, A., et al. (2003). Toward a communicative perspective of collaborating in research: The case of the researcher-decision-maker partnership. *Journal of Health Services & Research Policy, 8*(Suppl. 2), 20–25.

Heale, P., Hawks, D., & Lenton, S. (2000). Public awareness, knowledge and attitudes regarding the CEN system in South Australia. *Drug and Alcohol Review, 19*(3), 271–280.

Hunter, N. (2001). *Cannabis expiation notices in South Australia, 1997 to 2000* (Information Bulletin No. 27). Adelaide, Australia: Office of Crime Statistics, South Australia Attorney General's Department.

Kingdon, J.W. (1984). *Agendas, alternatives and public policies.* Boston: Little Brown.

Kingdon, J.W. (1995). *Agendas, alternatives and public policies* (2nd ed.). New York: HarperCollins.

Lavis, J.N. (2006). Research, public policymaking, and knowledge-translation processes: Canadian efforts to build bridges. *Journal of Continuing Education in the Health Professions, 26*(1), 37–45.

Lavis, J.N., Davies, H., Oxman, A., Denis, J.-L., Golden-Biddle, K., & Ferlie, E. (2005). Towards systematic reviews that inform health care management and policy-making. *Journal of Health Services & Research Policy, 10*(Suppl. 1), 35–48.

Lavis, J.N., Robertson, D., Woodside, J.M., McLeod, C.B., & Abelson, J. (2003). How can research organizations more effectively transfer research knowledge to decision-makers? *Milbank Quarterly, 81*(2), 221–248.

Lenton, S. (2004). Pot, politics and the press: Reflections on cannabis law reform in Western Australia. *Drug and Alcohol Review, 23*(2), 223–233.

Lenton, S. (2005). A framework for prevention. *Drug and Alcohol Review, 24*(1), 49–55.

Lenton, S., & Allsop, S. (2010). A tale of CIN – The Cannabis Infringement Notice scheme in Western Australia. *Addiction, 105*(5), 808–816.

Lenton, S., Ferrante, A., & Loh, N. (1996). Dope busts in the West: Minor cannabis offences in the Western Australian criminal justice system. *Drug and Alcohol Review, 15*(4), 335–341.

Lenton, S., & Heale, P. (2000). Arrest, court and social impacts of conviction for a minor cannabis offense under strict prohibition. *Contemporary Drug Problems, 27*(4), 805–833.

Lenton, S., Heale, P., Erickson, P., Single, E., Lang, E., & Hawks, D. (2000). *The regulation of cannabis possession, use and supply: A discussion document* prepared for the Drugs and Crime Prevention Committee of the Parliament of Victoria (NDRI Monograph No. 3). Perth: National Drug Research Institute, Curtin University of Technology.

Lenton, S., Heale, P., Humeniuk, R., & Christie, P. (2000). Infringement versus conviction: The social impact of a minor cannabis offence in South Australia and Western Australia. Drug and Alcohol Review, 19(3), 257–264.

Lenton, S., & Ovenden, C. (1996). Community attitudes to cannabis use in Western Australia. Journal of Drug Issues, 26(4), 783–804.

Lindblom, C.E. (1959). The science of 'muddling through.' Public Administration Review, 19(2), 79–88.

Martin, R. (1999, October 5). Minister holds firm on drugs hard line. The Australian, p. 8.

McGeorge, J., & Aitken, C.K. (1997). Effects of cannabis decriminalization in the Australian Capital Territory on university students' patterns of use. Journal of Drug Issues, 27(4), 785–793.

National Drug Research Institute. (2004). National Drug Research Institute strategic plan 2003–2008. Retrieved December 12, 2006, from http://www.ndri.curtin.edu.au/pdfs/ndri_strategic_plan_03-08.pdf

Reed, D., & Barnes, A. (2000, June 14). Relax drug penalties say experts. The West Australian, p. 5.

Sabatier, P.A. (1988). An advocacy coalition framework of policy change and the role of policy-oriented learning therein. Policy Sciences, 21(2–3), 129–168.

Sheldon, T.A. (2005). Making evidence synthesis more useful for management and policy-making [Editorial]. Journal of Health Services & Research Policy, 10(Suppl. 1), 1–5.

Single, E., Christie, P., & Ali, R. (2000). The impact of cannabis decriminalisation in Australia and the United States. Journal of Public Health Policy, 21(2), 157–186.

Sutton, A., & McMillan, E. (2000). Criminal justice perspectives on South Australia's cannabis expiation notice procedures. Drug and Alcohol Review, 19(3), 281–286.

Weiss, C.H. (1977). Research for policy's sake: The enlightenment function of social research. Policy Analysis, 3(Fall), 531–545.

Yeates, G. (2005). A journey into unfamiliar terrain. Journal of Health Services & Research Policy, 10(Suppl. 1), 55–56.

8 User-Led Reviews of Research Knowledge: Enhancing Relevance and Reception

DAVID A. GOUGH

Information is a source of power. High-quality, relevant information assists individuals with understanding and decision-making and can be used to persuade others to act or not to act in certain ways. Research evidence is one important type of information. Research methods vary considerably in their aims and techniques, but they share common rules for explicating methodologies that make the research evidence account-able and open to debate. Other forms of knowledge – for example, knowledge based on the experiences of individuals or organizations – are constructed differently and are often used in combination with research evidence.

In an increasingly complex world, research evidence is an important resource. Access to research evidence – and the ability to engage in debates about it – can enhance democratic participation and, thus, is an issue of citizenship. Those without access to research evidence or the skills to make use of it are at a disadvantage when making decisions, including decisions that affect both individuals and their communities. They are also less likely to influence the priorities that determine the nature of research and, thus, the nature of the research evidence used in future debates.

In this chapter I consider the problems of access to research knowl-edge and the power to influence the research agendas that construct that knowledge. I argue that systematic research synthesis provides a process to increase both access and engagement in research for all members of society. Anyone can be a user of research – as a policy-maker, professional practitioner, academic, service user, community group, or an individual member of society (Gough & Elbourne, 2002). In practice, research knowledge is defined and produced by select groups in society. Providing easier access to research and greater control of research agendas benefits the wider community in terms of having more knowledge that is relevant to their needs. Research agendas also benefit by having a wider and more receptive base in society.

Access to Research and Decision-Making

Researchers working in universities or other specialized facilities are the major contributors to most research. Most members of the public do not have the skills to evaluate the research designs and technical methods required by university departments and institutes. Studies' findings are typically reported in a disparate range of academic books and journals, often using technical language and scientific jargon. In addition, the quantity of studies now published means that even academic specialists have difficulty keeping up with the research results in their own fields. Furthermore, vested interests and other factors influence what research is undertaken and how it is reported, which may be hard to detect in specific studies.

The idea that research findings can directly solve practical problems has been regarded as a naive, rational approach to research-driven policymaking (Weiss, 1979). One would expect research results to inform decision-making, but it is naive to think that this would happen in a simple rational way. Research may be undertaken not only to increase knowledge but also for instrumental reasons; for example, in order to delay decision-making, divert attention, or with no real intent to apply the results or implement the findings. The results of research may be used selectively to support particular positions. Even researchers themselves may have vested interests to support findings that confirm their particular view of the world, or that support services or products with which they are associated. Just because research follows methodological rules does not mean that a particular method is appropriate, that the methodological rules are perfectly followed, or that the research itself is fair and equitable. Even if the findings of a study are of high quality and aim to increase knowledge for a decision that has wide-ranging implications, research evidence will often not be the crucial factor in making practical decisions. The evidence may indicate a solution to a problem that is simply too expensive, politically sensitive, or has practical barriers to implementation. There may also be quite appropriate ideological reasons why other knowledge sources predominate over research results in making decisions. There are indeed limits to the naive, rational approach to research use, but this does not mean that all research is necessarily of bad quality or badly used. In sum, we must be aware that there are many factors that must be considered along-side relevant evidence, such as access to research, instrumental uses of research, and other decision-making influences.

In order to understand how factors other than research influence decision-making, we also need to understand how research itself has various forms. There are many different ideological and theoretical assumptions that affect how research is undertaken; there are also many methodological approaches that can be applied to answer differ-ent questions. In many cases, research communities monitor the qual-ity of studies through peer review. To apply research, it is necessary to consider the values and assumptions employed, the methods used, the rigour and quality assurance applied to the study, and its transpar-ency and accountability. Considering these factors in assessing a single study is a significant undertaking. Discussing research evidence about a particular issue also requires consideration of not a single study, but rather whole bodies of research knowledge. Around the world, the output of research is enormous. It is unlikely that individual members of the public or community groups can keep up to date and evaluate the quality and appropriateness of studies without knowledge transfer mechanisms to aid this process.

Systematic Research Synthesis

One way to allow access to the breadth of what is known from research is through literature reviews. These consider many relevant studies, evaluate their relevance and methodological quality, and draw over-all conclusions about what is known. Until recently, many reviews did not have clear, explicit methodologies, so it was not possible to evaluate how well the review authors had considered and evaluated the available research literature. Now, however, the expectation is that reviews should have explicit, rigorous methods so that their conclu-sions are accountable (Oakley, Gough, Oliver, & Thomas, 2005). Meth-ods for undertaking systematic reviews are most frequently developed for reviews of research on the effects of medical interventions, such as surgeries, therapies, or medications. However, the logic of systematic methods of review applies to all research questions and methods, and they are being developed for wider use.

Systematic research reviews generally include the following stages: deciding on the research question; developing a conceptual framework and inclusion criteria; search strategy and screening; coding and mapping data; reconsidering the review question and scope; appraising the quality and relevance of the research; synthesizing findings and conclusions; and finally communicating, interpreting, and applying the findings. Both primary research and research reviews require judgments to be made based on ideological and theoretical assumptions and on accountable methodological approaches. Systematic reviews do not, therefore, avoid such judgments but make them explicit so that readers can understand why the review has been undertaken and the quality of the conclusions drawn.

Use of Research

The development of these systematic methods for determining what we do and do not know from research was intended to lead to more informed use of research by policymakers and practitioners. In practice, however, achieving evidence-informed policy and practice is difficult and complex (Graham & Tetroe, 2007; Grimshaw et al., 2004). Methods of knowledge translation (KT) that identify better strategies to enable the uptake of research findings are themselves an important focus of study.

Approaches to KT advocate simplifying review reports to make them more accessible. Strategies that encourage the uptake of research messages through knowledge brokers, change agents, early adopters, and communities of change are also growing (Greenhalgh, Robert, MacFarlane, Bate, & Kyriakidou, 2004; McCabe, this volume; Nutley, Walter, & Davies, 2007; Sudsawad, 2007). Nevertheless, there is relatively little theoretical work that informs the development of successful KT strategies (Graham & Tetroe, 2007; Grimshaw et al., 2004).

Generally, evaluating KT usually focuses on the uptake of research evidence produced by researchers. Typically, primary research is synthesized in reviews and then offered to potential consumers, such as policymakers and practitioners. When this does not work, strategies of KT are devised to increase uptake. In other words, it is a strategy that pushes knowledge rather than relying on a pull from consumer demand. How, then, is it possible to increase demand for the product of research reviews? One method is to increase user involvement in the production of the knowledge so that the product is more likely to be relevant and of interest to them.

Professional users of research, such as policymakers and service practitioners, may become involved directly in research projects. However, the involvement of these individuals is often limited in extent and degree because they are busy and unlikely to have all the technical skills of researchers. Even if users do become involved in the details of the research, their influence on the research focus and findings is likely to be relatively modest and limited to only a few projects. Involvement in systematic reviews, however, allows for a much greater influence on the interpretation of the results of many studies. The policymakers or practitioners do not need to possess all the skills of a systematic reviewer; rather, they need to understand the main processes of the review and have an opportunity to influence its focus and outcome. They can become involved in the process of reviewing literature to make it more relevant to their needs at any, or all, of its stages. These stages will be considered in the following section.

Question, Conceptual Framework, and Inclusion Criteria in a Review

For all research, implicit and explicit ideological and theoretical positions determine what is studied and influence what is found. Two projects with slightly different questions or analyses may come to different conclusions. Similarly, a review of the literature will be driven by a review question representing perspectives with specific theoretical and ideological assumptions. The issue here is how a wider range of users can be involved in directing research reviews (Oliver et al., 2004).

The starting point for a review is the question, *What do you want to know and why?* What this question means in practice is only understandable if the research questions and assumptions are sufficiently clear to inform practical decisions about what studies are included in the review and which are excluded. These criteria are operational definitions of the review question and its conceptual framework. A lack of clarity in research questions and assumptions make it difficult to know what studies to include in the reviews. If intended users are clear about their questions and assumptions, then the reasons for differences among reviews should be clear. An example of this is provided by six reviews of accidents in the elderly that reviewed 137 studies; however, only two studies were included in all of the six reviews (Oliver, Peersman,

Harden, & Oakley, 1999). If reviews are asking different questions and examining different studies, then it is not surprising if they produce different results and come to different conclusions.

User involvement in the process of defining the review question, conceptual assumptions, and inclusion criteria also needs to be considered in terms of the aims and methods of review. One aim might be for the users to be managers of the review and control all the major decisions. Researchers might assist by providing technical advice or undertaking the review, but this would be on behalf of the user drivers of the review. For example, one review undertaken by the Evidence for Policy and Practice Information and Co-ordinating Centre (EPPI-Centre) was controlled by school students (Garcia et al., 2006). They determined the focus of the review, whereas the EPPI-Centre staff did most of the practical work. The EPPI-Centre had suggested to the students that they might want to undertake a review of bullying, but the students were less interested in this topic. They were more interested in a review of the day-to-day issues in their lives related to how to make and maintain friendships. This focus for the review would never have been determined or used by the researchers. The perspective of the students had to be the driver of the process in order to produce a review relevant to their needs.

Another approach is for users to have an advisory or consultative role. Users might aim to provide advice on the direction of the review acting as consultants, using their experience and skills to suggest how the review should be framed. Alternatively, users may be consulted as a means of including particular perspectives in deciding the details of a given research question.

There are many ways that users might arrange to manage a research review team or be part of a collective management team (Carr & Coren, 2007; Oliver et al., 2004). Similarly, there are many ways that users could act as advisers. A common structure for involving users is an advisory group, although it may not be clear to what extent the users' advice must be followed or whether they are simply being consulted and the researchers make the decision. The use of advisory groups also raises issues about the training and support given to users to enable them to undertake such roles. Without support, the users' role may not be effective in influencing the review. Another fundamental issue is whether users are accurately representing a user constituency (e.g., Aboriginal adults) or the group from which they came (e.g., a particular Aboriginal cultural group) (Oliver et al., 2004).

One method for achieving user perspectives that can be more representative of the user community is to review research on users' views or to undertake new primary research on users' views. For example, in a review of the effects of travel on children, the reviewers undertook a telephone survey of the perspectives of individuals concerned with school travel, such as children, travel planners, policy, and teachers (Gough, Oliver, Brunton, Selai, & Schaumberg, 2001). This helped ensure that the preconceptions of the reviewers did not limit the scope of the review. The review considered the influence of factors such as exercise, pollution, and social and cognitive experiences on everything from illness, fitness, and cognitive maps, to social integration, and alertness at school. For example, children being driven to school by parents had positive social mixing effects that might not so easily occur in the larger areas with more seating choices provided by buses (Adler & Adler, 1984).

Search Strategy and Screening in a Review

Inclusion and exclusion criteria define what studies should be considered by a review, but there is still the task of finding the studies which are to be included. The search strategy is the plan that will be used to identify relevant studies. In many reviews, search strategies aim to be exhaustive in finding all studies in the literature that meet the inclusion criteria. Strategies may include searching bibliographic databases, researching online, researching hard copies of journals and books, or identifying unpublished reports. The strategy will depend upon the focus of the review, and user input may be critical to this process. If, for example, the review is on aspects of rural communities, then community knowledge could be critical to understanding the relevant literature indexed in libraries, keyworded on databases, or found in unpublished sources.

There can be problems in relying on a single source of advice on searching. For example, if academic specialists are searching for studies only in their own topic area, they may only locate studies with which they are already familiar. An exhaustive search attempts to find studies that meet the inclusion criteria that were not expected. An example is the review already referred to on the effects of travel on children (Gough et al., 2001). The search identified many 1960s studies in the United States on the policy of bussing children across cities to achieve racial mixing in schools. These studies were not expected by the reviewers but met the initial inclusion criteria and were found by the search strategy.

A strategy developed only by particular specialists may unwittingly miss relevant studies. This is part of a broader concern about the role of expert opinion. Experts may be highly skilled and experienced and know much about a particular subject, but the limits to their knowledge may not be clear to users. A systematic review should be explicit about its boundaries with both expert and user input being valued.

Data Coding and Mapping in a Review

The studies identified by the search strategy next need to be screened to ensure that they indeed meet the inclusion criteria. The studies included can then be described in specific ways. One reason for these descriptions is to provide an overall map of the whole group of studies selected. This is a useful product, as it describes a research field that may not have been previously delineated. Many descriptions of research fields are determined by the research discipline, but user input can reveal a unique grouping of studies relevant to user interests. For example, a narrowly focused, academic psychology review on the effects of travel on children would focus on cognitive or social effects of travel but would omit studies on larger social issues, such as racial bussing.

The mapping of the research field can also inform synthesis. Mapping provides an initial description of the studies included before more detailed data coding and analysis are undertaken. It can be used to select a subset of studies for synthesis. The mapping codes can be used as the basis for making the selection of a subsample of studies. The users' role in such a process is very powerful, as it is essentially a re-examination and refocusing of the original review question that determines the nature of the results of the synthesis of findings.

A second reason for providing an overall categorization of the studies included in the review is to provide data necessary for the synthesis of the results of the studies. This can have several components, including basic descriptive information and information to inform quality checks. The dimensions used to describe the studies will, of course, determine the nature of the review. User input is, thus, important in deciding what aspects of studies, methods, and results are included.

Quality and Relevance Appraisal in a Review

Once it has been decided whether all or just some of the mapped studies are synthesized, the next stage is to conduct the more detailed data coding and to rate the quality and relevance of the studies for the synthesis. Such judgments may exclude low-scoring studies from the synthesis or weight them lower in the synthesis. Many reviews only consider the methodological execution of the study to judge study quality, but there are two further dimensions that can be considered (Gough, 2007): the fit and relevance of research method for answering the review question. A study may be very well executed but not a good fit for addressing the review question. In many reviews, the type of primary studies to be included is often determined only at the inclusion criteria stage.

The second dimension is the relevance of the study for the review question. The inclusion criteria determine whether a study is relevant or not; but even within studies meeting these criteria, there can be variations in relevance. If, for example, a group is undertaking a review of effective approaches for increasing children's feeling of ownership of their communities, then studies that are sensitive to community participation may be more relevant to the review. If, however, the review is particularly concerned with policymaking in Canada, then only studies in Canada or similar countries may be relevant. Issues of study fit and relevance may also include ethical issues; for example, studies that are more ethical having more weight than others. These are clearly controversial issues, and people can differ in the criteria they apply and the judgments they make. The important points are to determine clearly whose voices are considered, that these determinants are made explicit so that the review methods are transparent, and that the review findings are accountable.

Synthesis in a Review

Once the parameters of how to include, exclude, or weight studies based on their quality and relevance have been decided, the findings can be synthesized. Synthesis involves bringing together the findings so that they create something greater than the individual studies. When the data are statistical, then the synthesis may also be statistical. When the synthesis is based on qualitative data (or on numbers that cannot be synthesized statistically), then the synthesis will be in words and so involve a rather different process.

Many reviews ask empirical questions; for example, what is the average, range, or size of certain types of communities, or whether a specific program is effective or not. These types of reviews tend to have their methodology decided in advance, with clear ways of combining data in the synthesis. Users' input at the initial question stage can help to determine the nature of the analysis and the synthesis as well as the results and the conclusions that are important.

There are also reviews that ask conceptual questions and synthesize conceptual data. For example, in a meta-ethnographic synthesis, the conceptual insights from individual studies may be combined to create new *meta* concepts (see, for example, Campbell et al., 2003). Such conceptual syntheses are interpretative and iterative and, thus have ongoing potential for user input during the synthesis.

Communication of Review Findings

A major aim of KT is to make the reports of systematic reviews accessible to potential users of that research. In being explicit about the methods used in systematic reviews, these reports tend to be very long and detailed. The way reviews are currently compiled necessitates other forms of more accessible communication. The EPPI-Centre, for example, has a four-layer method of communication for each study that includes an Internet database of the codings, a full technical report, a short user-friendly main report, and a two-page summary.

Each report refers to the others so that users who need either a more detailed or simplified report will know that other forms are also available. It is also possible to have a range of reports that target different user groups. For example, at the EPPI-Centre, we have experimented with asking different groups of users to provide user-led reports on reviews in education. Parents, teachers, and school students, for example, provided different one-page summaries of the reviews. These included a quick overview of the review aims and results and an interpretation of what these results meant for the user constituency that the writer was representing.

Interpretation and Application of Review Findings

Communicating the review is not the end of the process. First, a review can be interpreted in the contexts of practitioners, organizations, or users of services. Second, it can be interpreted in terms of its relevance to local contexts: some reviews provide findings that are more generalized than other review findings. Thus, user input at this stage is again significant. User interpretations can also feed future research. A review may have attempted to answer a specific research question, but most reviews will be unable to do this fully. The review can tell us what we know from research, but it can also highlight the limits of current knowledge. In this way, the people defining the initial review question can also influence where further research is needed. Thus, user involvement in research reviews can also influence wider research agendas.

When the interpreted results are used to make decisions, the application of a review is the final stage. Users can play a crucial role in evaluating the applicability of results and the barriers to implementation. In practice, it is users who interpret and apply research and determine what services are provided to whom, by whom, and under what circumstances. This process of interpretation depends upon how context-specific the research knowledge is, how it fits the particular context of the users making the interpretation, and what other non-research knowledge, including tacit practice knowledge (i.e., knowledge developed from practice that is not explicitly known or recorded yet may affect decision-making), that the user brings to the process. The application of this interpreted knowledge will depend upon the material facts on the ground and the knowledge and perspectives of others involved in making implementation happen, or not (see summary in figure 8.1).

In England, several intermediary organizations assist with the processes of interpretation and implementation of research reviews. For example, the National Institute for Clinical and Health Excellence (NICE, 2004) commissions research reviews and has formal methods for consultation with relevant parties who then determine what guidance to health practitioners arises from a research review (see Lavis, Oxman, Moynihan, & Paulsen, 2008, for a description of intermediary organizations in health).

Community Perspectives and Participation

In this chapter I have argued for the importance of user roles in reviewing research evidence for decision-making and of methods for being sure of what we know based on research evidence. Research knowledge, although scientific, is dependent on values and assumptions. Academics have many specialized skills and their knowledge includes insights into particular topic areas. Decision-making can also benefit from the insights and perspectives of users of research – those often affected by the research findings. Professional policymakers and practitioners are sometimes involved in these processes. The involvement

Figure 8.1 User input into interpretation and application

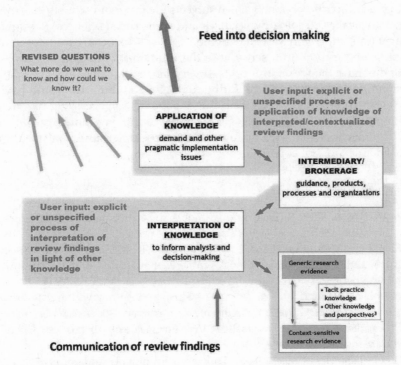

Source: Gough (2006).

of communities and individuals is less common. Enhancing involvement is a democratic process that is not easily achieved. In England, progress has been made by NICE, the National Health Service research and development program in health, and by the Social Care Institute of Excellence. Each of these organizations works to involve consumers in the research agenda and in research interpretation and application processes.

Although such developments are welcomed, these agencies are not always at the centre of knowledge production. Academic researchers and universities rarely offer a community focus. To the extent that they do, they may offer technical services or skills rather than engage on an equal footing with community members who have their own expertise to offer. More meaningful engagement between universities and the local communities can empower and encourage greater dialogue and participation. Science subjects are taught in schools in terms of physical and biological sciences and some social sciences. Research agenda-setting and research evidence needs to be a core aspect of citizen education. In a sense, it is the fundamental subject of how to understand the world around us. Everyone would benefit from understanding research evidence. Individuals and communities would have greater confidence and capacity for engagement in accessing research knowledge. Research might also benefit from being more attuned to the wider issues in society, rather than those determined only within academic areas of expertise.

REFERENCES

Adler, P.A., & Adler, P. (1984). The carpool: A socializing adjunct to the educational experience. *Sociology of Education, 57,* 200–210.

Campbell, R., Pound, P., Pope, C., Britten, N., Pill, R., Morgan, M., et al. (2003). Evaluating meta-ethnography: A synthesis of qualitative research on lay experiences of diabetes and diabetes care. *Social Science & Medicine, 56*(4), 671–684.

Carr, S., & Coren, E. (2007). *Collection of examples of service user and carer participation in systematic reviews* (SCIE Research Resource 02). London: Social Care Institute of Excellence.

Garcia, J., Sinclair, J., Dickson, K., Thomas, J., Brunton, J., Tidd, M., et al. (2006). *Conflict resolution, peer mediation, and young people's relationships* (Technical Report 1406R). London: EPPI-Centre, Social Science Research Unit, Institute of Education, University of London.

Gough, D.A. (2006, February). *User led research synthesis: A participative approach to driving research agendas.* Paper presented at the Sixth International Campbell Colloquium, Los Angeles, CA. Abstract retrieved July 16, 2010, from http://eppi.ioe.ac.uk/cms/Default.aspx?tabid=1919

Gough, D.A. (2007). Weight of evidence: A framework for the appraisal of the quality and relevance of evidence [Special Issue]. *Research Papers in Education, 22*(2), 213–228.

Gough, D.A., & Elbourne, D. (2002). Systematic research synthesis to inform policy, practice, and democratic debate. *Social Policy and Society, 1*(3), 225–236.

Gough, D.A., Oliver, S., Brunton, G., Selai, C., & Schaumberg, H. (2001). *The effect of travel modes on children's mental health, cognitive and social development: A systematic review.* London: EPPI-Centre, Social Science Research Unit, Institute of Education, University of London.

Graham, I.D., & Tetroe, J. (2007). Some theoretical underpinnings of knowledge translation. *Academic Emergency Medicine, 14*(11), 936–941.

Greenhalgh, T., Robert, G., MacFarlane, F., Bate, P., & Kyriakidou, O. (2004).
Diffusion of innovations in service organizations: Systematic review and
recommendations. *Milbank Quarterly, 82*(4), 581–629.

Grimshaw, J.M., Thomas, R.E., MacLennan, G., Fraser, C., Ramsay, C.R., Vale, L.,
et al. (2004). Effectiveness and efficiency of guideline dissemination and
implementation strategies. *Health Technology Assessment, 8*(6). doi:10.3310/
hta8060.

Lavis, J.N., Oxman, A.D., Moynihan, R., & Paulsen, E.J. (2008). Evidence-
informed health policy 1 – Synthesis of findings from a multi-method
study of organizations that support the use of research evidence.
Implementation Science, 3, 53.

National Institute for Clinical Excellence. (2004). *The guideline development
process – An overview for stakeholders, the public, and the NHS.* London:
Author.

Nutley, S.M., Walter, I., & Davies, H.T.O. (2007). *Using evidence: How research
can inform public services.* Bristol, UK: Policy Press.

Oakley, A., Gough, D.A., Oliver, S., & Thomas, J. (2005). The politics of evidence and methodology: Lessons from the EPPI-Centre. *Evidence & Policy,
1*(1), 5–32.

Oliver, S., Clarke-Jones, L., Rees, R., Milne, R., Buchanan, P., Gabbay, J., et al.
(2004). Involving consumers in research and development agenda setting
for the NHS: Developing an evidence-based approach. *Health Technology
Assessment, 8*(15).

Oliver, S., Peersman, G., Harden, A., & Oakley, A. (1999). Discrepancies in
findings from effectiveness reviews: The case of health promotion for
older people in accident and injury prevention. *Health Education Journal,
58*(1), 66–77.

Sudsawad, P. (2007). *Knowledge translation: Introduction to models, strategies,
and measures.* Austin, TX: Southwest Educational Development Laboratory,
National Center for the Dissemination of Disability Research.

Weiss, C.H. (1979). The many meanings of research utilization. *Public
Administration Review, 39*(5), 426–431.

PART THREE

Knowledge Translation in Indigenous
Contexts

9 Knowledge Translation and Adolescent Girls' Sexual Health Education in Indigenous Communities

DEBORAH L. BEGORAY AND ELIZABETH M. BANISTER

Research has shown that the health status of adolescent girls in North America has not improved in recent years (Canadian Federation for Sexual Health [CFSH], 2007). The major causes of morbidity in adolescence are related to health risk behaviours, such as unprotected sexual activity (Smith et al., 2009). In the United States, the Centers for Disease Control and Prevention (U.S. CDCP, 2006) identified risky sexual behaviour as being strongly associated with mortality, morbidity, and social problems among youth. There is a dire need for health education programs that reach adolescents 'where they are' (Begoray & Banister, 2007, p. 25). In this chapter, we argue that such programs would be more effective, especially with Indigenous adolescent girls, if they were founded upon community-based knowledge translation (KT) principles. We suggest these principles are contextuality, collaboration, reciprocity, relationality, and reflexivity, all established through effective communication processes. We then demonstrate how these principles are congruent with Indigenous ways of knowing. Finally, we describe the principles as demonstrated in a community-based research project entitled the Adolescent Girls' Sexual Health and Mentoring Program.

Adolescent Health Issues

Adolescent health issues can have long-term consequences for individuals, the community, and social and health systems (Health Canada, 2004). Early sexual intercourse increases the risk of sexually transmitted infections, termination of pregnancy (Wellings et al., 2001), and has been associated with depression and suicide (Hallfors et al., 2004). The rates of sexually transmitted infections in adolescent girls are among the highest of any age group and are continuing to rise (U.S. CDCP, 2004, 2006; Sex Information and Education Council of Canada [SIECCAN], 2004).

According to the 2005 Youth Risk Behavior Surveillance report (U.S. CDCP, 2006), many young people (aged thirteen to twenty-four) engage in a variety of health-compromising behaviours, such as having sexual intercourse at an earlier age. In the United States, 47 per cent of high school students (grades 9–12) report being sexually active and over 14 per cent report having more than four partners. Twenty-five per cent of sexually active youth use withdrawal to avoid pregnancy – an unreliable form of contraception (Smith et al., 2009).

Dating violence in adolescence is also a serious health issue (Cornelius, Shorey, & Kunde, 2009) and has been associated with other negative outcomes, such as STIs and HIV among sexually active adolescent girls (Decker, Silverman, & Raj, 2005), teenage pregnancy (Roberts, Auinger, & Klein, 2005), and substance use/abuse (Ellickson, Collins, & Bogart, Klein, & Taylor, 2005). One-quarter to over one-half of dating adolescents report physical or psychological abuse in their relationships (James, West, Deters, & Armijo, 2000), and significant numbers continue in these relationships despite the abuse (Smith & Donnelly, 2001).

Despite considerable funding, however, few intervention programs have shown a substantial influence on postponing sexual initiation or curtailing pregnancy among adolescents. Those studies that focus on changing young peoples' knowledge levels, attitudes, or risk behaviours fail to produce long-term sexual health improvements at the population level (Nahom et al., 2001; Shoveller & Johnson, 2006).

While the general adolescent population is already at risk for poor health, the problem is more pronounced in Indigenous communities. This disparity is particularly obvious for adolescent sexual health concerns, including risky alcohol use or sexual activity, risk for Fetal Alcohol Spectrum Disorders, unplanned pregnancy, and contracting STIs such as HIV, gonorrhoea, and chlamydia (CFSH, 2007). Indigenous persons are being infected with HIV at a younger age compared to non-Indigenous persons (Public Health Agency of Canada, 2004).

The suicide rate for Indigenous adolescent girls is eight times the national average (Health Canada, 2002). Higher levels of psychological distress among Indigenous youth are found in those adolescents who are younger, female, have lost parents or relatives, and have small social networks (i.e., fewer than five close friends or relatives) (Kirmayer, Simpson, & Cargo, 2003).

Despite these health disparities, little research has focused on the health concerns of Indigenous adolescent women. Even though advancements are being made in health services delivery for Indigenous women in Canada, significant inequities remain in relation to the general population (CFSH, 2007; Canadian Institute for Health Information, 2004).

In sum, research shows that adolescent girls, especially those in Indigenous communities, are at risk for poor sexual health. While all adolescents need developmentally and socially appropriate educational approaches, Indigenous populations need more specialized education that takes into account their cultural realities. One promising approach to reversing the heightened risk of poor health is through community-based KT processes.

Knowledge Translation

Within the social sciences, researchers are frustrated that research findings have not led to the alleviation of persistent social ills. The gap between research knowledge and practical application is called the know-do gap (Landry, Amara, Pablos-Mendes, Shademani, & Gold, 2006, p. 597). Narrowing this gap involves a shift of focus from taking or giving of knowledge – what might be termed knowledge transfer – to the transformational power of knowledge exchange (Norman & Huerta, 2006) or knowledge translation. Effective KT involves active participation between the producers and users of knowledge as well as reciprocal interactions between the two (Huberman, 1990, 1994; Lomas, 2000). We argue that there are five principles of effective KT: contextuality, collaboration, reciprocity, relationality, and reflexivity. We maintain that effective communication and other health literacy processes are paramount to the establishment of these principles.

Contextuality

Knowledge translation is a 'complex interaction process' (Landry et al., 2006, p. 597) within a specific context. It focuses on real problems within the community and emphasizes research done *with* the community rather than *to* the community (Nyden, Figert, Shibley, & Burrows, 1997). Researchers need to understand the context of the user group, including the group's perceived value of the research and its congruence with their objectives (Huberman, 1994). Understanding these factors can assist researchers in developing and translating knowledge that is accessible and useful (Bogenschneider, Olson, Linney, & Mills, 2000). Discovering contextual elements requires careful, long-term, participant observation with communities.

Collaboration

Collaboration is, literally, labouring together. Collaborative research draws upon both local community knowledge and the knowledge of academics, who have traditionally held the power to claim research authority. It is, therefore, important for university researchers to be aware of the power they hold and to engage in power-sharing processes (Tuhiwai Smith, 2005). In collaborative research, investigators do not assert authority by filling the community with knowledge; rather, they engage community members in the research and dissemination processes for mutual knowledge gain (see chapters by Moewaka Barnes, Henwood, Kerr, McManus, & McCreanor; Gough; and Smylie). Thus, the principle of collaboration necessarily involves a power shift.

Reciprocity

The researcher's awareness in a communal context must be synergistic and reciprocal (Mohatt et al., 2004). Within KT, synergistic relationships among researchers and community members are co-requisite to knowledge exchange and transformation among cultures with dissimilar knowledge bases. Garland, Plemmons, and Koontz (2006) defined partnership synergy as the process through which knowledge and expertise of diverse groups combine in effective ways to achieve goals, plan innovative programs, and enhance relationships with the wider community. To build synergy and reciprocity among research partners necessitates personal investment in the research endeavour (Bishop, 2005).

Relationality

Literature on KT emphasizes developing and nurturing mutually perceived trust and the strengthening of connectivity (Schulz, Israel, & Lantz, 2003). Building relationships can often be an overwhelming, time-intensive challenge for community partners. Personal investments

in the research endeavour (Bishop, 2005) are based on mutual understanding and goodwill. It is especially important for researchers to recognize 'the realities of working in the community, and sensitivity to the
burden research can place on community organizations. Attention to
these issues encourages the development of trusting, durable relationships' (Israel et al., 2006, p. 1030).

Reflexivity

Reflexivity is the process of becoming more self-aware and conscious of
the context within which the research takes place (Jacobson, Butterill, &
Goering, 2003). Team discussions and reflexive journaling can help
researchers to understand their own thoughts and feelings and those
of their community partners. All members of the research team need to
be conscious of their positions in the research context (Tuhiwai Smith,
2005). Reflexivity can only be accomplished through regular efforts to
consider one's thoughts and actions in light of new and often unfamiliar contextual information.

Effective Communication

The five principles – contextuality, collaboration, reciprocity, relationality, and reflexivity – are developed through effective communication processes. Health knowledge generated from community sources
arises through activities such as storytelling. Community members and
university researchers work together to build health literacy: the ability to access, comprehend, evaluate, and communicate health information (Begoray, Poureslami, & Rootman, 2007). Communication in
various forms (e.g., oral, written, visual, or multimedia combinations)
is essential to building and attaining effective knowledge translation
and exchange. Communication practices developed over time, in an
environment of mutual respect, can open spaces in which those who
are voiceless can share their stories and provide opportunities for others to hear those stories. Methods of Indigenous knowledge generation
and communication tend to be experiential, participatory, communal,
and congruent with local geography.

Ball (2004), for example, argues for education programs that are compatible with the community's values and world view. She describes a
'generative curriculum model' (p. 454) whereby Indigenous community
members become actively involved in the generation of knowledge,

experiencing it 'as alive, shared and collectively created' (p. 466). Smylie et al. (2004) maintain that knowledge generation begins with communication through storytelling. Stories form the 'base units of knowledge' (p. 141). Values are inherent in the stories. Knowledge and values result in wisdom. Those holding the wisdom as a result of hearing stories then retell them 'as a way of disseminating what they know' (p. 141).

Contextuality, collaboration, reflexivity, reciprocity, and relationality – all based upon effective communication – resonate with the tenets of Indigenous ways of knowing. Contextuality implies attention to the world view of Indigenous peoples based, for example, on the importance of the local history, land, or local geography (in this volume, see chapters by Moewaka Barnes et al. and Smylie). Collaboration takes into account the collective creation of knowledge. Reflexivity in Indigenous communities is shown in their belief in selected stories to teach specific knowledge. Relationality is found in Indigenous ways of bonding individual members to form a strong community group. Effective communication through stories mediates these processes.

Community-based approaches to KT may be important, in theoretical terms at least, to address the sexual health education concerns of Indigenous adolescent girls. We will now describe a project that demonstrates this approach in practice to KT research in an Indigenous community.

The Adolescent Girls' Sexual Health and Mentoring Program

We conducted a community-based study (2002–2006) that focused on adolescent girls' perceptions of their sexual health and on developing a mentorship program for exploring best practices in adolescent health education (Begoray & Banister, 2007). Our study used a respectful, participatory approach based on Indigenous ways of knowing and effective KT principles (see chapter by Smylie in this volume). We found both approaches to be complementary to each other.

With assistance from a local elder and the administration of a rural Indigenous secondary school in British Columbia, Canada, the researchers became acquainted with ten Indigenous girls, between the ages of fourteen and sixteen. During the first phase of the research, the girls participated in three consecutive focus groups that centred on their sexual health concerns. We designed the focus groups to create a space in which the girls could co-construct the meaning of their sexual health experiences. The girls' accounts generated rich qualitative data that guided the development of the mentoring and educational program used in phase two. During that phase, we delivered the program weekly to the same girls over a sixteen-week period in approximately ninety-minute group sessions.

The intervention group also included two female Indigenous school staff members (an administrative assistant aged thirty and a learning assistant aged twenty-seven) who were chosen as mentors. Each covered for the other when necessary, for example, when one was unexpectedly required to attend three weeks of traditional ceremonies held at the local band's Long House. We also included an elder who attended as many group sessions as possible. She said, 'I can encourage them. It's an opportunity for me to be able to speak to the girls, to share more. They're just young kids and they need to keep hearing from the older people.' The program provided education to the girls, and an opportunity for action research (Reason & Bradbury, 2007) on our instructional approaches. Follow-up individual interviews were conducted with the girls, mentors, elder, and school principal. A number of themes were detected from the group conversations and are reported elsewhere (Banister, Jakubec, & Stein, 2003).

We believe that the mentoring strategies used and evaluated in the Indigenous girls' group illustrate principles of effective KT. The community was involved in the conceptualization, delivery, application, and evaluation of the program.

The Mentoring Program

The program itself included feminist strategies designed to facilitate egalitarian relationships in the group, including (a) circling, where each person takes a turn to speak while others in the group listen in situations involving decision-making or conflict, and (b) closing, where participants share a critical reflection about the group's process at the end of a meeting (Chinn, 2007). Aspects of Grasley, Wolfe, and Wekerle's (1999) youth relationship project that used information, skill-building, and social action to empower youth to end relationship violence were also included, to increase learning about unhealthy power imbalances and visits to local community resources to gain information and report back to the group (e.g., the family planning clinic, sexual assault centre). We also adapted a multi-literate approach (New London Group, 1996) to enhance participants' learning (see Banister & Begoray, 2004) through a variety of sign systems (e.g., kinetics and visual design) for exploring multiple forms of self-expression. We used activities such as free writing and painting. The KT principles were demonstrated in the data collected during the mentoring program. Illustrative examples for each principle follow.

Contextuality

The community context demanded an experiential, active, and culturally appropriate program through which we could conduct our research. Gaining permission to access the community was facilitated in part by the elder. She cared about the maintenance of her culture which future generations would be responsible for, and how the project could positively influence youth behaviour in the community context. We encouraged girls' engagement in learning that was relevant and personally meaningful and that validated their sexual health experiences. The elder and mentors were invited to collaborate in constructing the sexual health curriculum activities that were contextually appropriate. We established an environment that helped to empower the girls and provide them with direction and self-efficacy.

For example, each student identified a personal goal that was revised throughout each lesson. The entire group linked their goals to successful graduation from school; many recognized that completing their education was central to establishing their own identity and would enhance their ability to give back to their communities. The importance of education was continually reinforced and translated to them through the elder's teachings.

Creating a space of relatedness and connection, both key components of Indigenous world views, helped to make possible the girls' shared goal of obtaining the necessary education to lead productive lives. The presence of community members helped to remind all of us about the Indigenous context within which we were working.

Collaboration

Our program provided a safe space for shared learning and reflection. The sexual health education program took place in a school located within the Indigenous community. The girls worked together in a group. Through a variety of activities, they discovered their common concerns; for example, they participated in dialogue with other girls, with mentors, with the elder, and with the researchers. They heard stories. They discussed new information, such as the differences among aggressive, assertive, and passive behaviour. They connected their own experience with this new knowledge and then acted upon it collectively, deciding, for example, what they could do in specific situations where aggressive behaviours were present. The girls also learned to become mutually supportive. As mentioned earlier, the researchers, mentors, and elder met regularly and worked collaboratively to brainstorm ideas for the sexual health curriculum that helped to make it culturally appropriate and responsive to the girls' issues as they emerged. Collaboration was a natural way to set and achieve group goals with community members.

Reciprocity

There were two main groupings within the program: the Indigenous community and the university researchers. However, the Indigenous community had sub-communities as well, for example, the adolescent girls and the adults, such as the elder, mentors, and the girls' parents. The girls became more knowledgeable about abusive relationships and about safe sexual health practices. A mentor describes KT processes that contributed to girls' absorbing this knowledge:

> And a lot of [the girls] didn't know [about safe sex] ... We'd take them to the workshop [on sexual health] and they didn't know about all the STIs and they have no mentor in the community ... But to come from the school or someone telling their story ... just the activities they did in the program ... [t]hey learned ... Hopefully ... they'll be able to help one of their own in a bad relationship.

Reciprocity among members of both groups strengthened the effectiveness of the program. Bonds were built among the groups that reinforced the KT processes.

The knowledge came from the university researchers and from the mentors who shared their stories about sexual health issues. Other community adults also became more aware of the problem of dating violence, the need for easily accessible condom machines, and the usefulness of consultants to continue sexual health education. The elder believed, however, that the circles needed to ripple out even wider. As she said,

> We spoke at conferences with some of the girls ... like we went up to
> [a conference] last year and did a group up there – but that's nothing
> compared to how much further in our communities this information
> needs to go. And it needs to reach the Chiefs in Councils ... It needs
> to reach the Child and Family Service Ministries in our Aboriginal
> Communities.

The reciprocal sharing and generation of knowledge helped create an
innovative sexual health program and served to strengthen relationships with the larger community.

Relationality

The ability to enter into and sustain meaningful relationships is an
important skill in Indigenous contexts and requires critical sensitivity by the researcher (Tuhiwai Smith, 2005). Frequent, face-to-face contacts and establishing roles that link the partners are strategies that
can help build trust (Jacobson et al., 2003). The relational aspect of the
partnership included the receptivity of the user group (Jacobson et al.,
2003). In this study, adolescent girls wanted information about healthy
relationships and ways to negotiate effective communication in their
peer relationships.

The project helped to maintain and enhance patterns of relationships in the community and extended benefits beyond that of the girls
themselves. The elder commented on developing a relationship with
the girls:

> Outside of the group they [the girls] would give me hugs ... they'd
> acknowledge me when they see me as part of hearing their stories and
> maybe a feeling a kind of bond. When you hear a person ... you don't
> really fully see them until you hear them share ... after they've shared
> their experiences of how they feel, who they are, their feelings – once they
> do that to you, you have a different kind of relationship.

Relationships built on trust are a challenge to build and easy to damage. In this case, the community had a philosophy of living commu-
nally and the program we introduced allowed them to discover what
was already in place. These girls discovered the power of friendships,
of elders, and of shared knowledge.

Reflexivity

Members of the community commented on their growth in self-awareness because of their participation in the program. We provided opportunities for the girls and mentors to reflect upon their learning in various ways, such as journaling, drawing, and painting activities. While delivering the curriculum, we posed critical questions to facilitate the girls' and mentors' reflections on how larger contextual factors influence sexual health experiences. We valued the girls' knowledge and their processes of translating this both within the group and to others within the Indigenous community. For example, as their daughters talked about their experiences, parents became more aware of some of their daughters' sexual health issues. The elder reported:

> One of the girls [who] fully participated and then was really speaking out, and then she was telling her mum about the group, so her mum was expressing to me how she thought the group really helped her daughter. She said, 'We need to keep on doing these and whoever's doing this – it's a good thing they're doing it.' So it's brought some awareness from the kids to the parents that this is what they're talking about. [Be]cause ordinarily, I think it's not something that girls share with either one of their parents.

It also was important for us to engage in reflection about the program. We did not attempt to become experts in Indigenous ways of knowing. We tried instead to be open to and, over time, to learn from realities that differed from our own.

Effective Communication

A variety of literacy practices, congruent with expressions of Indigenous ways of knowing, were used in the program to teach sexual health. Experiential, interactive learning among the girls developed their health literacy. The sharing of stories through listening and speaking, that is, oral literacy, took place in a discussion circle, where a feather was passed from hand to hand to denote the speaker. In keeping with Canadian Indigenous people's legacy of oral tradition, storytelling serves to translate information among and across generations about their history, origins, and spirituality (see the chapter by Smylie in this volume). For example, the elder shared stories about the imposed 'Indian Residential

Schools' program, that annihilated the 'legitimacy of thought, lifestyles, religions, and languages' (Ball, 2004, p. 457) of Indigenous peoples and ways this program contributed to intergenerational barriers to open communication.

> Some of our old people's parents sent them to residential school and they felt like they weren't wanted because they were sent away and they didn't want to go ... They learned that their parents had nothing to do with it, but ... there was no communication ... there was no way that the kids came home and said, 'why did you send me there?' All of them came home and didn't even talk – there was absolutely no communication whatsoever in that whole entire house. And I see it happening in the community ... even in my own family, where you can exist in a house and not have any kind of communication – you're just there. So when you're opening up you're letting people in and that's what this [program] has done. The girls have shared tears. They shared their sadness. They shared what happiness they had, which is not too much ... I hope for the girls, that when the girls sitting beside them are crying, that they'll have compassion for that ... they had not had really caring feelings towards others in the group before.

Storytelling was the most frequently reported and observed type of communication. The girls, the elder, and the mentors told stories to each other and to the university researchers. The elder modelled storytelling, listening, sharing, and ways to take positive action.

The power of communication through writing, creating artefacts, and telling stories invites everyone to participate in whatever way makes them feel comfortable. Then, as they practice new ways of sharing ideas, they empower themselves in a greater variety of situations.

Written communication was practised in journal writing. The girls wrote regularly to express their feelings about their sexual health including, for example, their intimate dating relationships. Visual literacy occurred in the creation of symbols such as necklaces that communicated the girls' authentic voices, membership in the group, and their support for one another. All of these practices developed health literacy over the period of the study. As the elder observed:

> They liked the journaling for sure, they liked the arts and the crafts, they liked the circles – after a while they got used to circles ... actually what they got was confidence out of that group to speak ... they were kind of shy and intimidated and couldn't ... then a change happened in them ... they were

looking forward to sharing and looking for the opportunity to hold the feather.

The elder and mentors reported on changes in the girls' behaviour as their communication abilities developed over the course of the study.

Discussion and Conclusion

In 2002, we entered a rural Indigenous community to interview Indigenous teenage girls about the perspectives they had of their own sexual health and, ultimately, to involve these girls and the community in a sexual health education curriculum. During our program, through synergy among the partners (Garland et al., 2006), effective KT was developed. Through storytelling in particular, knowledge that was shared helped to create networks that strengthened our relationship with the community.

Through storytelling and reflection, the mentors and elder used their authentic Indigenous voices to share knowledge connecting the girls' private lives with their public ones (Denzin, 1997). Community members, such as the elder, were convinced of the importance of the information sharing for future generations. She said: 'I think it's all of the information that's accumulated from this research and it's going to be translated into what it was all about . . . it's going to be looked at, listened to, heard, and then put down in record for the rest of eternity . . . and it's going to be kept as understanding that this is what happened.' Our program was congruent with methods of Indigenous knowledge generation in that it was participatory, relational, communal, and narrative-based (Smylie et al., 2004). We approached the program with the assumption that culturally appropriate and useful knowledge is rooted within the community (Ball, 2004). Involving members of the community in designing and delivering a sexual health curriculum that was culturally appropriate facilitated the multilayered KT process.

Unresolved and Problematic KT Issues

Sustainability is an important component of effective KT. We realized that, even though the project was congruent with the community's goal of educating youth about sexual health, the continuation of the program upon completion of the study depended on a number of factors, including the availability of school staff and financial resources. We returned to the community for two consecutive years to deliver the program as a way of giving back to the community. Our intent was to have the mentors continue running the groups with assistance from the elder. However, the school had limited resources, and staff shortages meant that the mentors were needed to fulfil their pre-existing organizational roles.

This project was collaboratively designed with input from community members. Even though the girls, mentors, elder, and community members reported on the success of the program, there was no guarantee that this success would transfer to another Indigenous context, given the 'heterogeneity of over 605 different First Nations in Canada, each with their own particular history, language dialect, culture, and social organization' (Ball, 2004, p. 458). Greenwood and Levin (2005) agree that KT is contextual and that investigators need to reflect upon ways in which knowledge generated from one context will be translated to another.

Some scholars would argue that as non-Indigenous researchers we were unable to critique sensitively what we observed and recorded in our research. It could also be argued that we needed to consider whose voice would be valued in our research reports and whether or not we might be guilty of appropriating Indigenous experience for our own research gains. Nevertheless, we believe that we achieved partnership synergy through implementing the five principles described above, thus largely avoiding these difficulties. We believe that through the processes of KT in this project we were changed for the better, for which we thank our community partners. More importantly, we believe that we had a positive influence on the health of the girls in this program. We look forward to learning more about KT approaches for the purpose of addressing health disparities.

REFERENCES

Ball, J. (2004). As if Indigenous knowledge and communities mattered: Transformative education in First Nations communities in Canada. *American Indian Quarterly, 28*(3/4), 454–479.

Banister, E.M., & Begoray, D.L. (2004). Beyond talking groups: Strategies for improving adolescent health education. *Health Care for Women International, 25*(5), 481–488.

Banister, E.M., Jakubec, S.L., & Stein, J.A. (2003). 'Like, what am I supposed to do?': Adolescent girls' health concerns in their dating relationships. *Canadian Journal of Nursing Research, 35*(2), 16–33.

Begoray, D.L., & Banister, E.M. (2007). Reaching teenagers where they are: Best practices for girls' sexual health education. *Women's Health and Urban Life, 6*(1), 24–40.

Begoray, D.L., Poureslami, I., & Rootman, I. (2007, Winter). Development of measures of health literacy for Canadian schools. *Health & Learning,* 11–13.

Bishop, R. (2005). Freeing ourselves from neo-colonial domination in research: A Kaupapa Māori approach to creating knowledge. In N.K. Denzin & Y. Lincoln (Eds.), *The Sage handbook of qualitative research* (3rd ed., pp. 109–138). Thousand Oaks, CA: Sage.

Bogenschneider, K., Olson, J.R., Linney, K.D., & Mills, J. (2000). Connecting research and policymaking: Implications for theory and practice from the family impact seminars. *Family Relations, 49*(3), 327–339.

Canadian Federation for Sexual Health (CFSH). (2007). *Sexual health in Canada: Baseline 2007.* Ottawa, ON: Author.

Canadian Institute for Health Information. (2004, February 25). *Improving the health of Canadians.* Retrieved July 22, 2010, from http://secure.cihi.ca/cihiweb/dispPage.jsp?cw_page=PG_39_E&cw_topic=39&cw_rel=AR_322_E

Chinn, P.L. (2007). *Peace & power: Creating leadership for building community* (7th ed.). Boston: Jones and Bartlett.

Cornelius, R.L., Shorey, R.C., & Kunde, A. (2009). Legal consequences of dating violence: A critical review and directions for improved behavioural contingencies. *Aggression and Violent Behavior, 14*(3), 194–204.

Decker, M.R., Silverman, J.G., & Raj, A. (2005). Dating violence and sexually transmitted disease/HIV testing and diagnosis among adolescent females. *Pediatrics, 116*(2), 272–276.

Denzin, N.K. (1997). *Interpretative ethnography: Ethnographic practices for the 21st century.* Thousand Oaks, CA: Sage.

Ellickson, P.L., Collins, R.L., Bogart, L.M., Klein, D.J., & Taylor, S.L. (2005). Scope of HIV risk and co-occurring psychosocial health problems among young adults: Violence, victimization, and substance use. *Journal of Adolescent Health, 36,* 401–409.

Garland, A.F., Plemmons, D., & Koontz, L. (2006). Research – practice partnership in mental health: Lessons from participants. *Administration and Policy in Mental Health and Mental Health Services Research, 33*(5), 517–528.

Grasley, C., Wolfe, D.A., & Wekerle, C. (1999). Empowering youth to end relationship violence. *Children's Services: Social Policy, Research, and Practice, 2*(4), 209–223.

Greenwood, D., & Levin, M. (2005). Reform of the social sciences and of universities through action research. In N.K. Denzin & Y. Lincoln (Eds.), *The*

Sage handbook of qualitative research (3rd ed., pp. 43–64). Thousand Oaks, CA: Sage.

Hallfors, D.D., Waller, M.W., Ford, C.A., Halpern, C.T., Brodish, P.H., & Iritani, B. (2004). Adolescent depression and suicide risk: Association with sex and drug behavior. *American Journal of Preventive Medicine, 27*(3), 224–231.

Health Canada. (2002). *Acting on what we know: Preventing youth suicide in First Nations* [Report of the Advisory Group on Suicide Prevention]. Retrieved July 22, 2010, from http://www.hc-sc.gc.ca/fniah-spnia/alt_formats/fnihb-dgspni/pdf/pubs/suicide/prev_youth-jeunes-eng.pdf

Health Canada (2004). *Canadian sexually transmitted infections (STI) surveillance report: Pre-release.* Ottawa, ON: Population and Public Health Branch, Health Canada.

Huberman, M. (1990). Linkage between researchers and practitioners: A qualitative study. *American Educational Research Journal, 27*(2), 363–391.

Huberman, M. (1994). Research utilization: The state of the art. *Knowledge and Policy: The International Journal of Knowledge Transfer and Utilization, 7*(4), 13–33.

Israel, B.A., Krieger, J., Vlahov, D., Ciske, S., Foley, M., Fortin, P., et al. (2006). Challenges and facilitating factors in sustaining community-based participatory research partnerships: Lessons learned from the Detroit, New York City and Seattle urban research centers. *Journal of Urban Health, 83*(6), 1022–1040.

Jacobson, N., Butterill, D., & Goering, P. (2003). Development of a framework for knowledge translation: Understanding user context. *Journal of Health Services Research & Policy, 8*(2), 94–99.

James, W.H., West, C., Deters, K.E., & Armijo, E. (2000). Youth dating violence. *Adolescence, 35*(139), 455–465.

Kirmayer, L.J., Simpson, C., & Cargo, M. (2003). Healing traditions: Culture, community and mental health promotion with Canadian Aboriginal peoples. *Australasian Psychiatry, 11*(3 Suppl. 1), 15–23.

Landry, R., Amara, N., Pablos-Mendes, A., Shademani, R., & Gold, I. (2006). The knowledge-value chain: A conceptual framework for knowledge translation in health. *Bulletin of the World Health Organization, 84*(8), 597–602.

Lomas, J. (2000). Using 'linkage and exchange' to move research into policy at a Canadian foundation: Encouraging partnerships between researchers and policymakers is the goal of a promising new Canadian initiative. *Health Affairs, 19*(3), 236–240.

Mohatt, G.V., Hazel, K.L., Allen, J., Stachelrodt, M., Hensel, C., & Fath, R. (2004). Unheard Alaska: Culturally anchored participatory action research on sobriety with Alaska natives. *American Journal of Community Psychology, 33*(3/4), 263–273.

Nahom, D., Wells, E., Morrison, D.M., Wilsdon, A., Gillmore, M.R., Archibald, M., et al. (2001). Differences by gender and sexual experience in adolescent sexual behavior: Implications for education and HIV prevention. *Journal of School Health, 71*(4), 153–158.

New London Group, The. (1996). A pedagogy of multiliteracies: Designing social futures. *Harvard Educational Review, 66*(1), 60–91.

Norman, C., & Huerta, T. (2006). Knowledge transfer & exchange through social networks: Building foundations for a community of practice within tobacco control. *Implementation Science, 1*(1), 20.

Nyden, P., Figert, A., Shibley, M., & Burrows, D. (1997). *Building community: Social science in action.* Thousand Oaks, CA: Pine Forge Press.

Public Health Agency of Canada. (2004). *HIV/AIDS Epi Notes – Understanding the HIV/AIDS epidemic among Aboriginal people in Canada: The community at a glance.* Retrieved July 22, 2010, from http://www.phac-aspc.gc.ca/publicat/epiu-aepi/epi-note/index.html

Reason, P., & Bradbury, H. (Eds.). (2007). *The Sage handbook of action research: Participative inquiry and practice* (2nd ed.). London: Sage.

Roberts, T.A., Auinger, P., & Klein, J.D. (2005). Intimate partner abuse and the reproductive health of sexually active female adolescents. *Journal of Adolescent Health, 36*(5), 380–385.

Schulz, A.J., Israel, B.A., & Lantz, P. (2003). Instrument for evaluating dimensions of group dynamics within community-based participatory research partnerships. *Evaluation and Program Planning, 26*(3), 249–262.

Sex Information and Education Council of Canada (SIECCAN). (2004). Adolescent sexual and reproductive health in Canada: A report card in 2004. *The Canadian Journal of Human Sexuality, 13,* 67–82.

Shoveller, J.A., & Johnson, J.L. (2006). Risky groups, risky behaviour, and risky persons: Dominating discourses on youth sexual health. *Critical Public Health, 16*(1), 47–60.

Smith, A., Stewart D., Peled, M., Poon, C., Saewyc, E., & The McCreary Centre Society. (2009). *A picture of health: Highlights from the 2008 BC adolescent health survey.* Vancouver, BC: McCreary Centre Society.

Smith, D.M., & Donnelly, J. (2001). Adolescent dating violence: A multisystemic approach of enhancing awareness in educators, parents, and society. *Journal of Prevention & Intervention in the Community, 21,* 53–64.

Smylie, J.K., Martin, C.M., Kaplan-Myrth, N., Steele, L., Tait, C.L., & Hogg, W. (2004). Knowledge translation and Indigenous knowledge. *International Journal of Circumpolar Health, 63*(Suppl. 2), 139–143.

Tuhiwai Smith, L. (2005). On tricky ground: Researching the native in the age of uncertainty. In N.K. Denzin & Y. Lincoln (Eds.), *The Sage handbook of qualitative research* (3rd ed., pp. 85–107). Thousand Oaks, CA: Sage.

United States Centers for Disease Control and Prevention (U.S. CDCP). (2004). Youth risk behavior surveillance – United States, 2003. *Morbidity and Mortality Weekly Report: Surveillance Summaries, 53*(SS-2), 1–96.
United States Centers for Disease Control and Prevention (U.S. CDCP). (2006). Youth risk behavior surveillance – United States, 2005. *Morbidity and Mortality Weekly Report: Surveillance Summaries, 55*(SS-5), 1–108.
Wellings, K., Nanchahal, K., Macdowall, W., McManus, S., Erens, B., Mercer, C.H., et al. (2001). Sexual behaviour in Britain: Early heterosexual experience. *Lancet, 358*(9296), 1843–1850.

10 Knowledge Translation and Indigenous Research

HELEN MOEWAKA BARNES, WENDY HENWOOD, SANDY
KERR, VERNE MCMANUS, AND TIM MCCREANOR

In the social sciences, the term *knowledge translation* (KT) has been used to describe processes by which research-based knowledge is taken up and used in social, policy, and community settings. The growing interest in KT signals a move beyond simplistic concepts of unidirectional dissemination, to more sophisticated theories that envisage flows of information through multiple stages of knowledge creation and utilization (Canadian Institutes of Health Research, 2004). However, acknowledging the complexity and contextuality of research processes – as well as the relational and iterative character of the generation, uptake, and application of research knowledge – is a necessary further step. Emerging literature on the subject supports these broader understandings of KT (Nutley, Walter, & Davies, 2007; Witten & Hammond, 2008), but there remains an emphasis on conventional definitions such as to *transmit* or *pass on*. These terms suggest processes of knowledge-rich research experts delivering outputs to knowledge-needing end-users (Witten & Hammond, 2008). Such expert-driven models fall short of meeting the complexity of the research-user interface, particularly in relation to Indigenous communities (Smylie et al., 2004; Tuhiwai Smith, 1999).

KT activities entail the introduction and explanation of research findings to user groups and their acceptance, endorsement, and use of the knowledge for the development of social life. KT may also involve temporal dimensions – as exemplified in Rich's (2001) knowledge cycle, in which different kinds and levels of information are used or highlighted at different stages – and interpretative practices, such as the 'local reconstruction of meaning' (Levin, 2007, p. 42).

One of the central contexts within which KT takes place is policy development, where decisions about policy formation are informed by multiple influences and interests, of which research is but one. Policymakers are seen as key drivers in the utilization of research findings. It has been suggested that if researchers understood policy processes better they might be more effective in both contributing to policy (Carroll, Blewden, & Witten, 2008) and providing research that is more relevant to the policy context (Social Sciences' Reference Group, 2005). However, other highly significant domains of interest in social science entail different dynamics and processes in knowledge creation and utilization practices.

As a Māori (Indigenous New Zealand) social science research group in Aotearoa New Zealand, we are interested in working with Māori communities and groups to inform, support, achieve, and understand their aspirations, initiatives, and actions. Conventional knowledge creation and transfer practices reflect cultural and political affiliations to the state and to settler society in diverse overt and covert ways. However, these usually fail to meet the expectations and accountabilities that many Indigenous Māori researchers experience as they engage in collaborative knowledge creation processes. *Kaupapa* (principle) Māori approaches to research are based on Māori theory and practices (Tuhiwai Smith, 1999); they naturalize Māori interests and concerns as the centre of inquiry and better serve Māori knowledge needs (Cram, McCreanor, Tuhiwai Smith, Nairn, & Johnstone, 2006; Pihama, Cram, & Walker, 2002; Reason & Bradbury, 2006; Tuhiwai Smith, 1999).

In this chapter, we explore the parameters of KT processes in three Māori research projects in which collaborative knowledge creation was a key feature (Cram, 2001; Tuhiwai Smith, 1999). We then discuss how such work is positioned in relation to policy agendas that may run counter to Māori aspirations of development and self-determination. We use these understandings to reflect on Māori concepts and practices of knowledge creation and transfer (Moewaka Barnes, 2006, 2008).

Background

Since the late eighteenth century in Aotearoa New Zealand, Māori self-determination, resistance to colonization, and efforts to uphold *te tino rangatiratanga* (sovereignty) have been a feature of relationships between the Indigenous peoples and European settlers. Adverse conditions of colonization that have impeded achievement include settler state-initiated warfare, large-scale land and other resource confiscation and alienation, imposition of a foreign culture, economic deprivation, and social marginalization. This systematic exclusion has produced disparities in health, education, income, and virtually all other indicators of well-being (Hill, 2008; Reid & Robson, 2007; Statistics New Zealand, 2007).

Māori development of land, resources, people, and institutions has continued in the face of barriers and injustices experienced through colonization (Ballara, 1986; R.J. Walker, 1990). Research, empirical observation, and theorizing have always been a part of Māori political, intellectual, and social organization, as have Māori aspirations for ongoing development in ways that reflect our origins, culture, and traditions (Durie, 2003; Royal, 2003; R.J. Walker, 1990). It is no surprise then, in the contemporary setting, to find vital embodiments of ways of analyzing, theorizing, planning, and implementing development (Durie, 2003; Tuhiwai Smith, 1999). Aside from the benefits of managed knowledge production and use, Māori are determined to be in control of these vital processes; we are aware of the value of research in shifting the often intransigent or overtly oppositional positions adopted by colonial politicians and bureaucrats in the face of Māori development plans and actions (Moewaka Barnes, 2006; Tuhiwai Smith, 1999). Māori also have an accumulated experience of damaging and unhelpful research, such as the Rākau studies that used inappropriate Western psychology in a misguided effort to measure Māori personality (Ritchie, 1956; Stewart, 1995). Research conducted outside of our control has been used to restrict, undermine, or reject our development aspirations (Cram, 2001; Pihama, 1993).

Considering a long and ongoing experience of Eurocentric colonialism, Māori methodologies have increasingly emphasized what can be referred to as Māori-centred frameworks that focus on Māori concerns, beliefs, and practices. Kaupapa Māori Research (KMR) is one such approach, whereby theorizing about research relationships, processes, and accountabilities (Cram, 2001; Jones, Crengle, & McCreanor, 2006; Moewaka Barnes, 2000; Pihama, 1993; Tuhiwai Smith, 1992) encourages Māori researchers to work in ways that address Māori aspirations to share, apply, and use research-based knowledge for the benefit of the people (see, for example, Cram et al., 2006; Moewaka Barnes, 2000; Pihama, 1993; Pipi et al., 2004; Tuhiwai Smith, 1992, 1999). KMR draws upon Māori theoretical frameworks for understanding the world as well as human activity and well-being within it that – in most formulations (Durie, 2000; Roberts, Norman, Minhinnick, Wihongi, & Kirkwood, 1995; Te Ahukaramū Charles Royal, 2003; Tuhiwai Smith, 1999) – are ecological, holistic, and communitarian, with important implications for approaches to research. 'Our world views have profound effects on how we view and use methodologies and methods; they are the frameworks that fundamentally shape our relationships to knowledge and practice' (Moewaka Barnes, 2006, p. 5).

In its focus on Māori concerns for Māori advancement, KMR adopts a theoretical position born of the need to interrogate and challenge colonizing power, norms, and assumptions so that Māori ways of knowing, thinking, and operating are central (Tuhiwai Smith, 1999; S. Walker, Eketone, & Gibbs, 2006). Moewaka Barnes (2000) emphasized three defining principles of KMR: it is by Māori for Māori, Māori world views are the normative frame, and the research done is for the benefit of Māori.

Ontology, epistemology, and methodology within Kaupapa Māori theoretical frameworks can be markedly different from conventional social science, critiquing positivist rationalism in favour of a Māori-centred social constructionism (Moewaka Barnes, 2006; S. Walker et al., 2006) with major implications for research interests, approaches, and practices (Te Ahukaramū Charles Royal, 2003; Tuhiwai Smith, 1999). A KMR approach naturalizes Māori theory so that we are not articulated as the *other* but are at the centre of research involving Māori. For the Whāriki Research Group, a Māori research organization comprised of social scientists based at Massey University in Auckland Aotearoa, these broad principles are translated into practical working realities in a diverse array of specific health and well-being projects, from national surveys and geographical information systems (GIS) mapping work, to qualitative explorations of sensitive issues, community action, and evaluation research. We are eclectic and pragmatic, drawing upon a wide array of research theories, methods, and styles to suit the context while steadfastly maintaining the KMR approach.

Kaupapa Māori frameworks frequently underpin research about Māori community assets, interests, or concerns while utilizing community personnel and skills, building capability, and pursuing transformational outcomes. In relation to knowledge and insights generated through such work, a key feature is a set of formal and informal practices, such as *kaitiakitanga* (stewardship), *manaakitanga* (hospitality), *whakapapa* (genealogy), and *whanaungatanga* (relationship-building), that achieve knowledge development through an interweaving of community, academic, and experiential expertise in 'common good' projects (Tuhiwai Smith, 1999).

Many Māori researchers work in ways that do not separate the users of research from the knowledge creators (Tuhiwai Smith, 1999). KT in Kaupapa Māori and other Indigenous settings (Smylie et al., 2004) links research and practice, juxtaposing knowledge creation and use by working in situ, inclusively and transparently (Moewaka Barnes, 2006). Knowledge creation in this setting requires that experience from many sources is brought together and looked at in ways that may not have occurred before; from these new directions, connections may be made that enable the use of the knowledge to bring about change. This process focuses on collaboratively developing and using research as a tool for social change and advancement, rather than as a mechanism of power and control. KT involves the input of key stakeholders, and is not unidirectional. Mutual respect, accountability, dialogue, finding common ground, and developing shared goals are key features of the kinds of relationships that Māori and other Indigenous researchers describe as central to effective and acceptable research-practice relationships (Cram, 2001; Greenwood & de Leeuw, 2007; Indigenous Health Research Knowledge Transfer Network, n.d.; Moewaka Barnes, McCreanor, Edwards, & Borell, 2009). Often, KMR processes are not written about or are only briefly described in the methodology or background sections of such articles. However, they are a central and routine feature of our research and evaluation practice and are crucial to the effectiveness of our research projects.

Such collaborative knowledge creation is also a difficult concept to convey to funders. Moving beyond dissemination of research as a mechanism for bringing about change, funding bodies may require a proposal to demonstrate that there are end-users of research knowledge. There is an apparent hierarchy of partners that funders prefer; some groups seem to carry greater weight than others do, with settler economic interests ranking high in contrast to community and Māori providers that are seemingly on the margins. Māori involvement may be needed in order for the research to be appropriate, but requiring evidence of Māori approval for a proposal rather than their engagement in the research is the norm. Processes that more fully engage partners and participants, such as participatory action, are extremely difficult to convey to funders as they cross Western science boundaries of objectivity, blur the divide between research and action, and are, by nature, not able to be fully predetermined and described.

Three Research Projects

The following stories describe research that uses the broad frameworks outlined and engages with the problematics introduced above, from within the research programs of the Whāriki Research Group (Whāriki Research Group / Te Rōpū Whāriki, n.d.). Knowledge creation and use has been at the heart of achieving social change for Māori communities. We discuss three projects – Māori Pathways to Health, Te Mauri o te Ū-kai-pō, and Ngāti Whātua Ngā Rima o Kaipara Marae Arataki Project – that are exemplars of the ways in which Māori aspirations for change and development drive knowledge creation and use.

Māori Pathways to Health

This participatory action research study (funded by the Health Research Council of New Zealand) was carried out between 2004 and 2007 using a three-phase process of qualitative data-gathering and analysis, action based on findings, and reflection on the impacts of the actions. The aim was to illuminate the experiences of Māori with ischemic heart disease (IHD) and contrast these with the understanding of health service providers in order to catalyze service changes to Māori patients and communities. Developed over several years of working with communities and providers, the project was set up in response to a widely perceived and shared concern about the health risks of Māori with cardiovascular disease (Penney, Moewaka Barnes, Kerr, & McCreanor, 2008; Penney, Moewaka Barnes, & McCreanor, 2006). The principal investigator was tribally linked to the area where the project was based, had worked there, and had built up considerable trust and credibility over time with a wide range of groups, including health care providers and communities. The stakeholders' commitment to the project was enhanced by it being nested within a Māori research group, ensuring that KMR perspectives would guide the project. The conceptualization and development of the project were carried out in collaborative and iterative ways, including discussions of ideas and the research proposal with stakeholders (local providers, organizations, patients and their families), informing them of the progress of the research, and involving them in making sense of the research results.

A critical KT process occurred at the end of phase one of the project, when findings generated from interview data were shared with patients, their *whanau* (extended family), and with providers. The process involved two sets of *hui*, facilitated by the principal investigator. *Hui* are types of meetings, usually conducted with certain understandings. They may be formal or informal; the more formal processes involve several stages of welcome and speeches that make connections between people and places. Shifts in power are part of the *hui* process; one understanding is that when the formal welcoming processes are complete, everybody has the right to speak and be heard. The first *hui* provided the participants with the findings. This was followed by a series of *hui* in which wider groups of providers and patients considered the findings together. Prior to these meetings, interviewee participants were sent a draft report on phase one findings and, if they wished for it, a full set of anonymous interview materials.

From these meetings, ideas and actions to improve service provision to Māori were developed, prioritized, and put in place by health professional groups including staff in primary, secondary, and tertiary service providers. These actions constituted phase two of the project, which generated significant changes and outcomes arising directly from the research (Penney et al., 2008) for the management of Māori IHD in the district. These included the development of the district cardiovascular disease strategy, implementation of Manaaki Manawa, and initiation of a community-based Kaupapa Māori cardiac rehabilitation program. Other outcomes were an analysis of barriers to Māori and non-Māori outpatient appointment attendance (funded from local health resources) and community placement of automated external defibrillation equipment, along with associated operator training. In addition, research input was used to develop an audio-visual resource to support Māori in cardiac rehabilitation, and a feasibility study of local provision of a pre-hospital fibrinolytic therapy service was completed. Improved access to coronary angiography through a new booking system was also achieved (Penney et al., 2008, 2006).

The final phase of the project entailed a series of follow-up interviews with as many of the patient and health professional participants as could be contacted one year after the completion of phase two. A number of participants, especially Māori, commented that the process had worked well for them. This was important, given the widespread Māori resistance to participation in conventional research. Data analysis confirmed that the changes outlined above had been locked into administrative and clinical systems and were making a real difference for Māori with IHD and for those providing care and services for them. One health professional summed up the experience as follows:

> I think one of the significant things for me was actually hearing the stories about patients' experience of the health services and on the other hand hearing the providers' stories about how they actually saw the situation with their Māori clients, and just the huge gulf between those two stories. That has given us a real challenge in terms of improving cultural competency of our providers; it's really the basis for a lot of the work that we're actually doing now.

We found that bringing Māori experiences of IHD directly to health providers and managers, which was only possible through the quality of research relations established by the team, was widely regarded as the impetus to change. As we have recorded elsewhere (Penney et al., 2008), there are numerous and ongoing impacts, including further projects, policy, and practice changes (e.g., the development of Māori cardiac rehabilitation programs) within health provider organizations.

Te Mauri o te Ū-kai-pō

Begun in 2005, this three-year, Health Research Council-funded project set out to explore the intersections between Māori notions of health and well-being and the physical and social environments with Te Rarawa, a major tribal grouping in the far north of Aotearoa. Tribal links and strong Whāriki and Te Rarawa relationships had developed through previous research collaborations over a number of years, particularly in the development of a community action project on youth and drugs. These connections underpinned the research with trust, respect, and cooperation.

Both tribal links and research relationships were important because the project relied on strong community buy-in and involvement. Tribal linkages carry with them generations of accountability and connections that cannot be ignored. When researchers acknowledge these connections, they acknowledge these accountabilities, thereby bringing an added dimension to the issue of trust.

When planning was underway for the Te Rarawa – Whāriki collaboration, Te Rūnanga O Te Rarawa (a tribal organization delivering health, education, and a range of other services) was refocusing its approach to research and development in an attempt to make better use of its limited financial and people resources. This resulted in a number of *rūnanga* (local Māori council) projects that have brought together elements of research and development under one banner – Ngā Tāhuhu o Te Taiao – and enabled a larger group of researchers to work as a team and share planning, training, and other research processes.

The first step of the project was to establish an advisory group to guide, monitor, and manage Ngā Tāhuhu o Te Taiao. The advisory group was comprised of tribal members with a range of skills and expertise and who were aware of how projects linked to wider tribal goals, developments, and aspirations. They enabled new projects and issues to be integrated in ways that added value to the other research projects and existing *rūnanga* initiatives. The advisory group also helped to manage competing tribal priorities and initiatives, such as conservation and sustainability imperatives against forestry and other resource-exploitative activities.

The second strategy was to align the research with building tribal research capacity. The starting point was the creation of a community researcher position within the *rūnanga* and building the community researcher's skills, as well those of the *iwi* (tribal group) and other interested tribal members, through mentoring by Whāriki researchers. With ongoing support from the advisory group, community interviewer training was conducted and several participants went on to become members of a pool of community interviewers. Some who undertook training chose not to be involved in the research but put their skills to good use interviewing *whanau* for their own purposes, such as genealogical research.

This capacity-building approach was also used to up-skill the researchers and other *rūnanga* staff in GIS and to develop analysis and writing skills. The active involvement of the advisory group in this process enabled associated issues that emerged from the research to be investigated, followed up, or flagged for future reference. For example, some interviews were suitable as oral history recordings, which led the group to develop an archival system for tribal information that complemented *marae* (Māori gathering places) and *whanau* systems. This included physical storage, data access and copyright protocols, and listings of materials.

The interview process provided an opportunity for the interviewees to (a) tell their stories about the areas of importance to Te Rarawa – be they traditional food sources, access to sacred sites, knowledge of family histories, or other features; (b) share what was important to them; and (c) recall experiences from the past, which generally rekindled interest in storytelling, and local knowledge and practices. Many interviewees did not regard their stories as being particularly important at the time; they took them for granted, seeing them as ordinary or just common sense. Therefore, having a reason to tell them and have them valued as knowledge was something new for them. In her seminal work on Indigenous research, *Decolonizing Methodologies*, Linda Tuhiwai Smith (1999) highlighted the importance of storytelling and the inherent value of sharing knowledge through recollection and testimony as valuable Indigenous research methods. Similarly, Smylie et al. (2004) referred to the telling of stories as central to a dynamic between collective Indigenous wisdom and personal knowledge.

The third key factor in this Indigenous approach to research concerned the utility of the research and the expectation of both Te Rarawa and Whāriki that it would make a difference; this was our underlying measure of success. The research provided practical examples of transformation at several levels: the interviewees had a platform from which to share their knowledge and were affirmed in providing valued information; the *runanga* had a raft of evidence to clarify their roles in relation to the aspirations of their people and inform their strategic directions for *iwi* development; the researchers were able to gather and explore new ways of recording information; and the agencies involved with Te Rarawa (e.g., territorial local authorities, government departments, and health providers) had local evidence and understandings presented that allowed them to be more inclusive of Māori interests.

Moreover, there were several examples of ways in which the project informed the approaches and policies of local and national organisations involved in Te Rarawa affairs. One instance was the evidence that experiential ways of learning were important in Te Rarawa; educational institutions could use this to inform school curriculum strategies in an endeavour to strengthen student achievement. Another instance arose from the fact that the Te Rarawa resource management expert attended our training workshop that highlighted practical uses of GIS for development and consent processes, which led to building up data for such purposes (W. Henwood, personal communication, November 11, 2008). It can also be argued that sharing some of the research findings with local authorities would increase their understanding about Māori issues of resource management. Although those possibilities have not yet been fully developed, they illustrate the scope and potential utility of people's stories.

Ngāti Whātua Ngā Rima o Kaipara Marae Arataki Project

Ngā Rima is a cluster of five *marae* belonging to the Ngāti Whātua ki Kaipara (situated north-west of Auckland) that have united to facilitate and synergize the health, well-being, and development of their people. The health and welfare of Māori in the location has been of concern to many, with high rates of morbidity and mortality, social fragmentation, and marginalization (ProCare Network North PHO and Ngāti Whātua Ngā Rima o Kaipara, 2008); as a result, the tribal leadership determined a strategy for change. As part of this effort, they accepted health promotion contracts with ProCare, a primary health organization, to deliver services to local Māori, particularly in the form of nutrition and exercise initiatives.

Whāriki had connections with project stakeholders reaching back over many years and agreed to provide a formative evaluation comprising advice, information, planning, and feedback on the development and progress of the health promotion activities. This required developing close relationships with the project workers to assist and support the program's development and planning. Verne McManus is an experienced Māori evaluator and Whāriki member who worked with *Arataki* (pathfinders) and the program coordinators at each *marae*. Her activities were those of a skilled, critical friend who could collaboratively support, question, theorize, and supplement the community's aspirations and initiatives. Her first steps involved strengthening or building relationships with key personnel in the funder and the community organizations. She took the time necessary to meet face-to-face with the people, acknowledge their struggles, share some of her own experiences, make the connections, and establish trust and good lines of communication. She was then able to help develop systematic evaluation plans, tools, and processes, and provide advice on documentation and guidance on disseminating information about the impacts of program activities (McManus, 2007).

The programs have been a great success, with high levels of involvement from within and beyond the *marae* communities. As well as formal program deliveries (information, enrolment, and ongoing provision of support) for *kai* (food) and nutrition programs, health education (*Tōku Oranga Pai*) and a local Green Prescription project, *Arataki* have initiated numerous other activities. There has been a rise in interest and participation in specific Māori health techniques, including *rongoa* and *mirimiri* (healing practices involving Māori medicines and massage). Group exercises, sports, games, and other physical activities have flourished; healthy eating projects have sprung up along with behaviours and practices that support better community health. A range of cultural activities and pastimes, such as *kapahaka, maurākau,* and *korikori* (skills involving song, dance, weaponry, and other physical activities), have been set up; walking groups, Māori Tai Chi, aerobics, and aquarobics (based at the local Parakai thermal pools) have been enthusiastically embraced. In addition, participation in general *marae* activities has increased with the production of *marae* newsletters and notice boards as well as fundraising for and renovation and redevelopment of the *marae* amenities.

The Whāriki approach to evaluation (Moewaka Barnes, 2000, 2008) is significantly influenced by the Kaupapa Māori theory outlined above; it differs markedly from conventional evaluation systems as applied to social development. Whereas the latter stress objectivity and measurement, we build our evaluations around the concept of *hikoi* (purposive journey) to encompass our vision of walking alongside others in respectful relationship; each brings different skills and perspectives but has the same direction towards community objectives. Ideally, relationships are developed so that contributions from all the parties can be sought, acknowledged, and respected. This is not always the reality; even with the best will, community and evaluators can easily get out of step. When the *hikoi* is not a shared one, obstacles appear and relationships are strained. There were challenges in this case arising from differences between the ideas of the people and the knowledge of *what works* on the part of the evaluator. However, the relationship quality, particularly the mutual respect of the parties, allowed these differences to be negotiated and resolved so the project could go forwards with workable and realistic innovations that met community aims.

The Ngā Rima project illustrates the importance of relationship-building, including the development of trust and rapport among the ProCare, Ngāti Whātua Ngā Rima o Kaipara, the *marae Arataki,* and the evaluators. The Whāriki notion of evaluation and research as a journey shared, especially between community and researcher, is critical; the collaborative, consensual, empowering set of relationships encourages the knowledge and strengths of the parties to flourish and bloom while remaining realistically grounded in what is doable. Without these relationships, the danger is that evaluation is seen as monitoring and surveillance in which authorities impose outcomes and accountability –

rather than as the supportive and process-based refinement and development of community-driven projects. A feature of this project was the commitment from the local funder, which had a Māori staffer who actively represented the project with management and was critical to driving the project forwards.

Following dissemination by the evaluator to other Māori groups, projects building on the successes of the Kaipara project were initiated in other areas. For example, funding of formative evaluation work in another cluster of *marae* in a location south-west of Auckland contributed to multiple community development outcomes, including the establishment of four primary health care clinics within the *marae* amenities.

Discussion of Examples

In all three examples, knowledge embedded in communities was focused and amplified by the evaluation and research activities that Whāriki was able to facilitate and provide. Training, up-skilling, new ideas, innovation, and an enthusiasm for the continuation of knowledge creation meant that knowledge was produced that had the salience and potency to bring about change. This knowledge, in turn, produced ongoing benefits and remains with the people who have an interest in maintaining and using the knowledge. The knowledge from the Pathways project continues to stimulate and produce change in IHD service provision. The Mauri database is in regular use for the benefit of the *iwi*, and the learnings from Ngā Rima have transformed the *marae* cluster into a functional institution and informed developments in other clusters. The knowledge lives longer than it might if had been produced and transmitted solely to policymakers faced with the competing, rapidly changing agendas of the political system.

The evaluation example differs from the other two in that there is greater distance between the evaluator and the evaluated; this is more explicit in process and impact evaluation roles (in which Whāriki was not involved) where the credibility of the assessment depends on some degree of separation. Although knowledge production was not the sole preserve of the researchers, KT had some salience; the evaluators drew out information about blockages or barriers to success in order to feed it back through another lens that framed such gaps as possibilities. In the other instances, the processes of knowledge creation were more interwoven and transfer was not reflective of the way that knowledge was shared or used. In the Mauri project, for example, the creation of a resource database involved empowerment and skills training that the *iwi* used (and continue to use) for their own purposes and aspirations.

Both the Pathways project and the Ngā Rima evaluation provided mechanisms for the organizations and communities to mobilize around issues of concern and to see demonstrable results, thus encouraging and supporting ongoing initiatives and action. Interestingly, the Mauri project came about through pre-existing relationships between that organization and Whāriki that had developed through earlier Te Rarawa initiatives.

As Indigenous people, we are interested in exchanging knowledge and practice both within Aotearoa and internationally. The projects that we have discussed started within local areas, gaining support and knowledge at that level before extending more widely. Discussions of evaluation models have begun with Māori and community groups in other areas and, as in the Ngā Rima evaluation, the program model was adapted to other areas, with the evaluator being a key person carrying the knowledge among the projects. More recently, Whāriki has been contracted via the University of Alaska at Fairbanks to carry out model evaluations for three programs with Alaska First Nations people and to provide an evaluation training course and follow-up workshops through 2009.

Locally and internationally, there is an interest in learning from each other in order to see what might be transferable to other areas and applications. For example, discussion about the Mauri project took place in recent meetings in Canada – *Health of the People: Health of the Land* (University of British Columbia Institute for Aboriginal Health, 2008) that Helen Moewaka Barnes and Wendy Henwood attended. Attendees, largely Indigenous people from academic and community organizations, expressed a sense of urgency about the state of environments and Indigenous health. Learning from each other in order not to reinvent the *waka* (canoe, boat) was seen as an important way forwards. These discussions were underpinned by the understanding that we have some shared visions and experiences as Indigenous peoples and, on this basis, we can learn from and support each other.

Policy Agendas and Knowledge Transfer

The divide between users and producers of knowledge became more relevant when talking of the policy environment at macro levels, where different relationships tended to emerge. In our examples, dissemination to policymakers was usually achieved through collaborative efforts. In the Pathways project, bringing the policymakers into the research loop meant that they were exposed to the data about patient experience and provider attitudes in ways that anchored the broader findings of the project for them, and thereby facilitated change. The organizations involved (including researchers where appropriate) strategically disseminated findings and challenges to policymakers at wider local and national levels. The successes in the Ngā Rima project were actively supported by the funder, who was impressed enough to fund the model for research in other communities within their catchment. The impetus and mechanisms for change were often built into these processes. In other words, the knowledge along with ideas for change were brought to policymakers, who were then more accountable to their constituents and thus less likely to consume and discard research knowledge according to their agendas.

The idea that understanding the needs of policymakers would enable the provision of more relevant research knowledge may be contrary to Māori needs. Within a Kaupapa Māori framing, transformation is high on the agenda. Understanding policymakers' needs is one important strategy. However, Māori aspirations often go beyond this and look at influencing the environment in which the policy agenda and, therefore, the policy priorities are set. The policy environment can change virtually overnight and may be either deeply ignorant of or determinedly hostile to Māori aspirations of development and self-determination. In 2004, for example, following criticism of Māori privilege, the New Zealand government took a number of steps, including attacking the Treaty of Waitangi,[1] which met with considerable opposition from Māori and others (Moewaka Barnes, McCreanor & Huakau, 2009). Aside from issues of funding and research time frames, providing information to meet these policy priorities is not necessarily consistent with Māori agendas. Rather, as the examples show, the priority is to work through particular pathways in order to develop ever-increasing spheres of interactions with policymakers. This process involves greater participation by research users and, potentially, greater advantage in that a range of constituents and stakeholders engage with policymakers.

Working collaboratively, for example, with the *rūnanga* to advance Māori knowledge and to develop strategies, intervention, and planning based on this knowledge, provides a basis on which to work with policymakers. Providing knowledge that meets policymakers' needs but may also influence their agendas can enhance Māori aspirations for change through a range of mechanisms, such as public opinion, community collective action, media, lobbying, and advocacy.

Despite much empirical evidence to the contrary, researchers tend to believe that transmitting evidence to policymakers is all that is needed to enable uptake of the findings. Although this is one approach, researchers may not always be in the best place to transfer knowledge in policy settings.

Conclusion

Why do Māori readily engage and seek to engage with research on their own terms? Māori have a history of creating and spreading knowledge within and among our communities; our distinctive institutions, social orders, and traditions attest to this. When faced with challenges to *tino rangatiratanga* (Māori sovereignty), knowing what provides leverage within the dominant cultural paradigms is an important skill. Depressing statistics related to our position under colonial rule tend to create a range of pessimistic views. However, in the examples given here, these challenges instead created a desire to do the best with the resources available in order to provide effective services and programs. These are internal desires, but external drivers also exist in terms of accountability for funding and in the intense scrutiny that Māori initiatives often face.

When the research or evaluation capability is within communities and groups, and particularly within an Indigenous cultural milieu, the parameters of KT are drastically altered. Often such dynamics of knowledge creation allow us to bypass or supplement conventional processes' knowledge uptake (e.g., via government or local authority policy) through the direct use of data and findings in Māori transformational work.

Many of the KMR and Whāriki processes we have described here breach Western quantitative scientific ideologies about objectivity and neutrality. Māori are variously, or severally, community, *whanau, hapu, iwi;* research is a role, not an identity. It is a task and a responsibility that plays out within Māori lives and within the identities as Māori. Conventional KT, then, is a challenge; Whāriki practice does not sit easily with this concept, as is often portrayed in contemporary Western theories and ideologies of knowledge. However, we are in an enviable position in that we are able to develop relationships that facilitate the effective creation and use of knowledge through research processes.

There is also a built-in accountability mechanism for us. Although not a motivation for working in the way that we do, our careers as researchers would be severely limited if our processes were unacceptable to our communities. Aotearoa is a small country, and Māori communities are closely linked through tribal and other connections. If we did not work in ways that are comfortable and successful for Māori communities, we simply would not be invited back, and the relationships we have described would not have developed as they did. We could still be academic researchers, but it is unlikely that we could call ourselves Māori researchers.

NOTE

1 The Treaty of Waitangi is an agreement between the British Crown and Māori signed progressively between 1840 and 1841. Contested interpretations range between cession and guarantee of Māori sovereignty.

REFERENCES

Ballara, A. (1986). *Proud to be white? A survey of Pākehā prejudice in New Zealand.* Auckland, New Zealand: Heinemann.

Canadian Institutes of Health Research. (2004). *Knowledge translation strategy 2004–2009: Innovation in action.* Retrieved October 10, 2008, from http://www.cihr.ca/e/26574.html

Carroll, P., Blewden, M., & Witten, K. (2008). *Building research capability in the social sciences (BRCSS): The social sciences and policy-research use.* Auckland, New Zealand: Massey University Centre for Social and Health Outcomes Research and Evaluation & Te Rōpū Whāriki.

Cram, F. (2001). Rangahau Māori: Tōna Tika Tōna Pono. In M. Tolich (Ed.), *Research ethics in Aotearoa New Zealand: Concepts, practice, critique* (pp. 35–52). Auckland, New Zealand: Pearson Education New Zealand.

Cram, F., McCreanor, T., Tuhiwai Smith, L., Nairn, R., & Johnstone, W. (2006). Kaupapa Māori research and Pākehā social science: Epistemological tensions in a study of Māori health. *Hulili, 3*(1), 41–68.

Durie, M. (2000). Māori health: Key determinants for the next twenty-five years. *Pacific Health Dialog, 7*(1), 6–11.

Durie, M. (2003). *Ngā Kāhui Pou: Launching Māori futures.* Wellington, New Zealand: Huia Publishers.

Greenwood, M., & de Leeuw, S. (2007). Teachings from the land: Indigenous people, our health, our land, and our children. *Canadian Journal of Native Education, 30*(1), 48–54.

Hill, S. (2008). Socioeconomic inequalities in health. In K. Dew & A. Matheson (Eds.), *Understanding health inequalities in Aotearoa New Zealand* (pp. 33–54). Dunedin, New Zealand: Otago University Press.

Indigenous Health Research Knowledge Transfer Network. (n.d.). *Homepage.* Retrieved August 6, 2008, from http://socserv.mcmaster.ca/ihrktn/

Jones, R., Crengle, S., & McCreanor, T. (2006). How Tikanga guides and protects the research process: Insights from the Hauora Tāne project. *New Zealand Journal of Social Policy, Nov.*(29), 60–77.

Levin, M. (2007). Knowledge and technology transfer: Can universities promote regional development? In A. Harding, A. Scott, S. Laske & C. Burtscher (Eds.), *Bright satanic mills: Universities, regional development and the knowledge economy* (pp. 39–52). Ashgate: Aldershot, UK.

McManus, V. (2007). *Ngāti Whatua Ngā Rima o Kaipara Marae Arataki Project: Formative evaluation report March 2006 – June 2007.* Auckland, New Zealand: Massey University Te Rōpū Whāriki.

Moewaka Barnes, H. (2000). Kaupapa Māori: Explaining the ordinary. *Pacific Health Dialog, 7*(1), 13–16.

Moewaka Barnes, H. (2006). Transforming science: How our structures limit innovation. *Social Policy Journal of New Zealand, July*(29), 1–16.

Moewaka Barnes, H. (2008). *Natural allies: A Māori take on ecohealth.* Manuscript submitted for publication.

Moewaka Barnes, H., McCreanor, T., Edwards, S., & Borell, B. (2009). Epistemological domination: Social science research ethics in Aotearoa. In D.M. Mertens & P.E. Ginsberg (Eds.), *The handbook of social research ethics* (pp. 442–457). London: Sage.

Moewaka Barnes, H., McCreanor, T., & Huakau, J. (2009). Māori and the New Zealand values survey: The importance of research relationships. *Kōtuitui: New Zealand Journal of Social Sciences Online, 3*(2), 135–147. Retrieved August 4, 2010, from http://pdfserve.informaworld.com/130811__921396589.pdf

Nutley, S.M., Walter, I., & Davies, H.T.O. (2007). *Using evidence: How research can inform public services.* Bristol, UK: Policy Press.

Penney, L., Moewaka Barnes, H., Kerr, S., & McCreanor, T. (2008). *It ain't what you do, it's the way that you do it! Action research gets results on heart disease services for Māori.* Manuscript submitted for publication.

Penney, L., Moewaka Barnes, H., & McCreanor, T. (2006). *New perspectives on heart disease management in Te Tai Tokerau: Māori and health practitioners talk.* Auckland, New Zealand: Massey University Te Rōpū Whāriki.

Pihama, L. (1993). *Tungia te Ururua, Kia Tupu Whakaritorito te Tepu o te Harakeke.* Unpublished master's thesis, University of Auckland, Auckland, New Zealand.

Pihama, L., Cram, F., & Walker, S. (2002). Creating methodological space: A literature review of Kaupapa Māori research. *Canadian Journal of Native Education, 26*(1), 30–43.

Pipi, K., Cram, F., Hawke, R., Hawke, S., Huriwai, T.M., Mataki, T., et al. (2004). A research ethic for studying Māori and iwi provider success. *Social Policy Journal of New Zealand, Nov.*(23), 141–153.

ProCare Network North PHO and Ngāti Whātua Ngā Rima o Kaipara. (2008, March 5). *Presentation to community public health advisory committee, Waitemata district health board.* Presentation to the Community Public Health Advisory Committee, Waitemata District Health Board, Auckland, New Zealand. Retrieved August 4, 2010, from http://www.waitematadhb. govt.nz/LinkClick.aspx?fileticket=rFgSVcS87AQ%3D&tabid=265&mid=815

Reason, P.W., & Bradbury, H. (2006). Introduction: Inquiry and participation in search of a world worthy of human aspiration. In P.W. Reason & H. Bradbury (Eds.), *Handbook of action research* (pp. 1–14). London: Sage.

Reid, P., & Robson, B. (2007). Understanding health inequities. In B. Robson & R. Harris (Eds.), *Hauora: Māori standards of health IV. A study of the years 2000–2005* (pp. 3–10). Wellington, New Zealand: Te Rōpū Rangahau Hauora a Eru Pōmare.

Rich, R.F. (2001). *Social science information and public policy making.* New Brunswick, NJ: Transaction Publishers.

Ritchie, J. (1956). *Basic personality in Rākau.* Wellington, New Zealand: Victoria University College.

Roberts, M., Norman, W., Minhinnick, N.K., Wihongi, D., & Kirkwood, C. (1995). Kaitiakitanga: Māori perspectives on conservation. *Pacific Conservation Biology, 2*(1), 7–20.

Smylie, J.K., Martin, C.M., Kaplan-Myrth, N., Steele, L., Tait, C.L., & Hogg, W. (2004). Knowledge translation and Indigenous knowledge. *International Journal of Circumpolar Health, 63*(Suppl. 2: ICCH 12), 139–143.

Social Sciences Reference Group. (2005) *Coming of Age, Social Science Research and its Contribution to Wealth and Well-being in New Zealand, 2006* (Report of the Social Sciences' Reference Group to the Ministry of Science and Technology). Wellington: Ministry of Research Science and Technology.

Statistics New Zealand. (2007). QuickStats About Māori; Census 2006 / Tatauranga 2006. Retrieved June 20, 2010, from http://www.stats.govt.nz/ census/2006-census-data/quickstats-about-maori/2006-census-quickstats- about-maori-revised.htm

Stewart, T. (1995). *Ka pu te ruha, ka hao te rangatahi: Contributions to 'indigenous psychology' in Aotearoa/New Zealand.* Unpublished master's thesis, University of Auckland, Auckland, New Zealand.

Te Ahukaramū Charles Royal (Ed.). (2003). *The woven universe: Selected writings of Rev. Māori Marsden.* Ōtaki, New Zealand: Estate of Rev. Māori Marsden.

Tuhiwai Smith, L. (1992). Kura Kaupapa and the implications for curriculum. In G. McCulloch (Ed.), *The school curriculum in New Zealand: History, theory, policy and practice* (pp. 219–231). Palmerston North, New Zealand: Dunmore Press.

Tuhiwai Smith, L. (1999). *Decolonizing methodologies: Research and Indigenous peoples.* London: Zed Books.

University of British Columbia Institute for Aboriginal Health. (2008, June 10). *The health of the people: The health of the land.* Retrieved July 5, 2010, from http://www.familymed.ubc.ca/__shared/assets/june10vc6269.pdf

Walker, R.J. (1990). *Ka Whawhai Tonu Matou: Struggle without end.* Auckland, New Zealand: Penguin.

Walker, S., Eketone, A., & Gibbs, A. (2006). An exploration of Kaupapa Māori research, its principles, processes and applications. *International Journal of Social Research Methodology, 9*(4), 331–344.

Whāriki Research Group / Te Rōpū Whāriki. (n.d.). *Homepage.* Retrieved July 5, 2010, from www.whariki.ac.nz

Witten, K., & Hammond, K. (2008). *What becomes of social science knowledge? New Zealand researchers' experiences of knowledge transfer modes and audiences.* Manuscript submitted for publication.

11 Knowledge Translation and Indigenous Communities: A Decolonizing Perspective

JANET K. SMYLIE

Knowledge translation (KT) has emerged as an international health research priority over the past decade. It has been described as the bridging of the know-do gap (Canadian Institutes of Health Research [CIHR], 2004). In the current literature, the *know* is primarily health-research-generated knowledge, and the *do* has focused on finding ways to help ensure that the behaviours and decisions of health practitioners and policymakers are aligned with the best of current health-research-generated knowledge. Only a fraction of work in this area has focused on the exchange and application of knowledge with or to the public, and a smaller amount has examined KT processes in Aboriginal community contexts (Smylie, Martin, Kaplan-Myrth, Steele, Tait, et al., 2004). For example, out of hundreds of clinical practice guidelines published for health care practitioners in Canada, only one has specific recommendations for Indigenous peoples (Canadian Diabetes Association, 2003, pp. S110–S111), and none provide direction on how to adapt generic models to local belief systems and practices.

This chapter explores the bridging of know-do gaps in Aboriginal community contexts from a decolonizing perspective. I begin with conceptualizing KT and give a theoretical framework. I then describe historic and current Aboriginal community approaches to health knowledge dissemination and application, including key mechanisms underlying knowledge development and translation strategies from biomedicine and clinical epidemiology and from First Nations, Inuit, and Métis contexts. I then summarize our team's community-based efforts to examine and develop Indigenous KT strategies within First Nations, Inuit, and Métis communities. Finally, I identify four key challenges for Indigenous KT that require further exploration and provide recommendations for how Indigenous KT work could move forward in an ethically sound way to improve the health of First Nations, Inuit, and Métis individuals and communities.

Definitions and Research Approach

In 2003, the Knowledge Translation and Indigenous Knowledge (KTIK) research group embarked upon a four-year, participatory, action-oriented, mixed-method study of knowledge translation in three First Nations, Inuit, and Métis communities in Ontario. Our developing conceptualization of Indigenous KT is a multidirectional process of knowledge synthesis, exchange, dissemination, and application that is intrinsically linked to knowledge development. This synthesis of knowledge development and transfer reflects an inherent practicality that underlies many Indigenous knowledge activities. Perception is pluralistic as each person's understanding is unique and rooted in his or her identity and experiences to date. The process of consensus-building collates individual perceptions to form a shared understanding within a group. Knowledge development is understood as a process of knowledge translation or the translation of knowledge that exists to the living being that now perceives it.

Within health-related contexts, our emerging working definition of Indigenous KT is 'Indigenously led sharing of culturally relevant and useful health information and practices to improve Indigenous health status, policy, services, and programs' (Kaplan-Myrth & Smylie, 2006, pp. 24–25). This definition is aligned with the principles of Indigenous self-determination – if it is to be an Indigenous process or activity, then Indigenous leadership is essential. In Indigenous community contexts, KT can be understood simply as *sharing what we know about living a good life* – a phrase easily translated into the mother tongue of my Métis-Cree grandmother. Another working definition for KT was generously shared with me by Cree scholar Willie Ermine (personal communication, February 2006): *kiskisamatotan ma miyo pimatisiwin* or collective blessing for good living every day. This definition is aligned with Indigenous assumptions of the metaphysical and secular characteristics of knowledge as well as with the collective knowledge development processes.

Our KTIK research group developed a decolonizing research framework for our community-based studies (Smylie et al., 2008). The framework draws on the Report of the Royal Commission on Aboriginal Peoples (RCAP, 1996), the United Nations Declaration on the Rights of Indigenous People (UN, 2007), and work of Indigenous scholars in Canada and internationally (Battiste, 2000; Brant Castellano, 2000; Little Bear, 2000; Tuhiwai Smith, 1999; Youngblood Henderson, 2000b). The key assumptions are as follows: (a) prior to colonization, Indigenous peoples had their own systems of health knowledge and services; (b) these systems were rooted in diverse, local ecosystems and, therefore, were diverse; (c) these systems were epistemologically distinct from modern biomedical scientific traditions, which purposefully decontextualize knowledge from local contexts in an effort to discover generalizable health principles and cures; (d) Indigenous systems of health were actively suppressed and outlawed as part of colonization; (e) the health of Indigenous peoples was and continues to be negatively affected by colonization; (f) contemporary health knowledge and health behaviour among Indigenous individuals and communities are influenced by an interplay of precolonial systems of health, historic, and ongoing processes of colonization, and exposure to non-Indigenous systems of health – the nature of this interplay is diverse and varies according to individual and community experiences, locations, migrations, and kinship systems; and (g) a decolonizing process involving critical examination and dismantling of individual and systemic assumptions and power relationships, including the suppression of Indigenous knowledge, is required to improve the health of Indigenous communities.

Indigenous Knowledge Systems, Knowledge Translation, and Colonial Processes

Notwithstanding the recent spotlight on KT by research institutions, the sharing and application of knowledge to improve the health and well-being of individuals and populations is not new. The transfer and successful application of specialized information about how to live healthfully on a particular land base using and sustaining the available natural resources was, and to different extents still is, an essential part of Indigenous life and culture. In many Indigenous knowledge systems, experiential demonstration and practice in real-life situations were the preferred mechanisms for sharing and transferring knowledge (Cajete, 2000; Kaplan-Myrth & Smylie, 2006). Storytelling was another important way that local knowledge, values, and skills were transferred within and among communities and across generations (Kaplan-Myrth & Smylie, 2006; Zimmerman & Molyneaux, 1996). More recently,

Indigenous communities around the world have articulated a preference for knowledge development and research processes that are linked to the betterment of their communities (CIHR, 2007; RCAP, 1996).

Unfortunately, the historically rich and diverse base of Indigenous knowledge and the systems in place for its dissemination, exchange, and uptake were purposefully and systematically disrupted by European colonization. Colonization included processes that suppressed Indigenous knowledge and language and imposed European knowledge and language in their place (Tuhiwai Smith, 1999). The assumption was that European knowledge and knowledge systems were superior. This has persisted over the past 500 years and is entrenched in present-day Indigenous health programs, services, and scholarship. A recent international meeting of Indigenous stakeholders, linked to the World Health Organization Commission on the Social Determinants of Health, highlighted the current lack of understanding of Indigenous cultures and world views and the need for increased respect for Indigenous peoples and their understandings of health and well-being (International Symposium on the Social Determinants of Indigenous Health, 2007).

The articulation of the need to respect Indigenous peoples and their cultures is linked to current ethical and human rights opinions regarding shared knowledge activities (including research) between Indigenous and non-Indigenous communities. For example, the first article of the CIHR Guidelines for Health Research Involving Aboriginal Peoples (CIHR, 2007) stipulates, 'A researcher should understand and respect Aboriginal world views, including responsibilities to the people and culture that flow from being granted access to traditional or sacred knowledge. These should be incorporated into research agreements, to the extent possible' (p. 3). Additionally, the recently adopted UN Declaration on the Rights of Indigenous Peoples (UN, 2007) states that Indigenous peoples have the right to maintain, control, protect, and develop their cultural heritage, traditional knowledge, and traditional cultural expressions as well as the right to be actively involved in developing and determining health, housing, and other economic and social programs affecting them.

The epistemological assumptions of modern-day biomedicine and epidemiology, combined with an emphasis on evidence-based clinical practice and health care decision-making, contribute to a hierarchy of health knowledge in which Indigenous knowledge is devalued and marginalized. In this knowledge hierarchy, knowledge derived from a randomized controlled trial (RCT) or quantitative meta-analysis is rated as superior compared to knowledge that is derived from a local experience or narrative (i.e., the case study). A commonly used scale for rating quality of evidence (Harris et al., 2001) appends an evidence grade that depends on the source of the knowledge. In this system, top grades are given to RCT-based knowledge and bottom grades are given to experiential or narrative knowledge. If the goal is to understand the efficacy of a simple intervention without the biases of the local contextual factor, the RCT is a useful tool. However, the application of health interventions occurs in real-world, local contexts. Difficulties arise when one tries to bridge the gap left by the decontextualization of RCT-derived knowledge and reintegrate this knowledge into real-life contexts so that it can contribute to improvements in health and well-being in particular communities. Indeed, one of the key drivers behind the recent emphasis of research institutions on KT may be a response to the limitations of RCT-derived knowledge with respect to its translation into practice and policy contexts. Most practitioners and policymakers require special tools to use RCT-derived knowledge products effectively.

Community-based Indigenous knowledge processes avoid the KT challenges created by the decontextualized knowledge processes because they are contextually situated and closely linked to knowledge application. The influence of local geographic contexts on historic Indigenous knowledge systems is well described by Youngblood-Henderson (2000a) and is a premise of our research team's theoretical framework. Scholar Willie Ermine eloquently described the applied and contextual nature of Indigenous knowledge:

> It is not abstract. It is right here, with the old people. How they work with the land, work with the family, work with the relationships. The active humanity that they do, that is Indigenous knowledge. Indigenous knowledge is not in a book or somewhere else. It is alive and it has to be practiced. (cited in Kaplan-Myrth & Smylie, 2006, p. 9)

What is required, however, is not a competition among different types of knowledge-development processes and their products but recognition by researchers, policymakers, and health professionals that multiple types are needed for effective health services, programs, and policies. The premise that multiple types of knowledge bring complementary contributions to problem solving has been recognized for years in business and more recently in health sciences KT discussions (Landry, Amara, Pablos-Mendes, Shademani, & Gold, 2006).

Within Indigenous contexts, Indigenous knowledge and knowledge processes need to be part of the knowledge toolkit. Most health interventions in Indigenous communities are complex and require contextual tailoring. Even the implementation of a drug treatment is a complex, contextually driven intervention in such settings. An RCT can help inform practitioners about whether they should prescribe drug A instead of drug B; but it offers little about practice behaviours, the acceptability of prescription drugs to those living in the community, the quality of the relationship between the provider and patient, or the financial and logistical accessibility of the prescription for the patient.

While the types of knowledge prioritized for KT and application by health KT scholars, practitioners, and policymakers appear to be primarily restricted to knowledge derived from RCT, there is a growing discussion on the limitations of this knowledge. The need for detailed information about the underlying theory and mechanisms of interventions in addition to outcome data – and for information about the specific contexts in which the intervention has worked – is increasingly recognized in scholarly and policy contexts (Pawson, 2006). This has led to new tools for the systematic review of interventions.

The limitations of RCT processes in the evaluation of community-based Indigenous health interventions are illustrated by considering ceremonial interventions such as the sweat lodge, a common and important traditional healing practice in First Nations and Métis communities in North America. How can one arrive at a standard scientific description of this therapeutic intervention that often includes the visitation of metaphysical beings? Each sweat lodge ceremony is considered a unique experience that naturally unfolds. How can one determine a common *dose*? Sweat lodge ceremonies are contextual and vary according to who is leading it, where it is occurring, and who is participating. These variables cannot be randomized to assess their effects; therefore, this important healing practice cannot be evaluated by an RCT. Does this mean it is less effective in treating a particular illness, for example depression, than a prescription drug that has received an 'A' grade evidence rating for treating depression? Of course, we do not know this – all we know is that one intervention is easier to evaluate by RCT than the other is.

Before moving on to community-based research examples, it is worth mentioning the work of Cree scholar Willie Ermine (2005, 2006) regarding the directionality of KT processes. Drawing on the work of philosopher Roger Poole, Ermine used the term 'ethical space' to describe the space between Indigenous (in his case Cree) and Western spheres of culture and knowledge (2005, para. 2). Ermine charted four models of KT, each built on a specific set of reference points or knowledge locations on his Indigenous/Cree – Western ethical space map (see figure 11.1). Model A, or the monocultural model, takes place completely within the Western sphere. According to Ermine (cited in Kaplan-Myrth & Smylie, 2006), this model

> is an established consciousness . . . that only western ideas, practices, and conventions will receive the light of day and be supported by discourses and . . . funding. What that states to Indigenous peoples is that their ideas do not register nor have value in the national health consciousness. (p. 34)

In Model B, the colonialism model, knowledge crosses from the Western sphere, over the ethical space, into Indigenous communities.

Figure 11.1 Mapping Indigenous knowledge translation onto the ethical space

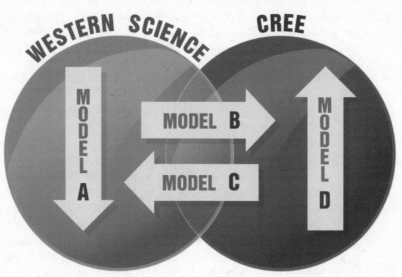

Source: Adapted from Ermine (2006) as quoted in Kaplan-Myrth & Smylie (2006, pp. 34–35).

Ermine asserted that this model displaces Indigenous knowledge and health practices since Western biomedical systems have not supported Indigenous philosophies, science, and healing practices.

Model C, the appropriation model, mirrors Model B in that knowledge crosses from the Indigenous sphere, over the ethical space, into the Western system. This model is problematic because, according to Ermine, Western-trained researchers are limited in their ability to understand Indigenous systems of knowledge and, therefore, how to translate Indigenous understandings and ideas. In the absence of adequate legal and ethical protection, Indigenous knowledge in this model becomes appropriated, distorted, and/or exploited by Western scholarship.

Model D, the Indigenous framework, takes place completely within the Indigenous sphere. Knowledge is developed, synthesized, and applied within Indigenous communities. This model is preferred by Indigenous communities because it allows for a postcolonial reclamation and rebuilding of Indigenous health knowledge and institutions. Unfortunately, it is the least resourced. Ermine (cited in Kaplan-Myrth & Smylie, 2006) proposed that

> once Indigenous communities reclaim their health knowledge base and have made significant progress in recapturing control of their lives and supporting institutions then knowledge translation and transfer can begin in earnest because the playing field would have been somewhat levelled. (p. 36)

Community-Based Research and Indigenous Knowledge Translation

There are several characteristics of Indigenous knowledge systems that make community-based, participatory, action-research approaches particularly relevant to contemporary Indigenous KT. These include the intrinsic and historic links between Indigenous knowledge systems and local geographic ecosystems; the diversity of both historic and present-day Indigenous communities in Canada with respect to language, culture, location, and experiences; and the persistent imbalance of Indigenous – non-Indigenous relations (including ways that Indigenous knowledge systems are perceived within the academe). A participatory action research approach can support the repositioning of Indigenous knowledge and conceptual frameworks from the margin to the centre of KT strategies. It contributes to matching theories and mechanistic assumptions underlying KT work with those operating in a particular Indigenous community context. Finally, it facilitates the integration of local Indigenous knowledge and experiences into KT strategies.

The latter two issues – the essential nature of contextually sound theory and the need for a formative understanding of community-specific knowledge and processes – have been articulated in the health promotion literature (Merzel & D'Afflittl, 2003). The repositioning of Indigenous knowledge from the margin to the centre of KT strategies aligns KT work with the processes of Indigenous self-determination. In the words of Brant Castellano (2004): 'Fundamental to the exercise of self-determination is the right of peoples to construct knowledge in accordance with self-determined definitions of what is real and what is valuable' (p. 204).

The KTIK research group's goal was to work in partnership with Indigenous communities to develop and evaluate Indigenous models of KT for health sciences research within Indigenous community contexts. The research team started with a formative exploration of existing pathways of health knowledge use and dissemination in one First Nations, one Inuit, and one Métis community in Ontario (Smylie et al., 2008). We applied a participatory action research partnership approach that drew on our research experiences as well as on successful models and recommendations regarding community-based, participatory, Indigenous health research (First Nations Centre, 2005; Fletcher, 2003; Inuit Tapirisat of Canada, 1998; Kahnawake Schools Diabetes Prevention Project, 1996; McShane, 2006; Schnarch, 2004; Smylie, Kaplan-Myrth et al., 2004; Smylie, McShane, & Inuit Family Resource Centre, 2006). Our approach attempted to balance the power relationships among community partners, community participants, collaborating Aboriginal organizations, and academic research team members from initiation to dissemination.

After developing academic-community research partnerships and formalizing these with a research agreement, we held two focus groups and five key informant interviews in each community to explore the following questions:

- If you wanted information on a physical, mental, emotional, or spiritual health issue, where or to whom would you go in this community?
- How would you decide if the health information that you received was good or not?

- What kinds of health information have you used in your day-to-day life and work over the past week?
- If you wanted to spread a health message in this community, how would you do it?

The results of this inquiry revealed that existing KT processes are diverse, distinct, and linked to local community structures, geography, history, and culture (Smylie et al., 2008). For example, there were significant differences in the ways in which the three communities were structured. These structures had an important impact on within-community information dissemination. For a cohesive community like the urban Inuit, word of mouth is an extremely effective means to disseminate information. In contrast, the First Nations community faced challenges with dissemination due to social fragmentation within the community. For the urban Métis community, identifying and engaging a dispersed population was a significant challenge for disseminating health information. Family and community networks were the most important sources of health information and mode of dissemination in all three communities. There was also a strong, cross-cutting preference for within-community messages; members of each community expressed an overall preference for health messages generated within their community and in which the messenger and/or medium reflected their specific Aboriginal ethnicity. A final, common theme was a shared valuing of experiential knowledge. Inuit, First Nations, and Métis community members emphasized that medicines, health care providers, programs, and services are evaluated based on evidence from personal experiences. As expressed by one Inuit community member: 'You try it out, it works, and they're going to tell somebody else and everybody's going to know.'

Building on these understandings of the use and dissemination of health information in each community, we tailored a specific KT strategy to address a health priority area in each community. With the urban Inuit community, we developed, piloted, and evaluated an interactive CD-ROM of an Inuit elder giving prenatal teachings (McShane, 2006; McShane, Smylie, Hastings, Martin, & Inuit Family Resource Centre, 2006). Among the urban Métis community, the KT vehicle took the form of cultural gatherings linked to the development of a Métis-specific health network (Smylie, Ottawa Council, Wellington, & Adomako, in press). Finally, in partnership with the First Nations community, we worked with youth on a mental health project that included the development, implementation, and evaluation of a youth drop-in facility and a mother-daughter group (Oosman, Smylie, Kauffeldt, & Pikwakanagan First Nation, 2007).

While a detailed discussion of these three projects is beyond the scope of this chapter and can be found elsewhere (i.e., in addition to citations by project in the preceding paragraph, see Smylie et al., 2008), it is worth highlighting the diverse, culturally distinct messages and mediums of Indigenous KT that developed in each participant community. These ranged from an Inuit elder sharing traditional Inuit teachings regarding the fetus and pregnancy in Inuktitut, to a young Métis woman teaching how to jig to fiddle music at a Métis community gathering, to First Nations youth doing Internet research for the health bulletin board at the youth drop-in centre. Considered together, the three community KT initiatives provide a vivid illustration of the diverse, dynamic, and transformative nature of Indigenous KT.

The guiding principles of our decolonizing framework and our community-based, participatory action approach provided the initial theoretical and operational structure of our KT model. The first key finding is that this approach was successful in its ability to engage three diverse Indigenous communities in KT research and activities. Further, this model facilitated a progression in the degree of community leadership and control in the area of Indigenous KT as applied to coordinated responses to emerging community health concerns.

The second key finding had to do with the outcomes of the community-based health knowledge interventions. In all three projects, we were able to demonstrate one or more tangible changes in health knowledge behaviour and/or health status at the completion of distinct KT interventions. In the Inuit community, we highlighted an elder giving prenatal teaching in Inuktitut on an interactive CD-ROM and were able to demonstrate that this tool was positively received in the community on all of our measurement scales. After using the CD-ROM, community members were more likely to recommend it to a friend, whereas before they had used it, they would not have made this recommendation compared to before they had used it (McShane, 2006). With the Métis, we organized a series of Métis-specific community cultural gatherings and a Métis health network. Following this intervention, we were able demonstrate with a pre– post-intervention survey that Métis participants had an enhanced sense of belonging to the Métis community and had increased self-rated access to Métis-specific health information and services (Smylie et al., in press). In the First Nations community, our interventions included a youth drop-in and mother-daughter group interventions, which included youth being assisted by their parents and youth workers in the preparation of their regalia for the annual community pow-wow. Following these interventions, we showed a reduction in the number of participants with high-risk profiles on the Children's Health Inventory Profile, Adolescent Addition, compared to before the intervention (Oosman et al., 2007). These findings are promising as there are very few Aboriginal health interventions in the published literature that have demonstrated tangible improvements in health knowledge behaviour and/or health status, despite a large number of ongoing health programs.

The KTIK study also explored the question of how Indigenous communities share information with each other. At a meeting of key Indigenous KT stakeholders from across Canada in November 2004, participants highlighted the importance of networks and gatherings and also the transmission of information by elders sharing oral stories. Essential to the success of this intercommunity sharing of information is recognition of and respect for each nation and their specific cultural heritage (Kaplan-Myrth & Smylie, 2006). As an example, Elder Maria Campbell described how Cree and Métis families lived on the land in extended family groups and how these groups would regularly gather for ceremonies and the exchange of knowledge and medicines. She described individuals who spent their time travelling between Métis communities in northern Saskatchewan, carrying information, stories, medicines as well as some trade goods from community to community (M. Campbell, personal communication, March 15, 2007).

Oral History as a Community-Based Indigenous KT Tool

Recognizing the historic importance of intergenerational oral transmission of Indigenous knowledge, we worked with community partners to develop another set of pilot studies in Saskatchewan and Ontario. These studies explored whether historic understandings and knowledge regarding infant wellness could be accessed through oral history interviews with elders, and whether this historic knowledge would include information that was of immediate relevance to health policy, programming, and practice. We interviewed seven elders in Ontario and over twenty elders in Saskatchewan, in partnership with the Ontario Federation of Indian Friendship Centres and the Tungasuvvingat Inuit Family Resource Centre, Canoe Lake First Nation, and Sagitawak Métis

Council. Participant communities and elders were enthusiastic about and engaged in the process. The oral history method, which builds on both the experience of Elder Maria Campbell and reports of oral history projects in other First Nations communities (Hart, 1995), was easily learned by both academic and community research team members. It was effective as well for gathering historic knowledge regarding Indigenous infant, child, and family health.

The pilot findings are very rich and elders shared much information that is relevant to contemporary policies, programs, and services. This includes insights into the underlying values and beliefs of reproductive health care as well as practical descriptions of ceremonies and traditional medicine, infant and maternity care practices, and parenting. For example, important themes in Canoe Lake First Nations included the support of female relatives and midwives before, during, and after birth; recommending physical activity; and the link between a diet of wild foods/garden vegetables and health (Indigenous Peoples' Health Research Centre, 2006). In the Ontario oral history study, the following key themes emerged: the need to transmit reproductive health information throughout the lifecycle and starting before conception; the link between the health of the unborn baby and the health of the mother during pregnancy; and the roles and responsibilities of the father in contributing to a healthy environment for the mother and baby (Anderson, 2006).

KT and Indigenous Contexts: Ongoing Challenges and Recommendations for Moving Forward

Like most research in developing fields, explorations of Indigenous KT raise more questions than answers. In this section, I describe four key challenges.

1. *Moving Indigenous health KT forward in ways that address rather than perpetuate existing imbalances between Indigenous and non-Indigenous approaches.* Moving forward will involve the ongoing repositioning of Indigenous knowledge at the centre of Indigenous communities. Community-based, participatory, action research is one way of ensuring that Indigenous communities regain control of health knowledge priorities, processes, and outcomes.

2. *Developing and revitalizing intrinsic community health KT strategies.* In consultations with Indigenous communities and Indigenous KT

stakeholders, this has emerged as the priority for health KT activities (Kaplan-Myrth & Smylie, 2006). In this model (Ermine's Model D), knowledge is developed, synthesized, and applied within Indigenous communities. The primary knowledge source is community-based Indigenous knowledge. Examples include Indigenous language programs, the revitalization of Indigenous health services (e.g., healing and midwifery), and support for the intergenerational transmission and application of local Indigenous knowledge using tools such as oral history, multimedia, community gatherings, and the intergenerational teaching of traditional skills. These types of activities are very common in Indigenous communities. Adequate resourcing and renewed respect for community-based Indigenous knowledge, processes, and capacities are essential for the further development of Indigenous community health translation strategies. We have been working in partnership with Indigenous communities to demonstrate that intrinsic community KT processes cannot only actively engage communities in KT work but also produce tangible improvements in health outcomes.

3. *Identifying and developing ethically sound and community relevant ways of harnessing specialized non-Indigenous knowledge for the benefit of Indigenous communities.* The translation of specialized non-Indigenous knowledge, such as biomedical research, into an Indigenous communities approach is the KT approach most closely aligned to the KT models currently purported by non-Indigenous health researchers and health research institutions. In our consultations with Indigenous communities and stakeholders, this type of knowledge activity was less of a priority than the development of intrinsic, community-based knowledge. Nevertheless, there are several examples of Indigenous communities incorporating Western European technologies into the fabric of their community, culture, and economy. The suggestion that Indigenous health messaging will be different from non-Indigenous health-research-generated messaging is not necessarily true. In my experience as a biomedically trained physician and public health researcher, more often than not, there is a synergy between non-Indigenous health research messages and local Indigenous health messages. For example, the prenatal messaging regarding self-care and physical activity given by the Inuit elder for the interactive CD-ROM in our KTIK project was well aligned with current biomedical and public health, evidence-based

recommendations for pregnancy and infant care. Key additional recommendations for future work in this area would be to build on articulated community priorities and recognize that non-Indigenous knowledge products may need to be transformed if they are to be relevant and useful in Indigenous community contexts.

4. *Identification and development of ethically sound and community relevant ways of evaluating Indigenous KT strategies.* The shared goal of improved Indigenous health and reduced Indigenous and non-Indigenous health disparities might be one with which both Indigenous and non-Indigenous stakeholders could agree. However, an agreed-upon definition of Indigenous health and of key pathways to achieve it would likely be more of a challenge to negotiate. It is well recognized that Indigenous models of health differ from non-Indigenous biomedical models in that they consider the health of the whole community and its surrounding environment (Stephens, Nettleton, Porter, Willis, & Clark, 2005). Likewise, the key pathways identified by Indigenous stakeholders for the achievement of health may be different from those that are the focus of biomedicine. For example, in the report from the International Symposium on the Social Determinants of Indigenous Health (International Symposium, 2007), the dismantling of colonial practices and policies and the restitution of Indigenous self-determination, through the implementation of UN instruments such as the UN Declaration on the Rights of Indigenous Peoples, was identified as a key pathway for the improvement of Indigenous health. In contrast, the bulk of the biomedical literature regarding health interventions focuses on pharmaceuticals and medical technologies developed outside these communities.

If the outcomes and pathways to Indigenous health differ from the outcomes and pathways established for non-Indigenous populations, it follows that the criteria by which we evaluate the success of interventions will also be different. The criteria for the evaluation of a health intervention in the non-Indigenous world may include clinical significance, reproducibility, generalizability, efficacy, and efficiency. Māori scholar Mason Durie (2006) proposed three very different criteria for Indigenous success. First, success is defined not only by individual achievement but also by the achievement of Indigenous collectives. Second, it involves a capacity to engage with Indigenous culture, networks, and resources as well as with global societies and communities. According to Durie, this 'recognizes the two worlds within which Indigenous peoples live and the skills needed to negotiate both' (p. 3). His third benchmark of Indigenous success is a capacity for self-management compatible with Indigenous world views and attuned to wider society.

Clearly, more work is required to evaluate success in Indigenous community contexts in ways that are relevant and useful to the diversity of Indigenous communities. One key assumption of the KTIK project was that before colonization, Indigenous knowledge systems were rooted in diverse, local ecosystems and, therefore, were themselves diverse. The need for underlying recognition of the diversity of local cultural knowledge systems in modern Indigenous health services and programs underpins the concluding remarks below. Both Durie's proposed criteria for success, which emerge from his context as a Māori scholar, and the success criteria of non-Indigenous scholars need to be revisited and revisioned to match the diversity of local Indigenous communities in what is now Canada. First Nations, Inuit, and Métis individuals and communities negotiate not in just two worlds but a multiplicity of worlds in their day-to-day lives and interactions; this complexity needs to be acknowledged in the assessment of their knowledge-sharing strategies.

Concluding Remarks

Effective health services and programs in Indigenous communities require an integrated understanding of local cultural knowledge systems and ways of knowing that are practised by Indigenous leaders and communities. Without these understandings, there will be predictable gaps in the promotion of health and provision of health services. Bringing Indigenous leadership, knowledge, and knowledge systems to the centre of health service development, implementation, and evaluation is critical for Indigenous health and success.

Community-based Indigenous knowledge and knowledge processes are essential to the improvement of Indigenous health and well-being. Further, Indigenous knowledge and processes provide important insights for current non-Indigenous KT initiatives. Recently, CIHR made a distinction between *End of Grant KT* and *Integrated KT*. Integrated KT is described as a way of doing research that is collaborative, action-oriented, and involves the co-production of knowledge with researchers engaging the stakeholders who are the end users (CIHR, 2008). In an integrated KT process, stakeholders are involved in shaping the research questions, deciding on the methodology, helping with data collection and tool development, interpreting study findings, crafting the message and disseminating the research results. This description sounds very similar to the community-based, participatory, action research model that has been evolving in Aboriginal health research over the past two decades and was fundamental to the community-based, Indigenous KT models that the KTIK research group has been working on in partnership with Indigenous communities. Both CIHR's integrated KT model and the Aboriginal community-based, participatory action research model can help address the know-do gap by building the perspectives of individuals and communities into all aspects of the research process. Both the Aboriginal health research community and the Indigenous KT initiatives have important experiences and insights to offer the broader KT research community in the area of integrated KT.

Such work will ease that practical challenge experienced every day by front-line health care providers – how to bridge what we know from our training and scholarship and the realities of the individuals and communities that we serve. The more that knowledge development and translation activities can create products and processes relevant to the contexts of our communities of practice, the more likely it is that these KT efforts will significantly contribute to enhancements in community health and well-being.

REFERENCES

Anderson, K. (2006). *Indigenous knowledge networks for infant, child and family health: A report on phase one.* Toronto, ON: Ontario Federation of Indian Friendship Centres.
Battiste, M. (Ed.). (2000). *Reclaiming indigenous voice and vision.* Vancouver, BC: UBC Press.
Brant Castellano, M. (2000). Updating Aboriginal traditions of knowledge. In G.J. Sefa Dei, B.L. Hall, & D.G. Rosenberg (Eds.), *Indigenous knowledges in global contexts: Multiple readings of our world* (pp. 21–36). Toronto, ON: University of Toronto Press.
Brant Castellano, M. (2004). Ethics of Aboriginal research. *Journal of Aboriginal Health, 1*(1), 98–114.
Cajete, G. (2000). Indigenous knowledge: The Pueblo metaphor of indigenous education. In M. Battiste (Ed.), *Reclaiming indigenous voice and vision* (pp. 181–208). Vancouver, BC: UBC Press.

Canadian Diabetes Association Clinical Practice Guidelines Expert Committee. (2003). Clinical practice guidelines for the prevention and management of diabetes in Canada. *Canadian Journal of Diabetes, 27*(Suppl. 2), S1–S140.

Canadian Institutes of Health Research (CIHR). (2004). *Knowledge translation strategy 2004–2009: Innovation in action*. Retrieved July 7, 2010, from http://www.cihr.ca/e/26574.html

Canadian Institutes of Health Research. (2007, May). *CIHR guidelines for health research involving Aboriginal people*. Retrieved July 7, 2010, from http://www.cihr-irsc.gc.ca/e/29134.html

Canadian Institutes of Health Research. (2008, May 30). *About knowledge translation*. Retrieved July 7, 2010, from http://www.cihr.ca/e/29418.html

Durie, M. (2006, December). *Indigenous resilience: From disease and disadvantage to the realization of potential*. Paper presented at the Pacific Region Indigenous Doctors Congress, Rotarua, New Zealand.

Ermine, W. (2005). *Ethical space: Transforming relations*. Paper presented at the Traditions: National Gatherings on Indigenous Knowledge, Ottawa, ON.

Ermine, W. (2006). Mapping of knowledge translation: Working in the ethical space. In N. Kaplan-Myrth & J.K. Smylie (Eds.), *Sharing what we know about living a good life: Indigenous knowledge translation summit report* (pp. 34–36). Saskatoon, SK: Indigenous Peoples' Health Research Centre.

First Nations Centre, National Aboriginal Health Organization. (2005). *First Nations regional longitudinal health survey (RHS) 2002/03: Results for adults, youth and children living in First Nations communities*. Ottawa, ON: Author.

Fletcher, C. (2003). Community-based participatory research relationships with Aboriginal communities in Canada: An overview of context and process. *Pimatziwin: A Journal of Aboriginal and Indigenous Community Health, 1*(1), 28–61.

Harris, R.P., Helfand, M., Woolf, S.H., Lohr, K.N., Mulrow, C.D., Teutsch, S.M., et al. (2001). Current methods of the U.S. Preventive Services Task Force: A review of the process. *American Journal of Preventive Medicine, 20*(3, Suppl. 1), 21–35.

Hart, E. (1995). *Getting started in oral traditions research* [No. 4 of Occasional Papers of the Prince of Wales Northern Heritage Centre]. Yellowknife, NT: Government of the Northwest Territories.

Indigenous Peoples' Health Research Centre. (2006). *Canoe lake community report – "Kokum, what makes a baby well?"* (Research project). Saskatoon, SK: Author.

International Symposium on the Social Determinants of Indigenous Health. (2007). *Social determinants and Indigenous health: The international experience and its policy implications.* Adelaide, Australia: Commission on Social Determinants of Health.

Inuit Tapirisat of Canada. (1998). *Negotiating research relationships: A guide for communities.* Nunavut: Nunavut Research Institute.

Kahnawake Schools Diabetes Prevention Project. (1996). *Code of research ethics.* Kahnawaka, PQ: Author.

Kaplan-Myrth, N., & Smylie, J.K. (2006). *Sharing what we know about living a good life: Indigenous knowledge translation summit report* [includes interactive DVD]. Saskatoon, SK: Indigenous Peoples' Health Research Centre.

Landry, R., Amara, N., Pablos-Mendes, A., Shademani, R., & Gold, I. (2006). The knowledge-value chain: A conceptual framework for knowledge translation in health. *Bulletin of the World Health Organization, 84*(8), 597–602.

Little Bear, L. (2000). Jagged worldviews colliding. In M. Battiste (Ed.), *Reclaiming indigenous voice and vision* (pp. 77–85). Vancouver, BC: UBC Press.

McShane, K.E. (2006). *Family health and parenting in an urban Inuit community.* Unpublished doctoral dissertation, Concordia University, Montreal.

McShane, K.E., Smylie, J.K., Hastings, P.D., Martin, C.M., & Inuit Family Resource Centre, Tungasuvvingat. (2006). Guiding health promotion efforts with urban Inuit: A community-specific perspective on health information sources and dissemination strategies. *Canadian Journal of Public Health, 97*(4), 296–299.

Merzel, C., & D'Afflittl, J. (2003). Reconsidering community-based health promotion: Promise, performance, and potential. *American Journal of Public Health, 93*(4), 557–574.

Oosman, S., Smylie, J.K., Kauffeldt, M., & Pikwakanagan First Nation. (2007, September). *CHIP-AE as a tool for evaluating a participatory youth mental health intervention in a First Nations community in Ontario, Canada.* Paper presented at the annual general meeting of the Canadian Public Health Association, Ottawa, ON.

Pawson, R. (2006). *Evidence-based policy: A realist perspective.* London: Sage.

Royal Commission on Aboriginal Peoples. (1996). Appendix E: Ethical guidelines for research. *The Final Report of the Royal Commission on Aboriginal Peoples. Vol. 5: Renewal: A Twenty-Year Commitment.* Ottawa, ON: Indian and Northern Affairs Canada.

Schnarch, B. (2004). Ownership, control, access, and possession (OCAP) or self-determination applied to research: A critical analysis of contemporary First Nations research and some options for First Nations communities. *Journal of Aboriginal Health, 1*(1), 80–95.

Smylie, J.K., Kaplan-Myrth, N., McShane, K.E., Ottawa Council, Métis Nation of Ontario, First Nation, Pikwakanagan, & Inuit Family Resource Centre, Tungasuvvingat. (2009). Indigenous knowledge translation: Baseline findings in a qualitative study of the pathways of health knowledge in three Indigenous communities in Canada. *Health Promotion Practice, 10*(3), 436–446.

Smylie, J.K., Kaplan-Myrth, N., Tait, C.L., Martin, C.M., Chartrand, L., Hogg, W., et al. (2004). Health sciences research and Aboriginal communities: Pathway or pitfall? *Journal of Obstetrics and Gynecology Canada, 26*(3), 211–216.

Smylie, J.K., Martin, C.M., Kaplan-Myrth, N., Steele, L., Tait, C.L., & Hogg, W. (2004). Knowledge translation and Indigenous knowledge. *International Journal of Circumpolar Health, 63*(Suppl. 2: ICCH 12), 139–143.

Smylie, J.K., McShane, K.E., & Inuit Family Resource Centre, Tungasuvvingat. (2006). Understanding knowledge translation in an urban Inuit community. In *Moving population and public health knowledge into action: A casebook of knowledge translation stories* (pp. 19–22). Ottawa, ON: Canadian Institutes of Health Research.

Smylie, J. K., Ottawa Council, Métis Nation of Ontario, Wellington, P., & Adomako, P. (2008). Resisting exclusion: Using culture to share health information among Métis in Ottawa. In *CIHR knowledge translation casebook 2008* (pp. 39–42). Ottawa, ON: Canadian Institutes for Health Research.

Stephens, C., Nettleton, C., Porter, J., Willis, R., & Clark, S. (2005). Indigenous peoples' health – why are they behind everyone, everywhere? [Comment]. *The Lancet, 366*(9479), 10–13.

Tuhiwai Smith, L. (1999). *Decolonizing methodologies: Research and indigenous peoples.* London: Zed Books.

United Nations. (2007). *Report of the human rights council: United Nations declaration on the rights of indigenous peoples.* New York: Author.

Youngblood Henderson, J.S. (2000a). Ayukpachi: Empowering Aboriginal thought. In M.Battiste (Ed.), *Reclaiming indigenous voice and vision* (pp. 248–278). Vancouver, BC: UBC Press.

Youngblood Henderson, J.S. (2000b). Postcolonial ghost dancing: Diagnosing European colonialism. In M. Battiste (Ed.), *Reclaiming indigenous voice and vision* (pp. 57–76). Vancouver, BC: UBC Press.

Zimmerman, L.J., & Molyneaux, B.L. (1996). *Native North America.* Boston: Little Brown.

12   Concluding Thoughts

ELIZABETH M. BANISTER, BONNIE J. LEADBEATER,
AND E. ANNE MARSHALL

As interest has shifted from defining what knowledge translation (KT) is to identifying how it works effectively, researchers and research users have been faced with questions about how to support the variety of mechanisms that serve to transfer, translate, manage, exchange, uptake, mobilize, adapt, and use research-based knowledge. The authors in this book describe the challenges involved with short-lived infrastructures within non-profit organizations (NPOs), brokering organizations, and communities that struggle to support the delivery of KT to improve individuals' health and social welfare. The authors demonstrate many mechanisms that do work in spite of these challenges.

In contrast to the large and highly regulated pharmaceutical industry, a great deal of health research does not result in intellectual property rights with profits for the developer. Often, research-based knowledge that benefits health and welfare accrues slowly over time, building a consensus across multiple settings and multiple studies. For example, the scientific processes for the development, dissemination, and ongoing review of children's mental health programs have, over time, established that these approaches are often preferable for treating children than widely used pharmaceuticals; however, to date these approaches rely on informal, often researcher-led, unfunded dissemination systems and communities of practice (Leadbeater, in press). The challenge we face is to share and promote KT strategies and practices that have been shown to be effective, while remaining sensitive to the contextual and cultural differences among stakeholders that define their particular needs and capacities. In this final chapter, we summarize the present authors' collective wisdom regarding such facilitators and barriers to effective KT.

Facilitators for Effective Knowledge Translation

Although we have argued that the contextual specificity of KT processes need to be recognized, common themes related to the success (or failure) of KT across contexts are evident in the chapters of this book. Notably, effective KT across contexts relies on establishing and sustaining positive relationships, ensuring relevance, attending to contextual factors, engaging facilitators, and opening lines of communication. Each requires an investment of time on the part of both researchers and research users. The preceding chapters describe effective KT experiences, including concrete examples of success.

Establishing and Sustaining a Positive Relationship

Successful relationships among researchers and research users require an investment of time and resources throughout all stages of the research (Landry, Amara, & Lamari, 2001). Researchers and users need to respect and be open to multiple perspectives while remaining focused on shared goals. Multiple exchanges, especially through personal contact, are needed to build and maintain meaningful connections. In addition to research skills, researchers need interpersonal skills, such as active listening, flexibility, self-reflexivity, conflict resolution, and a willingness to admit mistakes.

Ensuring Relevance

The relevance of the research to both the researcher and the community partner who hopes to use the research is essential for effective KT. Ensuring relevance may involve forming research collaborations in which users of the research are engaged in the various steps of the research itself and/or the KT mechanisms that provide access to research findings. Such engagement includes user involvement in the process of identifying the research questions or problems, having input into the methods used for KT, tailoring dissemination activities to their constituents, and ensuring relevance by evaluating the applicability of results and the barriers (see below) to implementation.

Attending to Contextual Factors

A community's background, history, habits, traditions, values, structures, and priorities influence how effectively research knowledge will be applied. For example, at the policy level, researchers or knowledge brokers need to be aware of the timing when brief windows of opportunity are *open* for research results to influence policy change.

Engaging Facilitators

Gatekeepers, or respected members of a community, can facilitate the formation of community-research partnerships. Knowledge brokers, or intermediaries, can facilitate both users' access to research-based knowledge and researchers' access to users. Knowledge brokers can also help influence practice, policy, and organizational decision-makers – they can facilitate access to relevant knowledge at strategic times (Landry et al., 2001). To support ongoing KT mechanisms, these facilitators often need to be part of organizations that have the capacity to pull research into action as well as have stable infrastructures and funding to build on this expertise.

Opening Lines of Communication

KT is an iterative, social process whereby researchers and research users co-construct knowledge to address problems. Constant and inclusive communication processes are vital to its success. Creative use of electronic technologies for document sharing, webcasts, and virtual conferences has made it possible for community partners in faraway communities to collaborate with researchers in ways and times that suit their particular needs and limitations. Nevertheless, it is important to note that face-to-face meetings can be critical for the partnership-building phase, particularly in Indigenous communities.

Barriers to Effective Knowledge Translation

Identifying the barriers to effective KT across contexts helps both researchers and users understand what to avoid in the KT process. Barriers identified relate to unidentified power imbalances, struggles, conflicting agendas, difficulties in sustaining needed KT partnerships, or in moving knowledge outside of existing partnerships. These are briefly described below; chapters in this book provide details of problematic KT experiences, including concrete examples of difficulties and how to resolve them.

Power Imbalances and Power Struggles

Community-based partners generally have fewer resources and less perceived status than university researchers, which can create barriers to establishing equitable partnerships – contributing to a 'hierarchy between those who "think" (i.e., academics) and those who "do" (i.e., CBRs)' (Cottrell & Parpart, 2006, p. 15). This problem generally does not arise or may be reversed when the partner is a decision-maker. Power imbalances can exist among academic researchers as well as between academics and decision-makers. Seeking symmetry between different sources of knowledge can lead to significant new knowledge and positive action (Fals-Borda, 2001).

Conflicting Agendas

Researchers and users may have conflicting agendas for the research. For example, participating in research activities may not be part of workplace expectations for some employees, and time requirements for the research may serve as a barrier to effective KT (Cottrell & Parpart, 2006). Community partners' goals tend to focus more on the immediate local problem whereas university researchers are more interested in generating new knowledge or in the big picture. Expectations for the partnership itself in terms of boundaries and roles also need to be collaboratively determined.

Lack of Sustainability

Resources such as time, finances, and personnel that are needed for sustainability of programs and effective use of research-based knowledge may not be available in sufficient amounts for successful KT. Research users, such as policymakers and service practitioners, may lack the time to develop research skills. Even when partnerships have been successfully established, it may be difficult to sustain the partnership long enough to achieve meaningful results. Given that many community partners are NPOs, their inability to obtain funding may be a barrier to sustaining research initiatives.

Difficulties Transferring KT Successes to Other Contexts

Given the contextual nature of KT, researchers need to consider ways in which research-generated knowledge can be transported across contexts. Lessons learned in one setting may be less or not at all relevant to other contexts; thus, an attempt to transfer not only research findings but also the KT processes may fail.

Conclusion and Next Steps

In conclusion, most approaches to KT have focused on the translation of research into policy and practice. Yet there has been increasing awareness of the importance of the users of research knowledge as key contributors to the process of KT. How-what-we-know-becomes-more-widely-known for the benefit of our health and social welfare is embedded in cultural value systems and in a host of informal and typically unspecified organizational infrastructures that support KT processes. Further research is needed in these underdeveloped and undertheorized areas. This book brings attention to a myriad of successful KT processes and to the infrastructures needed to support them.

Extensive research on improving the translation of academic research findings into practice now exists. However, this research is located in diverse places and can be hard to access. KT is a complex process involving the kind of knowledge being generated, its potential use, those involved in its generation, and the context. How knowledge is valued can vary from one context to another. Most importantly, individuals in research, policy, and community roles need to be involved in determining how best to engage in translating health knowledge into healthy lifestyles.

User-Driven Research

Traditional knowledge transmission methods such as producer-push methods are ineffective because they fail to take into account the complex social, economic, and cultural worlds that influence individuals' attitudes and decision-making processes. Davies and Nutley (2008) maintain that 'work that focuses on understanding research use in user communities may, ultimately, be better suited to an unpacking of the complex and highly contextual processes of knowledge creation and use' (p. 18). Emphasizing user focus has begun to explicate and, to a degree, evaluate the effectiveness of innovative mechanisms of KT.

KT Theory Development

Strategies that encourage uptake of research messages through knowledge brokers, change agents, early adopters, and communities of change are also growing (Nutley, Walter, & Davies, 2007; Sudsawad, 2007). Nevertheless, relatively little theoretical work informs the development of successful KT strategies (Graham & Tetroe, 2007; Grimshaw et al., 2005).

Evaluation of KT Mechanisms

Research evaluating the effectiveness of KT mechanisms is relatively undeveloped. Lavis et al. (2005) attribute this to a lack of both infrastructure and knowledge about effective evaluation methods. A necessary next step is to obtain evidence of the effectiveness of KT processes over time. There is a growing interest in methods such as evaluative inquiry (see McKegg, this volume) as a means for improved decision making (Cousins, Goh, & Clark, 2006). This form of inquiry has an explicit learning and action orientation, is highly participative, and focuses on quality, value, and performance (Preskill & Torres, 1999); for example, research reports that place the research experience within the local context, including descriptions of participants and their roles, illustrate the changes for those involved, including changes for the researcher (Smith, 1997). Creating opportunities whereby individuals and communities are viewed as assets capable of identifying social and health issues and developing solutions can be a mechanism for creating positive change.

In summary, the next steps in KT research include an investigation of user-driven research, KT theory development, and evaluation of KT mechanisms. User-driven research is better suited for understanding the influence of contextual factors in creating effective KT. The under-developed theoretical base for effective KT will benefit from new theoretical approaches such as evaluative inquiry. The field of KT is wide open for building upon previous work as well as the lessons gained from the chapters in this book.

REFERENCES

Cottrell, B., & Parpart, J.L. (2006). Academic-community collaboration, gender research, and development: Pitfalls and possibilities. *Development in Practice, 16*(1), 15–26.

Cousins, J.B., Goh, S.C., & Clark, S. (2006). Data use leads to data valuing: Evaluative inquiry for school decision making. *Leadership and Policy in Schools, 5*(2), 155–176.

Davies, H.T.O., & Nutley, S.M. (2008). *Learning more about how research-based knowledge gets used: Guidance in the development of new empirical research.* New York: William T. Grant Foundation.

Fals-Borda, O. (2001). Participatory (action) research in social theory: Origins and challenges. In P. Reason & H. Bradbury (Eds.), *Handbook of action research* (pp. 27–37). Thousand Oaks, CA: Sage.

Graham, I.D., & Tetroe, J. (2007). Some theoretical underpinnings of knowledge translation. *Academic Emergency Medicine, 14*(11), 936–941.

Grimshaw, J.M., Thomas, R.E., MacLennan, G., Fraser, C., Ramsay, C.R., Vale, L., et al. (2005). Effectiveness and efficiency of guideline dissemination and implementation strategies. *International Journal of Technology Assessment in Health Care, 21*(1), 149.

Landry, R., Amara, N., & Lamari, M. (2001). Utilization of social science research knowledge in Canada. *Research Policy, 30*(2), 333–349.

Lavis, J.N., Davies, H., Oxman, A., Denis, J.-L., Golden-Biddle, K., & Ferlie, E. (2005). Towards systematic reviews that inform health care management and policy-making. *Journal of Health Services & Research Policy, 10*(Suppl. 1), 35–48.

Leadbeater, B.J. (in press). The fickle fates of push and pull in the dissemination of child and youth mental health prevention programs. *Canadian Psychology.*

Nutley, S.M., Walter, I., & Davies, H.T.O. (2007). *Using evidence: How research can inform public services.* Bristol, UK: Policy Press.

Preskill, H.S., & Torres, R.T. (1999). *Evaluative inquiry for learning in organizations.* Thousand Oaks, CA: Sage.

Smith, S.E. (1997). Deepening participatory action research. In S.E. Smith, D.G. Willms, & N.A. Johnson (Eds.), *Nurtured by knowledge: Learning to do participatory action research* (pp. 173–264). New York: Apex Press.

Sudsawad, P. (2007). *Knowledge translation: Introduction to models, strategies, and measures.* Austin, TX: Southwest Educational Development Laboratory, National Center for the Dissemination of Disability Research.

Contributors

Elizabeth M. Banister is a professor in the School of Nursing, University of Victoria, and a professional research fellow in the Graduate School of Nursing, Midwifery and Health, Victoria University of Wellington, New Zealand.

Deborah L. Begoray is a professor in the Department of Curriculum and Instruction, University of Victoria.

Cecilia Benoit is a professor in the Department of Sociology and a scientist at the Centre for Addictions Research of BC, University of Victoria.

David Burns is the former executive director of the Child and Family Counselling Association, Victoria.

Lauren Casey is the former executive director of PEERS and the Canadian National Coalition of Experiential Women, Victoria.

David A. Gough is a professor of Evidence Informed Policy and Practice and director of the Social Research Unit and the EPPI-Centre, Institute of Education, University of London.

Francis Guenette is a PhD candidate and a sessional instructor in the Department of Educational Psychology and Leadership Studies, University of Victoria.

Budd Hall is a professor in the School of Public Administration and founding director of the Office of Community-Based Research, University of Victoria.

Wendy Henwood is a member of the Whāriki Research Group, Massey University, Auckland, Aotearoa New Zealand.

Mikael Jansson is a scientist at the Centre for Addictions Research of BC, University of Victoria.

Sandy Kerr is a member of the Whāriki Research Group, Massey University, Auckland, Aotearoa New Zealand.

Bonnie J. Leadbeater is a professor in the Department of Psychology, University of Victoria, and former co-director of the BC Child and Youth Health Research Network.

Simon Lenton is a professor and deputy director at the National Drug Research Institute at Curtin University, Perth, Western Australia. He was a former member of the Western Australian Ministerial Working Party on Drug Law Reform, which recommended the model of cannabis law enacted by the *Cannabis Control Act 2003* that became the *Cannabis Infringement Notice Scheme.*

Heather MacLeod Williams is the principal at MTM Research and Associates in North Vancouver, BC, and is a consultant in the recreation and physical activity field.

E. Anne Marshall is a professor in the Department of Educational Psychology and Leadership Studies, and director of the Centre for Youth and Society, University of Victoria.

Mary Ann McCabe is an associate clinical professor in the Department of Pediatrics at the George Washington University School of Medicine and an affiliate faculty in Applied Developmental Psychology at George Mason University. She is the former director of the Office for Policy and Communications of the Society for Research in Child Development in Washington, DC.

Tim McCreanor is a member of the Whāriki Research Group, Massey University, Auckland, Aotearoa New Zealand.

Kate McKegg is the founding director of the Knowledge Institute Ltd., Te Awamutu, New Zealand. She is also a lecturer at the Auckland

University of Technology and doctoral candidate at the University of Auckland.

Verne McManus is a member of the Whāriki Research Group, Massey University, Auckland, Aotearoa New Zealand.

Helen Moewaka Barnes is the director of the Whāriki Research Group, Massey University, Auckland, Aotearoa New Zealand.

Patti-Jean Naylor is an associate professor in the School of Exercise Science, Physical and Health Education, University of Victoria.

Rachel Phillips is a postdoctoral student in the Department of Anthropology and at the Centre for Addictions Research of BC, University of Victoria.

Janet K. Smylie, MD, FCFP, MPH, is a research scientist at the Centre for Research on Inner City Health, Keenan Research Centre in the Li Ka Shing Knowledge Institute of St Michael's Hospital, Toronto, and an associate professor in the Dalla Lana School of Public Health, University of Toronto.

Trina Sporer was the manager of Active Communities at the BC Recreation and Parks Association in Burnaby, BC.

Joan Wharf Higgins is a professor in the School of Exercise Science, Physical and Health Education, University of Victoria, and holds a Canada Research Chair (Health and Society).